Counselling for Stress Problems

Counselling in Practice

Series editor: Windy Dryden
Associate editor: E. Thomas Dowd

Counselling in Practice is a series of books developed especially for counsellors and students of counselling which provides practical, accessible guidelines for dealing with clients with specific, but very common, problems.

Counselling for Stress Problems

Stephen Palmer
& Windy Dryden

SAGE Publications
London • Thousand Oaks • New Delhi

First published 1995

SAGE Publications Ltd
6 Bonhill Street
London EC2A 4PU

SAGE Publications Ltd
2455 Teller Road
Thousand Oaks, California 91320

SAGE Publications India Pvt Ltd
32, M-Block Market
Greater Kailash – I
New Delhi 110 048

British Library Cataloguing in Publication Data

A catalogue record for this book is available from the British
Library.

  ISBN 0–8039–8862–1
  ISBN 0–8039–8863–X (pbk)

Library of Congress catalog card number 94-068660

Typeset by Mayhew Typesetting, Rhayader, Powys
Printed in Great Britain by Biddles Ltd, Guildford, Surrey

Contents

296144

To Maggie and Louise

Foreword

Stephen Palmer and Windy Dryden have written a splendid book! By stressing the need for a *multimodal* approach (instead of the more usual uni-modal, bi-modal or, at best, tri-modal orientations so widely practised), they clearly demonstrate how it is possible to employ a wide range of strategies in a rational and flexible manner for combating the ravages of stress. The systematic framework endorsed by multimodal practitioners enables one to embrace a series of methods that, as Professor Dryden has emphasized in many places, is 'challenging but not overwhelming'. The methods endorsed in this book are easy to understand, easy to apply and easy to remember.

The multimodal approach (Lazarus, 1989a) rests on the assumption that unless seven discrete but interactive modalities are assessed, treatment is likely to overlook significant concerns. Initial interviews and the use of a Multimodal Life History Inventory (Lazarus and Lazarus, 1991) provide an initial overview of a client's significant Behaviours, Affective responses, Sensory reactions, Images, Cognitions, Interpersonal relationships and the need for Drugs and other biological interventions. The first letters yield BASIC ID, an acronym that is easy to recall. These modalities exist in a state of reciprocal transaction and flux, connected by complex chains of behaviour and other psychophysiological processes.

The counsellor or therapist, usually in concert with the client, determines which specific problems, across the BASIC ID, are most salient. Whenever possible, the choice of appropriate techniques rests on well-documented research data but, as this book illustrates, multimodal counsellors remain essentially flexible and are willing to improvise when necessary.

The multimodal approach is essentially psycho-educational and contends that many problems arise from *misinformation* and *missing information*. Thus, as Palmer and Dryden indicate, with most outpatients, 'bibliotherapy', the use of selected books for home reading, often provides a springboard for enhancing the treatment process and content.

An assiduous attempt is made to tailor the therapy to each client's unique requirements. Thus, in addition to mastering a wide range of effective techniques, multimodal counsellors or clinicians address the fact that different *relationship styles* are also necessary. Some clients require boundless warmth and empathy; others prefer a more austere business-like relationship. Some prefer an active trainer to a good listener (or vice versa). Because the therapeutic relationship is the soil that enables the techniques to take root, it is held that the correct method, delivered within, and geared to, the context of the client's interpersonal expectancies, will augment treatment adherence and enhance therapeutic outcome.

In essence, this book contains an enormous amount of useful clinical information that can readily be translated into effective and efficient treatment and counselling procedures. I think it deserves a very wide readership.

Arnold A. Lazarus
Distinguished Professor of Psychology
Rutgers University

Preface

Stress counselling and stress management has become a new growth industry. Often in counselling or training settings the practitioner only uses one approach, such as non-directive counselling or relaxation training. Alternatively, an eclectic approach involving a confusing mish-mash of techniques is used. Either way, clients receiving stress counselling are not always given the most effective help for their individual problems (see Palmer and Dryden, 1994).

This book has been written to provide practitioners with a technically eclectic and systematic approach to stress counselling and stress management. The approach is technically eclectic as it uses techniques taken from many different psychological theories and systems, without necessarily being concerned with the validity of the theoretical principles that underpin the different approaches from which it takes its techniques. It agrees with London (1964: 33) who stated: 'however interesting, plausible and appealing a theory may be, it is techniques, not theories, that are actually used on people. Study of the effects of psychotherapy, therefore, is always the study of the effectiveness of techniques.'

The techniques are applied systematically, based on data from client qualities, the counsellor's clinical skills and specific techniques. The approach is underpinned by social learning theory, general systems theory, group and communications theory (Lazarus, 1987), and is based on the extensive work of Arnold Lazarus (1973b, 1981). It has been adapted to the field of stress by the authors (Palmer, 1992a; Palmer and Dryden, 1991). Experienced counsellors may be able to integrate this approach within their own working model.

Our approach to stress counselling and stress management incorporates Lazarus' thorough and comprehensive multimodal assessment procedures. These procedures involve the counsellor assessing a client from seven discrete modalities which Lazarus believes comprise the entire range of personality: Behaviour,

Affect, Sensation, Imagery, Cognition, Interpersonal, Drugs/ biology. Hence the approach's 'Multimodal' perspective. It uses techniques pioneered by Carl Rogers, Aaron Beck, Albert Ellis, Donald Meichenbaum and others.

This book will introduce counsellors, psychotherapists and trainers to multimodal assessment procedures and show them how these methods logically lead to the application of interventions for use with individual clients. Real examples are taken from the authors' clinical practice to show the model in action. In Chapter 1, we discuss a working model of stress; in Chapter 2, we explain the multimodal assessment procedures and therapeutic approach. From Chapter 3 we describe the different techniques that can be used in a multimodal approach to stress counselling. Chapters 3–8 each feature a different modality. Lazarus' seventh modality, Affect (emotion), has been integrated into the other chapters as Lazarus has argued that you cannot change affective reactions without using methods derived from the other six modalities (Lazarus and Lazarus, 1990a).

This book takes a pragmatic and empirical approach to stress counselling and can be used as a handbook of multimodal techniques. Even if counsellors, psychotherapists or trainers do not use the multimodal approach we describe in this book, it may nevertheless stimulate their thinking about how to approach stress counselling in a broad and comprehensive manner.

A note about pronouns: where no specific sex is intended, the use of 'he' and 'she' has been alternated for clients.

1

Stress: a Working Model

Before we explain our approach to stress counselling and stress management, it would be useful to share a working conceptual model of stress. A personal anecdote may illustrate some of the factors involved and help to highlight the complicated nature of stress.

Example of stress

It was an important day. I (S.P.) was about to start a series of lectures for a government agency which was due to close down. Even though, in the previous 12 months, the staff had received out-placement counselling and assistance to help them procure new jobs, this had been to no avail — a result of the recession, no doubt. Anyway, I got up promptly as I had a number of things to do before the lecture. Apart from putting my lecture notes in order and sorting out accompanying handouts, I also had to check my tax return and ensure it was posted that day to the Tax Office.

You may be thinking that I lack time management skills. Unfortunately, due to an unforeseen event, I had to leave work early the previous day without completing all my tasks. However, I knew that if I arrived at work early the next morning then I would have no difficulties in achieving my goals.

Little did I realize that the universe was conspiring against me! Being a creature of habit, I started the day as usual with a relaxing bath and then a slice of toast with my favourite mug of tea. Yes, things were going well. I managed to avoid any conflict with the teenagers. My partner had already left for work and it was my turn to go.

'Where the hell are my keys?' I exclaimed.

They were not in their usual place. I always put them on top of the bookcase in the hallway, by the front door. I knew if I did not leave promptly then I would be caught in all the traffic arriving at 8.45am bringing children to the school in my street.

'Damn it! I'll be late for work. Today of all days', I cursed.

Everything had been going so well up to this point. Where were my keys? I had no idea. I always left them in the same place. Perhaps my partner had tidied up the shelf.

'Damn her obsessive-compulsive disorder.' I had to find someone else to blame and not take responsibility for the loss of the keys! However, my partner just liked a tidy house. She didn't have a disorder. That was just 'therapist-speak'. As I thought about this I became angry.

'It's those bloody kids. They've knocked the keys off the shelf and they've fallen behind the books.'

I started taking the books off the shelf in great haste. Books landed everywhere. The keys were nowhere to be seen. Time was ticking by. The clock chimed. It was 8.45am.

'Damn it! I will be late now.' My level of frustration tolerance was gradually lowering.

However, I didn't want to come home to a row so I quickly tidied up the mess I had made all over the floor. Perhaps I had left my keys in my jacket. I furiously checked all the pockets. I couldn't find them. I could hear my partner's voice in my head telling me:

'You're incapable of looking properly for things. You couldn't even find socks if they were on your feet!' I had this clear image of my partner gesticulating at me too. By this time I noticed my stomach was feeling rather empty even though I had just eaten my breakfast. I decided to check slowly through my pockets again. Unfortunately, my luck had run out — no keys could be found.

I recalled having a spare set of keys somewhere. I had an image of them next to a box of pencils.

'They must be in my study', I thought. I almost fell down the stairs running to my bolt hole (the study). I found them.

'Thank God for that', I blasphemed. I dashed back upstairs, picked up my bag, and left the house.

I turned back because I couldn't remember if I had locked the front door. I put the keys into the lock and proceeded to unlock the lock. I *had* locked it when I left after all. I must have been on automatic pilot. I was wasting good time. I cursed myself.

I ran to where my car was parked. I noticed heavy traffic and that the weather was foggy and damp. I tried to open the car door. It wouldn't open.

'I don't believe this', I thought. The spare key doesn't fit properly. Why, oh why, hadn't I checked this out before? I collected myself and thought laterally. I was able to get entry through the passenger's door. I put the key in the ignition and turned it.

The car engine made a 'whirring' sound and then it died. Somehow, the damp atmosphere had flattened the car battery. The morning was ebbing away, I was still stuck outside my house, I had the tax return to complete, my lecture notes and handouts to put into order, and then attempt to travel into London by British Rail and London Underground to give a lecture on 'How to manage pressure and cope with redundancy'. It hadn't been a good start to the day. I wasn't feeling particularly calm either.

We can use this real example to demonstrate the complicated nature of stress. Initially, it appears that I became stressed because I could not find my car keys. They were not in the usual place as they 'should' have been. But there was no assailant about to attack me in my hallway. A knife was not at my throat. There was no need for my stress response to become activated. All that was happening was that I could not find my keys. I started blaming others, such as my partner or my teenagers, for allegedly moving the keys even though there was little evidence for this. As they had obviously moved the keys, as they 'shouldn't' have done, I became angry about the situation. In fact, I was also angry with myself as I anticipated that I would be arriving late for the important lecture.

The empty feeling in my stomach was part of the stress response or, more accurately, a physical component of becoming anxious about arriving late, which blatantly I felt that I 'must' not do. These internal dogmatic and absolutist beliefs such as my 'musts' and 'shoulds' (commonly known as 'musturbatory' beliefs) put more pressure on me and added to my emotional state. The feeling in my stomach could also have been triggered by the voice and image I had of my partner in my head chastising me as she has often done before when I have been unable to find my socks in the airing cupboard. My thoughts and exclamation, such as 'Damn it', did not help to lower my stress either as these phrases tend to be like a catalyst to the stress response and the anger they evoke stimulates the release of adrenaline and noradrenaline from the adrenal glands.

It is important to realize that a whole series of events occurred externally and internally in a very brief period of time. It involved my behaviour, affect (emotions), sensations, imagery, cognitions, interpersonal relationships and my biological/physiological response.

There was an interaction between internal and external demands, real or perceived, and the apparent stressor of mislaid keys only contributed to the scenario. My strong internal belief that I had to pay the tax demand and arrive at the lecture on time exacerbated my response to the situation. Although I may have been influenced by sociocultural rules to do things on time, I do have a choice in the matter. I was my own worst enemy. As I became more distressed, I then blamed others as the major cause of my problem rather than taking a calm rational approach to the situation. Pragmatically, if I had stayed calm I would probably have saved more time in the long run and actually achieved my goals of the day.

Multimodal transactional model of stress

The working model of stress we use in our approach to stress counselling is known as 'transactional'. This model provides a simple but realistic explanation of the complicated nature of stress as it addresses the inter-relationship between the internal and external world of individuals. We have modified the transactional models of stress proposed by Cox (1978) and Cox and Mackay (1981) to incorporate Lazarus' seven modalities. Figure 1.1 illustrates the new multimodal transactional model.

In the model, the psychological processes are of fundamental importance. How a person reacts to an event is more due to his or her perceptions of it and his or her perceived abilities to deal with it than the event or situation itself. Therefore the event can be considered as a potential 'trigger' to activate the stress response but not necessarily the main cause of its activation. Once the event has passed, the person may remain disturbed about it due to the action or interaction of the different modalities. For example, clients suffering from a chronic form of stress known as post-traumatic stress disorder may repeatedly see negative images of the event, may have many negative cognitions, may have physiological symptoms of severe anxiety, and may avoid anything that reminds them of the event. This response can still occur years after the stressful event. In other cases, clients who suffer an apparently harmless life-event, such as the death of a pet, become overwhelmed by immense grief, as the event takes on another personal meaning; for example, anxiety about their own death or memories of the loss of a close family member.

To help understand the multimodal transactional model, it can be broken down into five discrete stages.

In *Stage 1*, a pressure is usually perceived by the individual to be emanating from an external source in the environment, for example, having to meet an important deadline. In fact, there are also day-to-day physiological and psychological needs or demands an individual has in order to survive, such as food and water.

Stage 2 reflects the individual's perception of the pressure or demand and her appraisal of her ability to deal with it. If the

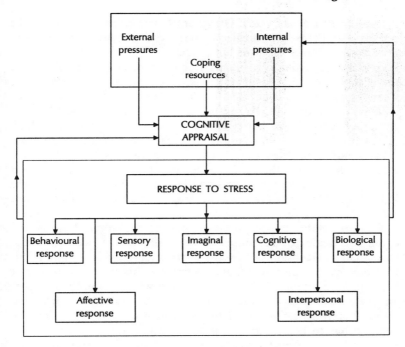

Figure 1.1 *Multimodal–transactional model of stress*

individual perceives that she can cope, even if she is being unrealistic, then she may stay in the situation; for example, working towards the deadline. If it happens that the person perceives that she cannot cope, then at that moment she may experience stress. However, added to this equation are social, family or cultural beliefs which the individual may have subsumed into her belief system. Thus, if the individual believes that she 'must' always perform well at work, an innocuous deadline may assume great importance. In reality, the 'must' is an internal and not an external pressure as the individual does not have to hold rigidly on to this belief. Many clients receiving stress counselling cognitively appraise experiences as 'very stressful' as a result of their beliefs which distort the importance of an actual or feared event. In this stage, then, the individual decides whether she has the resources to cope with the external and internal pressures of a specific situation. If she believes that she can deal with the situation then her stress response is less likely to be activated. However, if she perceives that she does not have the coping strategies to deal with the situation then she progresses on to Stage 3 of the model.

In *Stage 3*, psychophysiological changes occur. Taken together, these comprise what is generally known as the 'stress response'. There is usually an emotion or combination of emotions such as anxiety, anger or guilt. According to our multimodal model, these emotions may have behavioural, sensory, imaginal, cognitive, interpersonal and biological/physiological components (see Figure 1.1). In addition, there will probably be behavioural and cognitive attempts to change the environment or escape from the situation and thereby reduce the pressure. However, like animals, some individuals have been known to freeze with fear, which is not always helpful.

Stage 4 relates to the consequences of the application of the coping strategies or responses of the individual. Once again, the individual's perception of the coping strategies applied is important. Consequently, if an individual believes that his intervention is not helping, he may picture himself as failing which, in itself, becomes an additional strain in the situation. Actual failure to meet the demand is also detrimental if the individual truly believes that the demand has to be met in a satisfactory manner.

Stage 5 is concerned with the feedback system. Interventions may be made by the individual which may either reduce or alter the external and internal pressures. If this occurs then the organism may return to a neutral state of equilibrium. However, if the interventions are ineffective, then the individual may experience prolonged stress. This has many psychophysiological consequences which may even lead to mental breakdown or death in extreme cases. Death may be due to the prolonged effect of the stress hormones, adrenaline, noradrenaline and cortisol, on the body.

Individuals who have managed to cope with difficult life-events may view themselves as possessing coping skills which they can apply in similar situations. This is known as 'self-efficacy' and is a major cognitive component in the appraisal of future events as non-threatening and therefore *not* stressful. They may hold beliefs such as: 'I'm in control.' 'I know I can do it.' 'This will not be a problem.' 'This will be a challenge and not stressful.' These beliefs often prevent the person from going beyond Stage 2 of our multimodal transactional model. Coping is considered by researchers (e.g. Dewe et al., 1993; Lazarus, R.S., 1966; Lazarus, R.S. and Folkman, 1984) as an 'important part of the overall stress process' (Cox, 1993: 20) and, whenever possible, multimodal stress counsellors attempt to help clients improve their coping strategies.

The multimodal transactional model applied

If we now return to our stress example at the beginning of the chapter, we can show how this five-stage model applies to a real situation.

Stage 1 is usually an external pressure. In this case it was the need for Stephen to arrive on time to give a lecture on 'managing pressure' and also to pay his tax demand promptly. This in itself is not necessarily a stressor. He perceived it was a problem only when he could not find his car keys and he then realized that he might arrive late. In reality this still only becomes a stressful event when and if Stephen believes that he absolutely *must* arrive on time and he absolutely *must* pay the tax demand on time. Just because it is very strongly preferable to arrive on time and pay tax demands on time there is no law of the universe which states that Stephen *must* undertake these commitments on time. If there was a law of the universe then Stephen would always complete these commitments on time, whatever happened, whether he liked it or not! We return to this important issue in Chapter 3 when we look at cognitive interventions; more often than not, individuals suffer stress from the additional internal pressures they place upon themselves and not from the apparent external stressor.

Stage 2 reflects Stephen's cognitive appraisal of the situation. He thought that there was a possibility that he would arrive late for the lecture; something he believed he absolutely 'shouldn't do'. His exact phrase was 'Damn it! I'll be late for work. Today of all days.' He thought that the demand to arrive on time was not going to be achieved as he did not appear to have the resources to meet this demand. At this point he showed signs of stress.

Stephen's case highlights many different aspects of the 'stress response' in Stage 3 where psychophysiological changes occur. He experienced a number of emotions. He felt angry at others for allegedly moving the car keys and also at himself for 'wasting good time'. It is interesting to note that his anger had a cognitive component. He was anxious about possibly arriving late. He had an image of his partner gesticulating at him. He also had an empty 'sensation' in his stomach as the blood was diverted to other parts of his body due to the action of adrenaline and noradrenaline. Behaviourally, he attempted to change the situation by looking for the car keys, thereby hoping to arrive on time and reduce the demand.

In Stage 4 the individual considers the consequences of the application of any coping strategies or responses he or she has used. During our evolution, the 'stress response' may have been adaptive to help us cope with aggressive wild animals, other *Homo sapiens* or catastrophes such as flooding, but in a 'civilized society' fleeing from angry customers, bosses or one's family may not be so adaptive. Thus, individuals weigh up how they have dealt with specific situations. In this case, Stephen thought that he was doing his best in the circumstances, but he was anxious that his intervention was not going to be effective. He also attributed the cause of his problem externally by blaming members of his family for his mislaid keys. With these beliefs he became angry (affect). This did not help him stay calm and relaxed. Instead of being concerned about arriving late, he was anxious because of his internal 'must' demands. The emotional responses of anger and anxiety reduced his capacity to deal effectively with the problem. His 'headless chicken' behaviour included checking whether he had locked the front door which wasted precious time. However, he did realize that franticly checking his pockets for his keys was not necessarily useful and he decided to repeat the exercise more slowly. He did not exhibit the 'freezing with fear' response which can be likened to the 'ostrich sticking its head in the sand' (a useful analogy when discussing this subject with clients).

The example was not completed. It left out the ending which is relevant to Stage 4. On leaving the car parked near his house, Stephen decided not to rely on the buses. He walked to work and this gave him 15 minutes to challenge the beliefs that were causing his anxiety and anger. When he was no longer angry and was only concerned about arriving late, he was able to work out a new time schedule for the morning which included paying the tax demand, preparing the notes for the seminar, and finally just arriving on time. He was even able to base the introduction of the 'managing pressure' seminar on his experience of that morning which the audience was easily able to relate to. Stephen decided that his interventions to meet the demand had been successful and had even been helpful in demonstrating some of the difficult cognitive disputes at the seminar.

Stage 5 of the multimodal transactional model concerns the feedback system. In this case, Stephen's interventions had reduced and also altered the demand. When this occurred, Stephen became more relaxed about the situation. Once it was over, with the help of the parasympathetic nervous system (see next section), Stephen's body and mind returned to a neutral state of equilibrium. In fact, he was pleased to have a graphic example of stress and its management that he could now use at other seminars and workshops. He did not suffer from any of the common psycho-physiological consequences (see list on pp. 9–10) that can occur at this stage if the individual perceives that he or she has not successfully dealt with a stressful event.

Physiology of the stress response

The above description of the five-stage model of stress concentrates on the more psychological aspects of stress. In this section, therefore, we will highlight the physiological components. It is useful to inform clients as to the exact nature of the stress response as this can allay fears. Clients who are suffering from the effects of stress often fear that they are 'going mad'. An authoritative explanation of the psychophysiology of stress ensures that the client has confidence in the therapeutic programme that the counsellor or trainer will later negotiate.

If an individual in Stage 2 perceives that he is in a threatening situation or that he is unable to cope, then messages are carried along neurones from the cerebral cortex (where the thought processes occur) and the limbic system to the hypothalamus. This has a number of discrete parts. The anterior hypothalamus produces sympathetic arousal of the autonomic nervous system (ANS). The ANS is an automatic system that controls the heart, lungs, stomach, blood vessels and glands. Due to its action we do not need to make any conscious effort to regulate our breathing or heart beat. The ANS consists of two different systems: the sympathetic nervous system and the parasympathetic nervous system. Essentially, the parasympathetic nervous system conserves energy levels. It increases bodily secretions such as tears, gastric acids, mucus and saliva which help to defend the body and help digestion. Chemically, the parasympathetic system sends its messages by a neurotransmitter called acetylcholine which is stored at nerve endings.

Unlike the parasympathetic nervous system which aids relaxation, the sympathetic nervous system prepares the body for action. In a stressful situation, it quickly does the following:

- increases strength of skeletal muscles
- decreases blood clotting time
- increases heart rate
- increases sugar and fat levels
- reduces intestinal movement
- inhibits tears, digestive secretions
- relaxes the bladder
- dilates the pupils
- increases perspiration

- increases mental activity
- inhibits erection/vaginal lubrication
- constricts most blood vessels but dilates those in heart/leg/arm muscles

The main sympathetic neurotransmitter is called noradrenaline, which is released at the nerve endings. The stress response also includes the activity of the adrenal, pituitary and thyroid glands.

The two adrenal glands are located one on top of each kidney. The middle part of the adrenal gland is called the adrenal medulla and is connected to the sympathetic nervous system by nerves. Once the latter system is in action it instructs the adrenal medulla to produce adrenaline and noradrenaline (catecholamines) which are released into the blood supply. The adrenaline prepares the body for flight and the noradrenaline prepares the body for fight. They increase both the heart rate and the pressure at which the blood leaves the heart; they dilate bronchial passages and dilate coronary arteries; skin blood vessels constrict and there is an increase in metabolic rate. Also gastrointestinal system activity reduces which leads to a sensation of butterflies in the stomach.

Lying close to the hypothalamus in the brain is an endocrine gland called the pituitary. In a stressful situation, the anterior hypothalamus activates the pituitary. The pituitary releases adrenocorticotrophic hormone (ACTH) into the blood which then activates the outer part of the adrenal gland, the adrenal cortex. This then synthesizes cortisol which increases arterial blood pressure, mobilizes fats and glucose from the adipose (fat) tissues, reduces allergic reactions, reduces inflammation and can decrease lymphocytes that are involved in dealing with invading particles or bacteria. Consequently, increased cortisol levels over a prolonged period of time lower the efficiency of the immune system. The adrenal cortex releases aldosterone which increases blood volume and subsequently blood pressure. Unfortunately, prolonged arousal over a period of time due to stress can lead to essential hypertension.

The pituitary also releases thyroid-stimulating hormone which stimulates the thyroid gland, located in the neck, to secrete thyroxin. Thyroxin increases the metabolic rate, raises blood sugar levels, increases respiration/heart rate/blood pressure/and intestinal motility. Increased intestinal motility can lead to diarrhoea. (It is worth noting that an overactive thyroid gland under normal circumstances can be a major contributory factor in anxiety attacks. This would normally require medication.) The pituitary also releases oxytocin and vasopressin which contract smooth muscles such as the blood vessels. Oxytocin causes contraction of the uterus. Vasopressin increases the permeability of the vessels to water, thereby increasing blood pressure. It can lead to contraction of the intestinal musculature.

If the individual perceives that the threatening situation has passed then the parasympathetic nervous system helps to restore the person to a state of equilibrium. However, for many clients whom we see for stress counselling every day of their life is perceived as stressful. The prolonged effect of the stress response is that the body's immune system is lowered and blood pressure is raised which may lead to essential hypertension and headaches. The adrenal gland may malfunction which can result in tiredness with the muscles feeling weak; digestive difficulties with a craving for sweet, starchy food; dizziness; and sleep disturbance.

Responses to stress

It is useful to take a systematic approach to the responses that can be expected in a client requesting stress counselling or stress management. The following list places the responses to stress under headings which correspond to the multimodal model. This may help in the assessment and subsequent treatment stages of therapy. It may be an interesting exercise to refer back to our example at the beginning of the chapter to see the responses of S.P. in a stressful situation.

Responses to stress

Behaviour
  alcohol/drug abuse
  avoidance/phobias
  sleep disturbances/insomnia
  increased nicotine/caffeine intake
  restlessness
  loss of appetite/over-eating
  anorexia, bulimia
  aggression/irritability
  poor driving
  accident proneness
  impaired speech/voice tremor
  poor time management
  compulsive behaviour
  checking rituals

tics, spasms
nervous cough
low productivity
withdrawing from relationships
clenched fists
teeth grinding
type A behaviour, e.g. talking/walking/eating faster; competitive;
    hostile
increased absenteeism
decreased/increased sexual activity
eating/walking/talking faster
sulking behaviour
frequent crying
unkempt appearance
poor eye contact

Affect (emotions)
anxiety
depression
anger
guilt
hurt
morbid jealousy
shame/embarrassment
suicidal feelings

Sensation
tension
headaches
palpitations
rapid heart beat
nausea
tremors/inner tremors
aches/pains
dizziness/feeling faint
indigestion
premature ejaculation/erectile dysfunction
vaginismus/psychogenic dyspareunia
limited sensual and sexual awareness
butterflies in stomach
spasms in stomach
numbness
dry mouth
cold sweat

clammy hands
abdominal cramps
sensory flashbacks
pain

Imagery
Images of:

helplessness
isolation/being alone
losing control
accidents/injury
failure
humiliation/shame/embarrassment
self and/or others dying/suicide
physical/sexual abuse
nightmares/distressing recurring dreams
visual flashbacks
poor self-image

Cognition
'I must perform well'
'Life should not be unfair'
self/other-damning statements
low frustration statements, e.g. 'I can't stand it'
'I must be in control'
'It's awful, terrible, horrible, unbearable' etc.
'I must have what I want'
'I must obey "my" moral code and rules'
'Others must approve of me'
cognitive distortions, e.g. all or nothing thinking

Interpersonal
passive/aggressive in relationships
timid/unassertive
loner
no friends
competitive
puts other's needs before own
sycophantic behaviour
withdrawn
makes friends easily/with difficulty
suspicious/secretive
manipulative tendencies
gossiping

Drugs/biology
  use of drugs, stimulants, alcohol, tranquillizers, hallucinogens
  diarrhoea/constipation/flatulence
  frequent urination
  allergies/skin rash
  high blood pressure/coronary heart disease (angina/heart attack)
  epilepsy
  dry skin
  chronic fatigue/exhaustion/burn-out
  cancer
  diabetes
  rheumatoid arthritis
  asthma
  flu/common cold
  lowered immune system (reduction in lymphocytes and
    eosinophils)
  poor nutrition, exercise and recreation
  organic problems
  biologically based mental disorders

An individual may have been suffering from stress for a long time and this may lead to problems of a physiological nature, such as diabetes, hypertension or ulcers. Stress counselling and management can involve helping a person to deal with the stressors in life as well as hypertension. Unlike many other approaches to counselling, multimodal stress counselling and therapy does not overlook the *whole* person and is concerned with much more than just dealing with the emotional disturbances an individual may have.

The linking of modalities

In the multimodal approach to stress counselling, the counsellor is always aware of the ways in which the different modalities can interact with each other. For example, a client may become disturbed about an image and then may have thoughts about it in the cognitive modality. Then in the sensation modality muscular tension occurs when neurotransmitters directly act on different muscle groups via nerves and their synapses.

The modalities can be seen as linked together to produce an emotional/affective response. The drugs/biology modality is involved with each link in the chain by the action of the neurones, neurotransmitters, stress hormones and other chemicals released into the

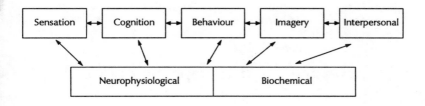

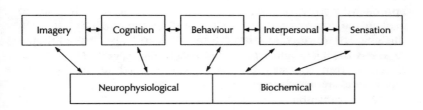

Figure 1.2 *Possible relationships between the modalities*

organism. Figure 1.2 illustrates two possible relationships between the modalities and the biological nature of stress. Other combinations are possible depending upon the individual and the nature of the stressor. 'Tracking' (see Chapter 2) is a multimodal technique that is used to analyse the firing order of the modalities and helps to provide a uniquely tailored therapeutic programme for clients who suffer from stress in certain situations, for example, panic attacks on social occasions.

2

Assessment and Therapeutic Approach

In Chapter 1 we looked at a model of stress which underpins our approach to stress counselling and stress management. It helps to explain the complex nature of stress and its possible resolution. In this chapter we provide a basic framework to help the practitioner to assess the client and negotiate a flexible therapeutic programme. Excerpts from counselling sessions will be used to highlight the multimodal approach.

The fundamental premise of this approach is that clients 'are usually troubled by a multitude of specific problems that should be dealt with by a similar multitude of specific treatments . . . the multimodal approach stresses that all therapy needs to be tailored to the individual requirements of each person and situation' (Lazarus, 1981: cover). However, a problem may arise when choosing what technique or intervention to make for a specific problem (Palmer and Dryden, 1991). Karasu (1986) estimated that over four hundred forms of psychotherapy exist; careful consideration is therefore required to ensure that the client receives the most suitable set of interventions.

Examples of technique specificity range from exposure treatment programmes for phobics (see, for example, Marks, 1986), and response prevention for obsessive-compulsive disorders (see, for example, Grayson et al., 1985), to the other end of the spectrum where, perhaps, an unfit individual may simply require a fitness programme. The study by Smith et al. (1980) on the meta-analysis of different treatments has often persuaded counsellors that all forms of psychotherapy are of equal effectiveness. However, later studies (see Shapiro and Shapiro, 1983; Butler et al., 1991) indicate that some approaches and techniques are more effective than others.

Counsellors may reduce their effectiveness if they only use a restricted range of techniques. Maslow summed this up in a concise statement when he wrote 'If you only have a hammer you treat everything like a nail.' We have seen many individuals who have received counselling and years later still suffer from the original phobia. Unless some form of exposure programme to the phobic situation is encouraged by the counsellor, even if the roots of the phobia emanate from childhood, the client is not likely to overcome the problem. Beitman (1990: 65) also believes that 'counselors must build flexibility into their approaches to their clients. This flexibility may be imagined as the counselor's moulding around the other, a fitting with the client rather than forcing the patient into the therapist's own theoretical bed.'

Case study
John had been going through a stressful period at work and started to develop a phobia about making presentations to clients. He explained his problem to a counsellor who then spent the next four 50-minute counselling sessions exploring John's childhood. John kept on asking the counsellor 'Is this relevant?' He was told 'Yes it is.' John told his counsellor that he did not find this approach helpful. He wanted 'a more positive approach'. In fact, his condition was becoming worse as he was now beginning to have panic attacks while driving to work. Although he agreed with his counsellor that the cause 'might' lie in his childhood, he needed to overcome his problem 'now' and wanted advice on how to cope and control the panic attacks. John decided to ask a friend who had been a 'nervy person since childhood' which therapist he had seen for counselling. On recommendation, John saw a multimodal counsellor and, on explaining his previous experience of counselling, was relieved to discover that a 'practical, here and now' approach would be used. The counsellor took the role of an expert who clearly understood panic attacks. Knowing that the counsellor had previously 'cured his friend from a lifetime of anxiety' John was very happy to undertake his exposure assignments which initially included imaginal exposure. John could also relate to the counsellor disputing his irrational beliefs, such as 'I must not lose control; it's awful; I can't stand it' that apparently heightened his anxiety.

Comment
The multimodal stress counsellor elicited from John at the initial assessment what he expected from the therapist. The counsellor decided that taking the role of an expert was worth the risk in this case as it appeared that John would be more responsive to such an approach. In addition, a 'here and now' approach would help strengthen the therapeutic alliance especially as John's first experience of counselling had been negative. John considered that the previous psychodynamic counsellor had had her own agenda, i.e. exploring John's childhood would help him overcome his phobia, which was very

much at variance with his own wants (i.e. practical help to deal with panic attacks in the 'here and now').

Rationale for therapeutic approach

Lazarus believes that the entire range of human personality can be included within seven specific modalities. As mentioned previously the modalities are:

Behaviour
Affect
Sensation
Imagery
Cognition
Interpersonal
Drugs/biology

This is known by the acronym BASIC ID and the assessment of clients usually involves a thorough and systematic examination of each modality. In addition, the interaction between the different modalities is also closely examined. For example, in the personal example in Chapter 1, when S.P. became stressed he could hear his partner's voice (cognitive modality) in his head telling him 'You're incapable of looking properly for things. You couldn't even find socks if they were on your feet.' Then he had a clear picture (imagery modality) of his partner gesticulating at him. He then had an empty feeling (sensation modality) in his stomach even though he had just eaten. The order of interaction between the modalities is important as the subsequent therapeutic programme will often take these factors into account (see 'Tracking' below).

Essentially, the multimodal view is that to achieve an effective therapeutic outcome a comprehensive assessment of all the modalities is necessary, and suitable interventions across the modalities need to be applied. This will enable long-lasting gains to be achieved. Matching the therapeutic approach to the needs of the client helps multimodal counsellors to attain this goal. One of the challenges for the counsellor is in determining the correct match. The more the client can learn in counselling, and subsequently put into practice in everyday life, the more the odds of any possible relapse are reduced. The approach is psycho-educational and this is often reflected in the therapeutic programme. This allows it to be used easily in an individual or group stress management training programme as well as in counselling.

Assessment procedures

In line with many other approaches to counselling, in the initial counselling session a multimodal counsellor will be concerned with establishing a good therapeutic alliance, assessing presenting problems and considering possible therapeutic interventions. At the initial session the counsellor derives thirteen determinations (based on the twelve determinations of Lazarus, 1987):

1 Are there signs of 'psychosis'?
2 Are there signs of organicity, organic pathology or any disturbed motor activity?
3 Is there evidence of depression, or suicidal or homicidal tendencies?
4 What are the persisting complaints and their main precipitating events?
5 What appear to be some important antecedent factors?
6 Who or what seems to be maintaining the client's overt and covert problems?
7 What does the client wish to derive from counselling, therapy or training?
8 Are there clear indications or contraindications for the adoption of a particular therapeutic style (e.g. is there a preference for a directive or a non-directive style)?
9 Are there any indications as to whether it would be in the client's best interests to be seen individually, as part of a dyad, triad, family unit and/or in a group?
10 Can a mutually satisfying relationship ensue, or should the client be referred elsewhere?
11 Has the client previous experience of counselling, therapy or relevant training? If yes, what was the outcome: was it a positive, negative or neutral experience and why?
12 Why is the client seeking counselling/therapy/training at this time and why not last week, last month or last year?
13 What are some of the client's positive attributes and strengths?

At this stage of counselling the multimodal counsellor is not only collecting information but is looking for underlying themes and problems. Additionally, the counsellor tries to ascertain whether a judicious referral may be necessary to a medical practitioner or a psychiatrist if the client presents problems of an organic or psychiatric nature. A referral may also be necessary if it is clear that a productive match between client and counsellor is not possible. Additionally, at the end of the initial session it may become abundantly obvious that, for example, couples counselling, family therapy or the help of a co-therapist may be required. This issue can be explored at this point in the counselling process or at a later date depending upon the time left in the session.

We have found it helpful to agree initially a short-term contract of five counselling sessions with a client. This allows both the counsellor and the client to review progress and to decide whether there is a need to extend counselling beyond the agreed term or perhaps refer the client elsewhere. If counselling is extended then goals can be renegotiated if necessary. However, some clients may only require one or two counselling sessions in total, so it is important to maintain a flexible approach to contracting.

Multimodal stress counsellors take a 'Sherlock Holmes' approach to investigating a client's declared problem. The counsellor analyses the problem across the entire range of modalities. The following excerpt from the initial counselling session with John (the previous case study) illustrates the counsellor making a mental note of the modalities involved. This is an important exercise as the therapeutic programme is underpinned by suitable interventions being matched to the different modalities.

Counsellor: What happened next?
John: I stayed on the road because I thought that if I give into this I wouldn't drive again [*cognition*]. I thought it may be a 'one-off'. I hoped it was but it wasn't. I did exactly the same thing at exactly the same point again.
Counsellor: On the next journey?
John: Yes.
Counsellor: So just to clarify, you made another journey to visit your client [*behaviour*]. Did you have a panic attack on the way down?
John: No. But I felt anxious again [*affect*] about driving on that road [*behaviour*] and on the return journey it happened again. I was overwhelmed by this feeling [*affect*] and this time I stopped the car [*behaviour*]. I could picture me [*imagery*] crashing the car.
Counsellor: What was the effect on you this time?
John: I'm now completely avoiding visiting my clients [*behaviour*].
Counsellor: Anything else?
John: I won't be able to go anywhere soon [*laughs*].
Counsellor: No wonder you were late today!
John: [*Laughs*].

The first session may last longer than the usual 50–60 minutes as a large amount of relevant information is sought. The client should be told that this may be an extended session before the appointment is made. However, the counsellor needs to be flexible as sometimes, especially with stress counselling, the client may arrive in a very distressed state. If so, it may not be helpful to elicit all thirteen determinations in the first session; rather, it would be far more useful to help the client deal with the immediate presenting problem. The case study below illustrates this point. (See Chapter 9 for an in-depth analysis of this counselling session.)

Case study

Rachel suffered from panic attacks in situations where she had to meet strangers. She was dedicated to her work and had been recently informed that she was to be transferred to another branch for a couple of months. Although she was excited at the prospect of the transfer, the move would involve living away from home and working with people she had never met before. She was convinced that she would have panic attacks and wanted immediate help. On seeing the counsellor, she explained the problem and that she needed an 'instant cure' as she was departing within days. She would not be able to see the counsellor for some months. The counsellor did a very brief BASIC ID assessment of the specific problem. Irrational beliefs (cognitive modality) were elicited, i.e. 'It's awful; I can't stand it', and then disputed (see Chapter 3). A list of relevant rational coping statements was devised and the Benson relaxation response (sensation modality) was taught (see Chapter 6). The rationale of an exposure programme was explained to illustrate that gradually anxiety habituates in stressful situations and avoidance behaviour (behaviour modality) would prolong the problem (see Chapter 5). The extended counselling session was recorded and she was instructed to listen to the tape in the comfort of her home as a lot of material had been covered and she may need to remind herself of the techniques and rationale of the approach. The counsellor told Rachel that he would be willing to undertake telephone counselling with her if the need arose when she was working away from home.

Comment

Rachel went to the other branch and was able to cope without suffering from panic attacks. The brief multimodal assessment procedure covering the entire seven modalities allowed the counsellor quickly to design an individual programme for Rachel that dealt with the relevant modalities. The approach made sense to Rachel too.

The case study highlights the need for counsellors to be flexible to the needs of the client. It also indicates that to be as effective as possible counsellors may need skills covering the entire seven modalities. The counsellor was still able to cover the majority of the thirteen determinations in the session but noted the information as it arose as opposed to seeking it in a more systematic manner.

If we assume that the client is not in an immediate crisis, then a thorough assessment of the modalities is undertaken. Some of the questions (based on Lazarus, 1981; Lazarus and Lazarus, 1991) asked are as follows:

Behaviour
What behaviours are preventing you from being happy?
What would you like to start or stop doing?
Are 'significant others' doing things you would like to do?
What is holding you back from doing things that you want to do?
What skills would you like to develop further?
How does your behaviour affect your relationships (or images, or emotions, or sensations, or thoughts, or health)?

Affect
What do you laugh about?
What do you cry about?
What do you get angry about?
What do you get anxious about?
What do you get sad about?
What do you get depressed about?
What do you get guilty about?
Do you persistently have a recurring negative emotion?
How do your emotions affect your relationships (or behaviour, or images, or sensations, or thoughts, or health)?

Sensation
What do you like to see?
What do you like to taste?
What do you like to hear?
What do you like to smell?
What do you like to touch?
What do you dislike seeing?
What do you dislike tasting?
What do you dislike hearing?
What do you dislike smelling?
What do you dislike touching?
What unpleasant sensations do you suffer from, if any? (e.g. pains, light-headedness, shakes, etc.)
How do you feel emotionally about any of your sensations?
How do your sensations affect your emotions (or behaviour, or thoughts, or images, or relationships, or health)?

Imagery
Can you describe your self-image (or body-image)?
What do you picture yourself doing in the immediate future?
What do you picture yourself doing in two years' (and/or five years') time?

What images do you have that you like?
What images do you have that you dislike?
Do you have any recurrent dreams or nightmares?
How do these images affect your emotions (or behaviour, or thoughts, or sensations, or relationships, or health)?

Cognition
What are your main musts, shoulds, oughts, have/got tos?
What are your main beliefs you believe are important?
What are your main values you believe are important?
What are your major intellectual interests?
How do your thoughts affect your emotions (or behaviour, or sensations, or images, or relationships)?

Interpersonal
What expectations of others do you have?
What expectations do you think others have of you?
What expectations do you think society has of you?
What people are important in your life?
What people have been important in your life?
Who has been the most significant person in your life?
How do the significant people in your life affect you?
How do you affect the significant people in your life?

Drugs/biology
What are your worries about your health?
Are you on medication?
Do you take drugs?
Can you describe your diet?
What type of exercise do you do?
Are you interested in improving your general health?

It is not essential to cover all of these points in the first interview as some of the relevant information can be gleaned over a period of time. A useful 15-page *Multimodal Life History Inventory* (MLHI, see Postscript, p. 228) can be used to elicit the majority of the required details. At the end of the first session the client is asked to complete the questionnaire at home. We normally tell the client that completion of the MLHI saves therapeutic time (and their fees if they are paying for counselling) as they can answer the questions in their own time. They do not have to complete all the sections if they don't want to and if any queries arise, we can look at them in the next session. As it is a detailed questionnaire, we suggest that they don't have to complete it in one sitting. If the client is not up to undertaking the task due to inadequate skills or severe depression, the counsellor can use the MLHI questions as a guide in the session.

The initial session is also used to decide what is the most helpful approach that the counsellor can take with the client. This is important as the therapeutic alliance can be negatively affected if the counsellor's approach and interpersonal style do not meet the client's expectations or therapeutic needs. Thus the counsellor needs to:

1 Monitor the client's response to directive and non-directive interventions.
2 Discover whether the client responds well to humour.
3 Decide whether the client prefers a formal or informal relationship (see excerpt with John).
4 Establish how the client responds to counsellor self-disclosure.

Matching counsellor behaviour with client expectations in this (and other) ways may prevent early termination of counselling. Counsellors should even consider what they wear with particular clients; for example, suits may be very off-putting to young clients who associate them with authority figures. The environment may also be important. Formal office surroundings may be indicated for some clients and absolutely contraindicated for others.

The MLHI also explores the client's expectations of therapy and his or her beliefs about the ideal therapist. Some clients want a 'no-nonsense' approach, whereas others prefer a 'warm, gentle' approach. On completing the 'Expectations Regarding Therapy' section of the MLHI one client, Sue, responded to the questions as below:

Q: In a few words, what do you think therapy is all about?
A: Having the opportunity to talk through problems with a non-partial listener. Hopefully be given a new way of thinking about things/ rationalizing problems.
Q: How long do you think your therapy should last?
A: As long as it is useful to me and productive.
Q: What personal qualities do you think the ideal therapist should possess?
A: Warmth and friendliness, and be non-judgemental, sincere and professional.

Not only did the above information help with the therapeutic alliance, it also suggested that the client was aware of how her thoughts were involved with her problems. The counsellor decided to take a fairly cognitive approach with Sue (see Chapter 9 for an in-depth illustration of her therapy). Initially, she found the ABCDE paradigm of Ellis and the associated logical, empirical and pragmatic disputes very helpful (see Chapter 3 for details of these types of interventions).

Basic therapeutic ingredients of change

In 'The Essential Arnold Lazarus' (Dryden, 1991a: 132) Lazarus sums up briefly the 'main hypothesized ingredients of change' when using a multimodal approach:

Behaviour: positive reinforcement; negative reinforcement; punishment; counter-conditioning; extinction.
Affect: admitting and accepting feelings; abreaction.
Sensation: tension release; sensory pleasuring.
Imagery: coping images; changes in self-image.
Cognition: greater awareness; cognitive restructuring.
Interpersonal: non-judgemental acceptance; modelling; dispersing unhealthy collusions.
Drugs/biology: better nutrition and exercise; substance abuse cessation; psychotropic medication when indicated.

This list gives a brief indication of the main thrust of the interventions in each modality. Chapters 3–8 look in depth at the main techniques used to achieve these ingredients of change.

Modality Profile

Information obtained from the initial interview and a completed MLHI helps the counsellor to produce a comprehensive Modality Profile (or BASIC ID chart). This underpins the assessment and subsequent therapy. The Modality Profile initially consists of a modality analysis of identified problems. Many adults are able to compile their own Modality Profile if they are given a typewritten instruction sheet (see Box 2.1) describing each modality of the BASIC ID (adapted from Lazarus, 1981: 76–7).

Compiling a Modality Profile can be set as a homework assignment and later compared in counselling with the counsellor's initial assessment. The profile serves as 'working hypotheses' which can be revised or modified as new information arises. The revision can form part of regular reviews. Each specific problem on the Modality Profile may need a specific treatment intervention. The Modality Profile is completed with specific interventions written adjacent to the problems. Table 2.1 shows a completed Modality Profile (see Palmer, 1992a).

The therapeutic programme should be negotiated with the client; if client expectations are met, this will lead to a better outcome (Lazarus, 1973a). If a client really believes that hypnosis will deal with his or her level of anxiety then this should be offered instead of relaxation techniques. If a client thinks that a 'healthy body' will

Box 2.1   *Modality Profile*

Behaviour: This refers mainly to overt behaviours such as acts, habits, gestures, responses and reactions that can be observed. Write down which behaviours you would like to increase and which ones you would like to decrease. What would you like to stop doing? What would you like to start doing?

Feelings: This refers to emotions, moods and strong feelings. What emotions do you experience most often? Write down your unwanted emotions (e.g. anger, anxiety, depression, embarrassment, guilt, shame etc.). Note under 'Behaviour' what you tend to do when you feel a certain way (e.g. avoid friends when depressed).

Physical sensations: Seeing, hearing, touching, tasting and smelling are our five basic senses. Make a list of any negative sensations that apply to you (e.g. blushing, butterflies in the stomach, dizziness, pain, sweating, tension etc.). If any of these sensations cause you to act or feel in certain ways, ensure you note them down under 'Behaviour' or 'Feelings'.

Imagery: Write down any recurring dreams, and any vivid memories that may be bothering you. Include any negative features about the way you see yourself (your self-image). We are looking for 'pictures', or vivid scenes from your past, present or future, that may be troubling you. If your images arouse any significant actions, feelings or sensations, ensure that these items are added to 'Behaviour', 'Feelings' and 'Physical sensations'.

Thoughts: What sorts of ideas, values, opinions and attitudes get in the way of your happiness? Make a list of unhelpful things you tell yourself (e.g. 'I'm useless and worthless', 'I must be perfect at all times', 'I'm a bad person'). What are some of your most irrational ideas? We are also interested in auditory memories that you keep on hearing and that constitute a problem (e.g. sad music etc.). Note down how these thoughts and ideas influence your 'Behaviours', 'Feelings', 'Physical sensations' and 'Images'.

Interpersonal relationships: Write down any problems with other people (e.g. friends, relatives, work colleagues, lovers, acquaintances etc.) that bother you. Any concerns you have about the way other people treat you or how you treat them can appear here. Check through the items under 'Behaviour', 'Feelings', 'Physical sensations', 'Imagery' and 'Thoughts', and try to determine how they influence, and are influenced by, your 'Interpersonal relationships'.

Continued

Box 2.1   *continued*

Biological factors: Make a list of all drugs, whether prescribed by a doctor or not, that you are taking. Include any health and medical concerns, and illnesses you have or have had. Write down whether you want to improve your diet, lose or gain weight, or take more exercise.

Table 2.1   *Modality Profile (or BASIC ID chart)*

Modality	Problem	Proposed treatment
Behaviour	Avoidance of social events	Exposure programme and cognitive restructuring
	Avoidance of public transport	Exposure programme
	Sleep disturbance	Self-hypnosis tape or Benson relaxation response
Affect	Anger and irritability	Anger management; self-calming statements
	Anxiety attacks	Breathing exercises
	Guilt	Dispute irrational beliefs
Sensation	Tension	Biofeedback; relaxation training (or massage)
Imagery	Images of physical abuse	Imaginal exposure
	Recurring nightmares	Mastery imagery intervention
Cognition	Must perform well	Cognitive restructuring and disputing irrational beliefs
	Life should not be unfair	
	Self-damning statements	
	Low frustration statements, e.g. 'I can't stand it'	
Interpersonal	Passive–aggressive in relationships	Assertion training
	Few close friends of long-standing	Friendship training
Drugs/biology	Smokes 10 cigarettes daily	Behavioural: stop smoking programme; self-hypnosis
	Lack of exercise	Fitness programme
	Aspirin for headaches	Relaxation training
	Unhealthy diet	Nutrition programme

help him or her to a healthy mind, the counsellor may need to discuss the possibility of the client joining a local sports club or fitness centre. The counsellor does not need to know everything about fitness programmes if the client can be referred elsewhere for help. A 'healthy body' may also involve changing diets and require referral to a nutritional specialist. However, multimodal stress counsellors should consider receiving training in these areas as the seventh modality (drugs/biology) invariably includes consideration of exercise and diet.

In the following case study the counsellor thought he knew best before becoming a multimodal practitioner and failed initially to listen to his client.

Case study

Nancy was 18 years old and retained a habit that she had had since she was a baby. At school and anywhere she was feeling either bored or absorbed and not using her hands, she would suck her thumb.

She told her counsellor that she thought that hypnosis would definitely work, but Nancy's counsellor told her that a behavioural intervention called habit control had a 96 per cent success rate and this would be the recommended treatment. However, there was only a partial success with a relapse within a couple of weeks. Nancy reminded her counsellor that she did not think that habit control would work, and persuaded her counsellor to use hypnosis. Her counsellor agreed but only grudgingly. Much to the counsellor's surprise, Nancy ceased to suck her thumb. As Nancy was so pleased about her success she later referred her friends to the counsellor for a variety of behavioural problems.

Comment

If it was not for Nancy's keenness to overcome her problem, it is likely that she would have left counselling prematurely when asked to undertake the behavioural intervention. Nancy had seen stage hypnosis work on television with willing members of an audience and was convinced it would stop her thumb sucking. This conviction made her a very receptive subject for hypnosis. The counsellor adapted a simple hypnosis script (see Chapter 6) which basically included all the instructions that he had previously given Nancy for the behavioural intervention. If the counsellor had done the hypnosis in the first session, as requested by Nancy, it is likely that subsequent counselling would have been unnecessary.

This case study indicates how important it is to 'sell' the technique or intervention to the client. In Nancy's case, however, she had to 'sell' the technique to the counsellor! A working knowledge of the 'right' technique by the counsellor is not sufficient, even if the counsellor sounds confident to the client and is proficient in its use. Encouraging the client to adhere to the therapeutic programme is even more important. The ability to present techniques in ways that are acceptable to clients is a core skill that needs to be learned by multimodal stress counsellors (see Lazarus, 1989c).

Second-order BASIC ID

Occasionally, a counsellor may find that the techniques or interventions applied to help a specific problem do not appear to have resolved it. In this situation a second-order BASIC ID may prove useful. This is a Modality Profile which solely concentrates on the different aspects of the resistant problem (Lazarus, 1986). For example, Jack attempted to use a relaxation exercise to reduce muscle tension, but this did not work. To investigate the problem in greater depth, the counsellor produced a second-order BASIC ID (see Table 2.2) focusing specifically on any issue that may have been the cause of Jack's muscle tension.

A number of different problems were discovered that could have led to muscle tension. Jack's 'hard-driving' did not allow him much time to unwind and relax. On analysis, when he drove his car he tended to be hunched over his steering wheel. His behaviour and attitudes often irritated his staff which led to interpersonal difficulties. This hostile, 'hurry-up' approach to life is sometimes known as Type A behaviour and is characterized by: explosive speech, free floating hostility, hyper-alertness, impatience, quick talking/eating, aggressive driving, competitiveness, feeling pressured by time constraints, need for recognition, few interests outside work, and tendency to finish a slow talker's sentence. This general hostility and attitude to time-constraints can regularly trigger the stress response and may be responsible for individuals who exhibit Type A behaviour having a higher incidence of coronary heart disease. Type A behaviour can also lead to interpersonal problems.

Jack's imagery made him angry even before any staff difficulties arose. He thought that the muscle tension was indicative of a serious illness so that whenever he did the relaxation exercise he concentrated on his physical symptoms and then, not surprisingly, found it difficult to relax. This misinterpretation needed to be challenged first. The counsellor used cognitive restructuring and rational disputation to challenge his other negative thoughts. After these interventions Jack found it much easier to use the relaxation exercises to reduce his muscle tension.

Table 2.2   *Jack's second-order BASIC ID to reduce muscle tension*

Modality	Problem	Proposed treatment
Behaviour	'Hard-driving' behaviour, e.g. drives car fast, walks/eats fast, always in a rush (Type A behaviour)	Discuss advantages of 'slowing down'
Affect	Easily angered	Anger management involving disputation of irrational beliefs
Sensation	Physically tense, especially at work and not at weekends	Relaxation exercises; self-massage
Imagery	Images of getting angry with staff	Coping image of staying calm and assertive when dealing with staff
Cognition	Thought muscle tension indicative of serious illness	Health education
	Awful to have a serious illness; staff must perform well; lack of self-acceptance	Cognitive restructuring; dispute irrational beliefs
Interpersonal	Passive–aggressive with staff	Assertion training; role play
	Withdraws from supportive relationships	Discuss whether withdrawing from relationships is helpful or not
Drugs/biology	Hypertension	Receiving medication; relaxation and biofeedback techniques

In Chapter 8 we use second-order BASIC ID Modality Profiles to focus on specific health-related problems such as high blood pressure (Table 8.1), and stop smoking programmes (Table 8.3).

Vividness in portraying activating events

Traditional assessment procedures through verbal dialogue do not always yield the desired information from some clients. However, multimodal stress counsellors may use evocative imagery to stimulate the client's memory about specific events or fears. The client is encouraged to focus on relevant evocative images in the session to help gain access to cognitive processes below the level of awareness. Dryden (1990: 49–50, adapted) demonstrates this assessment procedure with Marjorie, who was terrified that her mother might die, which led her to be very unassertive with her mother. The counsellor used evocative imagery to bring the future event into the present.

Counsellor: So you feel you just can't speak up to her. Because if you did, what might happen?

Marjorie: Well, she might have a fit.

Counsellor: And what might happen if she did?

Marjorie: She might have a heart attack and die.

Counsellor: Well, we know that she is a fit woman, but let's go along with your fear for the moment. OK?

Marjorie: OK.

Counsellor: What if she did die?

Marjorie: I just can't think . . . I . . . I'm sorry.

Counsellor: That's OK. I know this is difficult, but I really think it would be helpful if we could get to the bottom of things. OK? [*Client nods.*] Look, Marjorie, I want you to imagine that your mother has just died this morning. Can you imagine that? [*Client nods and begins to shake.*] What are you experiencing?

Marjorie: When you said my mother was dead I began to feel to feel all alone . . . like there was no one to care for me . . . no one I could turn to.

Counsellor: And if there is no one who cares for you, no one you can turn to . . .?

Marjorie: Oh, God! I know I couldn't cope on my own.

Encouraging clients to imagine vividly something they have been avoiding often leads to the underlying cause of the anxiety. This assessment procedure is sometimes related to the client's central problem.

Feeling identification

Often in stress counselling clients are unsure how to define different emotions or physical sensations and have difficulty exploring and expressing the issues involved with the counsellor. A common remark a client may make is 'I'm stressed'. This is not very helpful clinically as 'stress' is a term that is used globally by individuals to describe a wide range of emotions or physical sensations.

To aid assessment, the counsellor should ensure that he or she has adequately explored the emotion or sensation that the client is expressing so they can reach a mutual understanding. To the client who states, 'I'm stressed', the counsellor can respond by asking, 'Do you mean: anxious stressed; angry stressed; depressed stressed; guilty stressed; tense stressed etc.?' However, even this may not be sufficient as the client may state that she is depressed when in fact she means severe shame: by eliciting the thoughts that are connected to the emotion, the counsellor may gain greater insight into the precise nature of the client's emotional disturbance (see Chapter 3).

Structural Profile

To obtain more clinical information and also general goals for counselling, a Structural Profile is drawn (Lazarus, 1989a). This can be derived by asking the client to rate subjectively, on a scale from 1 to 7, how she perceives herself in relation to the seven modalities. The counsellor can ask a number of different questions that focus on the seven modalities:

Behaviour: How much of a 'doer' are you?
Affect: How emotional are you?
Sensation: How 'tuned in' are you to your bodily sensations?
Imagery: How imaginative are you?
Cognition: How much of a 'thinker' are you?
Interpersonal: How much of a 'social being' are you?
Drugs/biology: To what extent are you health conscious?

To save therapeutic time, the *Multimodal Life History Inventory* has an entire section (p. 14) given over to asking the client about how she perceives herself with reference to the seven modalities. The client is also asked to rate herself in each modality. Assuming the client has returned the MLHI to the counsellor by the second counselling session, then the counsellor can clarify that the client has understood the questions in the MLHI and confirm that the rating is correct. Then in the session the counsellor can illustrate these scores graphically by representing them in the form of a bar chart on paper. We have found that graph paper is useful for this exercise. Figure 2.1 shows Natalie's Structural Profile. It can be seen that this client perceives herself as a 'doer' as she has rated herself at 7 on the behaviour modality. This suggests that Natalie will probably be keen to undertake behavioural homework assignment tasks.

Once the Structural Profile has been discussed with the client, a 'desired' Structural Profile can be considered. The client is asked in what way she would like to change her profile during the course of counselling. Once again, the client is asked to rate subjectively each modality on a score from 1 to 7. The desired Structural Profile can be thought of as another way of expressing general goals a client may wish to attain in counselling, while the Modality Profile lists specific target problems. Figure 2.2 illustrates Natalie's desired Structural Profile. The counsellor needs to be cautious at this point

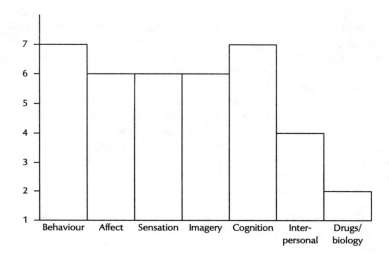

Figure 2.1   *Natalie's Structural Profile*

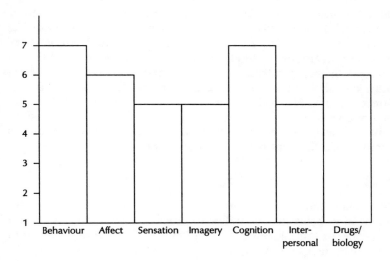

Figure 2.2   *Natalie's desired Structural Profile*

in case the client wants to modify factors that cannot be readily altered. This client believed that if she improved her general physical health, then her mental health would also improve. In counselling, while the counsellor worked on the major presenting problems, time was also spent looking at interventions in the drugs/ biology modality.

If it has been agreed to review the counselling every five sessions, then comparing the actual Structural Profile and the desired Structural Profile will form part of that review. Clients will often want to revise their desired Structured Profiles when reviewing their therapy. We have frequently noticed that clients may not initially wish to improve their drugs/biology modality. However, as they start benefiting from the different interventions, they become more convinced that improving this modality would be helpful. For example, as smokers learn to increase their frustration tolerance towards different aspects of their life, then giving up smoking is gradually perceived as less of an ordeal. A stop smoking programme becomes a new desired intervention. Another common example is when procrastinators start to reap the benefits of actually getting down to the work that they have been avoiding for some time. Later, when reviewing their desired Structural Profile, they then decide to increase their desired behaviour modality rating up to 7.

Multimodal counsellors who are involved with marital or couples counselling have also found that using Structural Profiles can provide a wealth of useful clinical information (Lazarus, 1981). For example, if one partner has a high interpersonal rating, while the other partner has a low score, their interpersonal needs are often in direct conflict. The high scorer may be very keen to socialize with family and friends, while the low scorer may avoid social events. This can lead to resentment with both parties. The counsellor can compare the different profiles and discuss them with both partners.

Tracking

The multimodal counsellor will always be looking out for interaction between the different modalities and any particular sequence or 'firing order' of the modalities that a client may experience in any specific problem situation (Lazarus, ed., 1985). This is important when considering the most suitable interventions for a particular problem. This is best illustrated with an example.

Case study
Peter wanted promotion at work. However, he never applied to be upgraded as his next step up the ladder would regularly involve making

presentations to a number of staff at meetings. When he had last attempted to speak to a group of people he had encountered difficulties. He was asked to present a prize to the winner of an annual sports event at his club and also make a short speech. Just before the presentation he had an image of himself being unable to speak, with his friends looking at him (imagery modality). He then experienced a rapid heart beat, clammy hands, shallow breathing and a dry mouth (sensation modality). As he stood up to speak he then thought 'This is awful. What's wrong with me. I'm going to really mess this up and look stupid' (cognitive modality). He quickly gave the prize to the winner and then made a speech that lasted under 30 seconds (escape–behaviour modality). Since that occasion, he had avoided (behaviour modality) giving speeches whenever possible. He tried using a relaxation exercise to help him deal with this problem but he did not find this useful.

Comment
Peter experienced an imagery–sensation–cognition–behaviour 'firing order' sequence. This is usually written in an annotated form, i.e. I–S–C–B. When analysing the sequence of the modalities it is useful to write them down as follows:

Firing order	Modality
1	Imagery: Self-image of being unable to speak with friends looking on
2	Sensation: Rapid heart beat, clammy hands, shallow breathing, dry mouth
3	Cognition: 'This is awful. What's wrong with me? I'm going to really mess this up and look stupid'
4	Behaviour: Escape

Peter agreed with his stress counsellor to take up the next offer of either speaking publicly or making a presentation. The therapeutic programme was linked to the sequence of the firing order of the modalities. The type and order of the interventions were as follows:

Intervention sequence	Modality	Intervention
1	Imagery	Coping image of performing reasonably well
2	Sensation	Breathing relaxation exercise (Benson relaxation response)
3	Cognition	Rational coping statement: 'It's unpleasant but not awful. It's just the effect of my body's stress response. It's unlikely

| | | that I will totally mess this up. If I do then it's not the end of the world and it does not mean that I am stupid |
| 4 | Behaviour | Stay in the situation |

The rationale for the use of the techniques was explained to Peter, particularly the order in which to use them. The stress counsellor advised Peter to practise the techniques daily before making a presentation, ensuring that he could easily apply them in the real situation. He practised imagining coping with the situation and seeing himself able to speak to a group of colleagues (imagery modality). He also practised a relaxation technique known as the Benson relaxation response (sensation modality). He regularly read his rational coping statement until he was able to remember it without reading from a card (cognitive modality). The counsellor explained that in his personal and clinical experience, prolonging the length of a presentation, and not avoiding or escaping from it prematurely, eventually helps to lower a person's overall anxiety about the task (behaviour modality).

Thirty minutes before the next presentation, Peter countered his negative imagery by picturing himself successfully making the presentation and just as he was about to give it, he started his relaxation technique. He still felt some bodily sensations so as he started to have a few negative thoughts he reminded himself of his rational coping statement. He remembered not to try to bring the presentation to a premature end, thereby receiving more exposure and practice. By the end of the presentation, much to his surprise, he was actually enjoying the experience.

Counsellors trained in other approaches often do not consider the firing order of the different modalities for a problem that a client presents. Thus, for anxiety, they may indiscriminately train every client to use a relaxation exercise in stressful situations. If a client experiences the firing of other modalities earlier in the sequence, relaxation exercises may not be helpful. In Peter's case, it was his image of not coping that initially greatly contributed to his stress response being activated and not the situation itself. The multimodal approach to stress counselling and stress management calls for the therapeutic programme to be matched to the individual needs of the client. Tracking is one of the methods that helps the multimodal stress counsellor to attain this goal. In our experience, if the initial firing order is elicited and a suitable intervention applied at the start of the sequence, then some clients find that they do not need to apply other interventions targeted to modalities fired later in the sequence. With other clients, as with Peter, the counsellor will need to help them use interventions targeted at each 'fired' modality in the order it is 'fired'.

Peter's case is an example of an 'imagery reactor': Peter would initially experience the firing of the imagery modality in a variety of stressful situations. Individuals often favour one or two modalities and may, for example, be known as a 'sensory reactor', a 'behavioural reactor' or a 'cognitive reactor', depending upon the modality that generally fires first. This information helps the counsellor determine the most suitable intervention for a particular client.

Bridging

A client may have one or two preferred modalities which he uses to communicate with the counsellor, but this may not help the counsellor to explore the other modalities. For example, a counsellor may ask a client how he feels (affect modality) about an event and the client responds by describing what actually happened and not how he felt. The client may have a clear image in his mind's eye of the event. A multimodal stress counsellor would not want to threaten the therapeutic alliance by confronting the client directly on this issue, i.e. by repetitively asking the client how he felt about the event in question. Indeed, the client may not even realize that he has unintentionally avoided the question. Here, the client is given the benefit of the doubt.

The counsellor may need to be creative in his or her approach to exploring the other relevant modalities. 'Bridging' involves a counsellor initially 'keying into' the client's preferred modality and then taking an indirect route via a second (and sometimes third) modality and then finally arriving at the avoided modality. The following example demonstrates the technique of 'bridging'.

Counsellor: When you heard the news, how did you feel about it?
Client: I remember the telephone ringing. I answered it and it was James. He told me how it happened. Jill had run out of school and straight out into the road and there just wasn't enough time for the car to stop. Fortunately, the ambulance came quickly and she was rushed off to hospital. I left for the hospital immediately. When I arrived, my daughter was there too. [*This story continued.*]
Counsellor: Jan, as you described what happened, you looked very tense. I wonder if you have any sensations in your body at the moment?
Client: Funny enough, I do! I have a vague headache. It's at the back of my head.

Counsellor: If you don't mind, I would like you just to concentrate on your headache for the moment. [*Pause*] How does if feel now?
Client: It feels much worse. I feel that it's going to explode.
Counsellor: Do you recall having this sort of headache before?
Client: Yes. [*Pause*] In fact, I've had it since James told me the news.
Counsellor: How's your headache now?
Client: It's getting worse.
Counsellor: Are you feeling any emotion at the moment?
Client: [*Pause*] I'm sad about what happened [*Cries*].
Counsellor: It may be helpful if we explore your sadness.

Comment

The counsellor allowed the client to tell her 'story' as she saw it without interruption. Bridging started when the counsellor asked the client if she was feeling any sensations. This helped to shift the client away from the cognitive modality. Exploring the sensation modality allowed the counsellor eventually to 'bridge' into the affect modality. This 'through the back door' method did not directly challenge the client and still led to the exploration of the desired modality. By focusing on one modality, another modality will often be triggered.

Multimodal counsellors will not insist that their clients must 'get into their gut feelings'. Some clients may find this direct approach unhelpful and sufficiently disturbing to leave counselling prematurely. For example, adult clients who have suffered from abuse in their childhood may be unable to or unwilling to go directly into their affect modality. By insisting that they 'get into their gut feelings' against their wishes the counsellor may unwittingly stimulate a re-enactment of the earlier trauma where the abuser held the power. This can seriously damage the therapeutic alliance and may be perceived as a further abuse of the client.

Bridging helps counsellors to make progress with clients who may sometimes be unfairly described as 'resistant' or 'difficult'.

Resistance

With some clients progress may either slow up or grind to a complete halt. Sometimes it may never seem to get off the ground! The counsellor occasionally perceives this as a form of 'resistance', whereby the client is intentionally or unintentionally frustrating the work of the counsellor. Sometimes the client may not undertake agreed homework assignments, forget the appointment, turn up late, or even withhold important information. This can also be seen as client 'resistance' by counsellors. But is it (see Lazarus and Fay, 1982)?

The multimodal stress counsellor would not necessarily hold this view. If an *impasse* appears to have been reached then the counsellor should ask him or herself a number of questions:

1 Was the intervention or technique I used suitable for this client? Did I apply it incorrectly?
2 If the client does not wish to undertake the homework assignment what is holding her back or preventing her from doing it? Can this barrier be circumnavigated?
3 Does the client understand why a certain intervention or technique was chosen?
4 Does the client trust me? Do I need to work on strengthening the therapeutic alliance before we tackle more difficult issues?
5 If the client improves and overcomes her target problems would this detrimentally affect relationships with significant others as perceived by the client?
6 Is the client avoiding certain issues because they are so painful to even think about or discuss?
7 Is the client ashamed to express emotion in the counselling session?
8 Was the homework assignment perceived by the client as relevant?
9 Is a significant other interfering or undermining the client's goals of counselling?
10 Is there a client–counsellor mismatch? Is a referral necessary?
11 Have I misunderstood the client's problems?
12 Am I demanding too much change, too soon?
13 Have I assessed the client incorrectly? Have I identified the antecedents or maintaining factors correctly?
14 Does the client wish to be in counselling? Was she sent by a court order, her parents, her teacher etc.? If so, can she be shown any benefits of staying in counselling?

The concept of client 'resistance' effectively blames the client for not complying or performing as well as the counsellor believes she should. It does not take into account the multi-faceted nature of the client–counsellor relationship or the meaning of change to the client. The social context is also often overlooked. Some counsellors, who inflexibly adhere to a specific therapeutic orientation, may decide that it really is an example of 'resistance' and as their intervention, according to their theory, is suitable, then they will carry on using it. Even though the client's condition may be getting worse, they reassure themselves that they are not deviating from their theoretical base and it is acceptable to continue. Meanwhile, the client may become very disturbed. This may be an extreme example but unfortunately it does occur. In some cases, a counsellor can become sufficiently angry about his or her so-called 'resistant' client that he or she can threaten the therapeutic alliance. By taking the multimodal view of 'resistance' this outcome is less likely to occur.

Structure of therapeutic session

We have found that the session format used in cognitive therapy is also very helpful in stress counselling or stress management (see Blackburn and Davidson, 1990). The structure allows the client to negotiate a working agenda for the session with the counsellor so that the time available is maximized. It allows the client and the counsellor to raise issues that they think are relevant to the therapeutic programme. It also helps to underpin the problem-focused approach and usually ensures that the counsellor is concentrating on the client's issues.

It is not assumed if a client arrives at a session feeling, for example, angry that he wishes to explore this topic. He may just have had an argument with somebody on the way to the session and a counsellor who spends the whole of the time on this issue may later wonder why the client has become angry or resentful towards him or her too. The counsellor may incorrectly come to believe that there is a problem of transference when in reality the client is quite rightly annoyed with the counsellor for wasting his time. The client may wish to discuss other more important issues than something that occurred on the way to the session.

The following list gives the basic format of a session in six steps:

1 Review client's present state
2 Set agenda
3 Review homework assignment(s)
4 Target problem
5 Negotiate homework assignment(s)
6 Session feedback

This is only a guide. In some circumstances it may be more appropriate to respond immediately to the problem that the client has presented. For example, if the client has a panic attack on entering the counselling room, insisting on using the structure may not help the client or the therapeutic alliance. However, in our experience, briefly setting the agenda may still be very helpful to ensure that the client achieves the most out of the session. This helps to prevent the counsellor's agenda coming to the fore.

Review client's present state
The session starts with the counsellor asking the client how he has been since the last session. It is essential to keep this as brief as possible as otherwise valuable therapeutic time may be wasted. If difficulties have arisen then the counsellor can ask the client whether he wishes to put it on the agenda. If the client has previously received a more non-directive form of counselling, then he may believe that he is expected to spend the next 30 minutes telling the counsellor about the nature of the problem.

Set agenda
The agenda for the session is then negotiated with the client. Each session lasts between 45 and 60 minutes depending upon what was initially agreed. Normally 60 minutes provides plenty of time to cover steps 1 to 6. However, we have found that a number of clients are unable to concentrate usefully for 60 minutes and prefer to have a 30-minute session. The multimodal approach emphasizes adapting the therapy to the client and not vice versa.

Generally, it is important not to explore each issue raised by the client in any depth at this stage. If the client starts recounting a recent event that he feels disturbed about then the counsellor can ask him whether he would like to put it on the agenda and remind him that they will return to it shortly. It is usually agreed to review any homework assignments that the client has undertaken since the last session and this is normally scheduled near the top of the agenda as the outcome of the homework assignments may affect the latter part of the counselling session. Thoughts and feelings about the last session may also be put on the agenda. If the client raises a number of different problem(s) to be covered in the session then putting them in order of priority is essential. If the counsellor does not believe that all the different issues can be successfully discussed in one session then this should be shared with the client so that they can mutually agree to transfer one or more of the issues to the following session. This can help to avoid possible resentment that could occur if the client thinks that all his important issues are not being covered in every session. This negotiation also helps to involve the client in 'his' therapy and in taking some responsibility for it.

Review homework assignment(s)
The next step in the sequence is to review the homework assignment(s) that were agreed in the previous session. This should not be overlooked as the client can become disheartened if the counsellor does not take an interest in homework. Such neglect can lead the

client to downplay the importance of completing his assignments and he may stop doing them. Important information is often gleaned from looking at the client's assignment tasks, especially when he has not managed to achieve the agreed targets. Any difficulties that he may have encountered will usually highlight different aspects of the overall problem and will help both client and counsellor to form a more accurate mutual understanding of the client's world.

The counsellor may need to explain to the client that sometimes there is insufficient time to examine every assignment the client may have undertaken. If thought or behavioural exposure diaries are used, it is likely that the client will present the counsellor with one for each day since the last session. When this happens, client and counsellor can choose together the diaries that they think are the most relevant. As previously, it is important not to spend too long discussing the homework tasks as this may leave insufficient time to look at the session targets. However, in the early stages of counselling it is often useful to schedule more time for this part of the session as the counsellor can often gain a clearer insight into the client's problems and difficulties from discussing the homework assignments.

Target problem

In the agenda-setting stage (step 2) the client may have raised certain targets that he wishes to cover in the present session. Usually in stress counselling the client's target is to become less stressed or disturbed about a problem situation. At this stage, the problem can be defined and then explored from the seven modalities of multimodal counselling. The client's main problems would have been transferred to the Modality Profile (or BASIC ID chart) in the early stages of therapy. The Modality Profile may be referred to in this step as the possible intervention(s) may have already been worked out. However, a second-order Modality Profile may be needed if specific problems are not being resolved and this would also be carried out at this point.

Negotiate homework assignment(s)

Depending upon the issues worked on in step 4, relevant homework assignment tasks are then negotiated between the counsellor and the client to help the client to put into practice what he has learned from work done in step 4. As these tasks are an essential part of multimodal stress counselling, the relevance and rationale for the task will need to be explained to ensure compliance. If the counsellor is unsure whether the client understands the reason for undertaking a specific homework assignment it is usually a good idea to ask the client to explain in his own words the relevance of the task and how it might help him to overcome or manage his session target.

We have found it a useful exercise not only to discuss with clients any problems they think they may encounter in undertaking the task but also to get them to complete an Assignment Task form (see Chapter 9, Box 9.1). In their own handwriting they write the nature of the agreed task, why, when and where they are going to undertake it, including any obstacles they may encounter in carrying out the task, and also how they may overcome such obstacles. We have found that if the client has a thorough understanding of how this assignment task may help him to overcome his problem then he is far more likely to undertake it. If the discussion of the rationale for the task is rushed, the client will be unlikely to grasp these important issues. Consequently, the counsellor needs to take responsibility for managing time in the session. Adequate time should be left to negotiate and explain the assignment tasks. While most counsellors refer to these tasks as 'homework', we have found that the word 'homework' can have negative connotations for some clients due to childhood experiences. Using a different phrase such as 'assignment tasks' can help overcome this problem.

Session feedback

In our experience of supervising counsellors, many do not leave sufficient time to receive feedback from the client on the session. It is important to ascertain whether the counsellor has said or done anything in the session that the client may have become upset about or if any aspect of the session was unclear. When they are stressed, it is common for clients to misunderstand or misinterpret comments, or instructions about interventions. These issues should be resolved before the client leaves the session otherwise they may impede future therapeutic progress. It is also useful to ask the client what he found helpful and unhelpful in the session.

Asking the client directly whether he has any additional comments or queries can help to clarify any points that he is bothered about. If an important issue is then raised and there is insufficient time to deal with it there and then, it can be rescheduled for the following counselling session. If this occurs, it is crucial for the counsellor to put it on the agenda for the following session and not discuss it in any depth as this can prolong the counselling session and, once allowed, it can establish a bad precedent. If the counsellor allows the session to be prolonged in this way, he or she is not serving as a good time-keeping role model. And if the session is prolonged, waiting clients may quite rightly feel aggrieved.

3

Cognitive Interventions

This chapter is in two parts. The first part focuses on the basic theory of cognitive therapy (Beck, 1976) and rational emotive behaviour therapy (Ellis, 1977). This will help the reader to understand the rationale for the application of the interventions and techniques described in the second part of the chapter.

Basic theory of cognitive therapy

> People are disturbed not by things but by the views which they take of them
>
> (Epictetus)

The words from the first-century philosopher Epictetus underpin the central tenet of cognitive interventions and techniques. When a person's beliefs are overly negative and/or unrealistic about an event she may be sufficiently disturbed to develop a psychological disorder such as anxiety, depression or obsessive-compulsive behaviour. Consider the example of an individual who has failed her exam. In behavioural terms, she has only failed an exam. However, if, in addition, she is telling herself, 'I've failed my exam. This proves I'm a total failure. I'm no good for anything anymore' then it is very likely that she will feel depressed and possibly ashamed too. Often the individual will also see in her mind's eye a negative image. In this example it could be a picture of her friends and relatives ridiculing her. Both the thoughts and the negative image contribute to her emotional distress. Aaron Beck (1976) describes these thoughts and images as 'automatic thoughts' which occur involuntarily. In addition, Beck's model focuses on the necessity of modifying deeper-level cognitive structures called 'schemas', the content of which lie dormant until triggered by relevant life-events (see Weishaar, 1993).

Albert Ellis has been described by Dryden (1991b: 7) as the 'Father of Rational-Emotive Therapy and the Grandfather of Cognitive-Behavioural Therapy'. Ellis (1962) hypothesized that 'irrational beliefs' are the major contributing factor in emotional disorders. These beliefs are evaluative and involve dogmatic and absolutist 'musts', 'oughts', 'shoulds', 'got tos' and 'have tos', which can lead to the following evaluative derivatives:

I am worthless because . . .
It's awful that . . .
I can't stand it that . . .

Ellis (1977) described an ABC model where A represented an Activating event which the individual had certain Beliefs about at B. This can lead to behavioural, emotional and physiological Consequences at C. If the previous example is now analysed in greater depth using this ABC model the picture becomes clearer:

A =	Activating event	Failing exam
B =	Beliefs	
	(a) Inference	'I didn't work hard enough'
	(b) Evaluation	'I absolutely should have passed'
		'I am a total failure and worthless because I failed'
		'It's awful that I failed'
		'I can't stand it that I failed'
C =	Emotional consequence	Depression
	Behavioural consequence	Future avoidance of relatives and friends
	Physiological consequence	Difficulties with digestion

A mathematical formula can be used to highlight the relationship between A, B and C:

$$A \times B = C$$

However, a more complex formula is probably required to express the relationship fully (see Dryden, 1991a).

Beck et al. (1979) and Burns (1980) both believe that thought or cognitive distortions are a major feature of emotional disturbance. However, Dryden (1991a: 17) asserts that the distortions are almost always derived from 'musturbatory' beliefs. The following are the most frequent:

1 All-or-none-thinking: 'If I fail at any important task, as I must not, I'm a total failure and completely unlovable!'
2 Jumping to conclusions and negative non-sequiturs: 'Since they have seen me dismally fail, as I should not have done, they will view me as an incompetent worm.'

3 Fortune-telling: 'Because they are laughing at me for failing, they know that I should have succeeded, and they will despise me forever.'

4 Focusing on the negative: 'Because I can't stand things going wrong, as they must not, I can't see any good that is happening in my life.'

5 Disqualifying the positive: 'When they compliment me on the good things I have done, they are only being kind to me and forgetting the foolish things that I should not have done.'

6 Allness and neverness: 'Because conditions of living ought to be good and actually are so bad and so intolerable, they'll always be this way and I'll never have any happiness.'

7 Minimization: 'My good shots in this game were lucky and unimportant. But my bad shots, which I should never have made, were as bad as could be and were totally unforgivable.'

8 Emotional reasoning: 'Because I have performed so poorly, as I should not have done, I feel like a total nincompoop, and my strong feeling proves that I am no damned good!'

9 Labelling and overgeneralization: 'Because I must not fail at important work and have done so, I am a complete loser and failure!'

10 Personalizing: 'Since I am acting far worse than I should act and they are laughing, I am sure they are only laughing at me, and that is awful!'

11 Phoneyism: 'When I don't do as well as I ought to do and they still praise and accept me, I am a real phoney and will soon fall on my face and show them how despicable I am!'

12 Perfectionism: 'I realize that I did fairly well, but I should have done perfectly well on a task like this and am therefore really an incompetent!'

In counselling, clients are helped to recognize their cognitive distortions and challenge them.

In certain circumstances, many individuals believe that it is appropriate to experience an emotion. For example, a father may feel very guilty about shouting at his daughter as he is breaking one of his own moral codes. We have found it very useful to explore with clients whether they believe another more appropriate, more healthy and helpful negative emotion would enable them to cope with their situation more effectively and constructively. If the client cannot find an alternative then the options in Table 3.1 are discussed.

If we return to the previous example, the evaluative belief usually involved with guilt is: 'I should not have broken my moral code. I

Table 3.1   *Unhealthy and healthy negative emotions and their cognitive correlates*

Inference[1] related to personal domain[2]	Type of belief	Emotion	Healthiness of emotion
Threat or danger	Irrational	Anxiety	Unhealthy
Threat or danger	Rational	Concern	Healthy
Loss (with implications for future); failure	Irrational	Depression	Unhealthy
Loss (with implications for future); failure	Rational	Sadness	Healthy
Breaking of own moral code	Irrational	Guilt	Unhealthy
Breaking of own moral code	Rational	Remorse	Healthy
Breaking of personal rule (other or self); other threatens self; frustration	Irrational	Damning anger	Unhealthy
Breaking of personal rule (other or self); other threatens self; frustration	Rational	Non-damning anger (or annoyance)	Healthy
Personal weakness revealed publicly	Irrational	Shame/ Embarrassment	Unhealthy
Personal weakness revealed publicly	Rational	Regret	Healthy
Other betrays self (self non-deserving)	Irrational	Hurt	Unhealthy
Other betrays self (self non-deserving)	Rational	Disappointment	Healthy
Threat to desired exclusive relationship	Irrational	Morbid jealousy	Healthy
Threat to desired exclusive relationship	Rational	Non-morbid jealousy	Healthy

[1] Inference = an interpretation which goes beyond observable reality, but which gives meaning to it. It may be accurate or inaccurate.
[2] The objects – tangible and intangible – in which a person has an involvement constitute his/her personal domain (Beck, 1976).

am a rotten person for doing so.' In this case the person is not accepting the reality as he did break his moral code. If he changes his belief to: 'I would very strongly prefer not to break my moral code but as I am a fallible person, there's no law that states that I must not break it', he is more likely to feel remorse. He may still feel bad but less damning of himself. Remorse is also less self-defeating as an emotion as he may still interact with his child instead of avoiding her. He is more likely to react with a short fuse if he continued staying guilty than if he suffered remorse. In Table 3.1 unhealthy emotions involve evaluative beliefs such as 'musts' and their evaluative conclusions such as 'therefore I'm worthless'.

Dryden (1990) believes that one major way individuals can perpetuate their psychological disturbances is when they further disturb themselves (secondary disturbance) about their original disturbance. In the previous example the parent was guilty about his anger and later could possibly have become depressed about his guilt. This can be expressed:

Primary disturbance   = Anger
Secondary disturbance = Guilt
Tertiary disturbance = Depression

In counselling, these disturbance chains need to be assessed and discussed with clients in case they are unable to work on their primary disturbance in the counselling session as they find the secondary disturbance too upsetting. In this example, if the parent wanted help to control his anger, he might find that he felt so guilty thinking about what he had done that he would not be able to concentrate on the counselling session unless the guilt were dealt with first.

The techniques and interventions described in the next section help the counsellor to dispute and challenge inaccurate inferences, cognitive distortions, and evaluative beliefs which contribute to an individual's level of psychological distress.

Bibliotherapy and bibliotraining

In bibliotherapy/bibliotraining the client uses relevant self-help books, manuals, videos and audio-tapes at the counsellor's suggestion. This helps her to understand the cause and subsequent management or cure of her emotional distress. The counsellor suggests that the client reads literature on the relevant topic that will aid her recovery. This is usually set as a homework assignment.

It has been found that if individuals suffering from mild depression or anxiety, who are on a waiting list for counselling, are sent suitable self-help books (for example, Burns, 1989; Marks, 1980), then often they will not need to receive formal therapy. This highlights the effectiveness of self-help literature without any input from the counsellor. We have successfully used bibliotherapy on a wide range of subjects including stress management, anger management, asthma, assertion, backache, diet, exercise, massage, problem-solving, public speaking, relaxation, safer sex, self-hypnosis, smoking cessation, and sulking. Counsellors will need to maintain a collection of different articles, leaflets and books on a variety of subjects.

Indications and contraindications

Assuming that the counsellor provides relevant and suitable literature, this intervention is probably indicated with most clients. If a client is unable to read, then audio-cassettes or videos may be the preferred choice of bibliotherapy. During counselling the intervention is contraindicated if the counsellor does not allow sufficient time for the client to discuss any problems or mis-understandings that may have arisen from reading the literature.

Challenging cognitive distortions

Cognitive distortions commonly occur in inferences (see next section). The client can be given a list of the common cognitive distortions with examples (see pp. 46–7). Then the client can be asked if he recognizes any distortions that he regularly makes and whether they help him deal with a situation more effectively. The counsellor highlights that cognitive distortions do not usually help a person deal with problems or events.

Burns (1989) lists ten ways that clients can help themselves to 'untwist' their thinking. Initially, the counsellor can use the techniques in the counselling session to show clients how to apply them. With regular practice, clients can start using the techniques without the counsellor's help. The following are adapted from Burns (1989: 118–19):

1 *Identify the distortions.* The client is asked to monitor his negative thoughts and write down any cognitive distortions that he can recognize. Once the client can label the thought as a cognitive distortion or a 'twisted' thought it can help the client to see the problem more realistically.

2 *Examine the evidence.* The client is encouraged to assess the actual evidence for his negative thought and not to automatically believe that it is true. For example, if a parent believes that his teenage child never helps around the house, he can make a list of the things that the teenager actually does contribute.

3 *The double-standard method.* If a client heavily condemns himself for some action, he is asked to consider how he would

treat a friend in the same situation. Would he condemn his friend? It is also sometimes useful to ask the client why he is so special to deserve harsh treatment whereas his friend would be spared his complete condemnation?

4 *The experimental technique.* Undertake an experiment to test the validity of a negative thought. For example, clients who are phobic of lifts and believe that they could not stand being in one for more than 30 seconds could attempt to stay in a lift for 90 seconds.

5 *Thinking in shades of grey.* Instead of thinking of problems in all-or-nothing terms the client can assess the situation on a 0–100 scale. For example, instead of thinking of an experience as an absolute failure, all the different aspects of it could be rated on a 0–100 success scale.

6 *The survey method.* The client is encouraged to ask his friends and colleagues whether they agree with the client's negative thoughts and general beliefs. For example, is it unnatural to feel anxious about taking a driving test? Will they see the client as a complete failure if the driving test is failed?

7 *Define terms.* If clients use emotive terms such as 'fool', 'idiot', 'loser', 'bastard' etc. to describe themselves or others the counsellor can ask questions that help the client focus on the exact meaning of the label. For example, 'What exactly is the definition of an "idiot"?' 'Would a complete idiot ever manage to get up in the morning?' 'Is it just a description of one aspect of a person's behaviour?' 'Can one aspect of a person's behaviour make them a complete "idiot"?' 'Would a complete idiot ever manage to turn up for a counselling session?'

8 *The semantic method.* The client is encouraged to substitute extreme and emotive language with beliefs that are less evocative. For example, 'I must give a good speech' could become 'It's preferable to give a good speech.'

9 *Re-attribution.* Instead of self-blame or blaming others for a particular problem, the client is encouraged to think about all the different factors that may have contributed to it. Then he is asked to concentrate on solving the problem as opposed to feeling guilty or angry about it.

10 *Cost-benefit analysis.* The client is asked to list the pros and cons of having a particular feeling, negative thought, negative image or behaviour. For example, becoming angry in traffic queues; thinking that he is absolutely useless or 'I must be a good parent'; persistently picturing himself performing badly; binge eating or avoiding friends.

Fennell (1989: 225–31, adapted) suggests that clients can ask themselves a number of different questions to help challenge negative thinking:

What is the evidence for my belief?
Am I jumping to conclusions?
What alternatives are there to my belief?
Am I assuming my view of things is the only one possible?
What is the effect of thinking the way I do?
What are the advantages and disadvantages of thinking this way?
Am I asking questions that have no answers?
What thinking errors am I making?
Am I thinking in all-or-nothing terms?
Am I using ultimatum words in my thinking?
Am I totally condemning myself (or somebody else) on the basis of a single event?
Am I concentrating on my weaknesses and neglecting my strengths?
Am I blaming myself for something which is not really my fault?
Am I taking things personally which have little or nothing to do with me?
Am I expecting myself to be perfect?
Am I using a double standard?
Am I only paying attention to the negative side of things?
Am I overestimating the chances of disaster?
Am I exaggerating the importance of events?
Am I fretting about how things should be, instead of accepting and dealing with them as they are?
Am I assuming I cannot do anything to alter my situation?
Is the outcome really going to be catastrophic?
Am I predicting the outcome instead of experimenting with it?

It is helpful if the client has a list of these questions and uses them to challenge negative thoughts and cognitive distortions. With slight changes, counsellors can also use these questions to challenge their client's thinking.

Indications and contraindications
Assuming that the client understands how challenging his thinking errors or cognitive distortions may help to reduce his level of distress, then the techniques used and questions asked are suitable for most clients. However, a good therapeutic alliance is essential otherwise it is easy for clients to believe that they, rather than their cognitive distortions, are being challenged. Humour can be effectively used to help dispute beliefs, but it is important to ensure

that clients realize that their thoughts and not themselves are the target of the humour.

Clients with particular disorders such as severe depression or paranoid schizophrenia may require drug therapy to alleviate or stabilize their condition before these techniques can be safely used. In the case of severe depression, clients may also benefit initially from a behavioural programme to encourage them to become more active before cognitive interventions are applied. Clients suffering from personality disorders may benefit from these techniques too, but once again, they can become disturbed about the questions asked and this can affect the therapeutic relationship.

Challenging faulty inferences

In any situation, an individual is likely to make accurate or inaccurate inferences about what is happening and what other individuals involved may be thinking. Clients often reach the wrong conclusions and this can exacerbate their emotional disturbance. As cognitive distortions commonly occur in inferences, the techniques described in the previous section may prove helpful.

Trower et al. (1988: 3) outline a simple ABC analysis of a situation where A is the Activating event, B is the client's Beliefs about A, and C is the emotional and behavioural Consequences mediated by B.

A = Activating event		Work colleague fails to acknowledge the person
B = Beliefs		
	(a) Inferences	'My colleague has ignored me' 'He must be angry with me' 'He probably dislikes me'
	(b) Evaluation	'It's awful if someone dislikes you'
C = Emotional consequence		Depression
Behavioural consequence		Future avoidance of colleague

In this example, Trower et al. suppose that the client is walking down a road and a work colleague walks past without acknowledging him. After writing down the ABC analysis, the counsellor explores the three inferences with the client and helps him to consider alternative inferences that may be more accurate: perhaps the colleague was day-dreaming or deep in thought and was unaware of the client; perhaps the colleague was upset and normally ignores everybody when in this state. The colleague's behaviour may not be due to her being angry with the client or disliking him. The evaluation 'it's awful' can also be disputed (see 'Disputing irrational beliefs' below).

Listed below are some examples of questions that are useful when challenging and disputing negative inferences. The questions are targeted on the inference from the example of Trower et al. (1988) 'My colleague has ignored me':

Where is the evidence that she ignored you?
What else could explain her behaviour?
Could she have been absorbed in her own thoughts?
Could this be an example of you mind-reading?
Is it possible that you could be jumping to conclusions?
Have you ever unintentionally not seen a colleague?

Indications and contraindications

Challenging inferences is indicated for most clients. As the technique does not necessarily challenge the underlying irrational beliefs or assumptions, it is generally less confrontational and therefore more acceptable. However, Ellis (Dryden, 1991b) advocates disputing the evaluations before the inferences as he believes that the main emotional disturbance is due to the underlying irrational evaluative beliefs.

Cognitive focusing

Cognitive focusing is adapted from an intervention developed by a person-centred therapist, Eugene Gendlin (1981). The technique is used to help clients to identify the underlying cause of their personal unhappiness (see McMullin, 1986) and, in addition, it can have a desensitizing effect. The counsellor asks the client to make himself comfortable, and then to relax. The client is then asked passively to observe any spontaneous thoughts, images and feelings. If and when a specific feeling arises that the client becomes absorbed with, she is encouraged to concentrate on it for a couple of minutes. She is then asked if she can discover something new from the emotions, images and sensations. By using this technique, the client's irrational or core beliefs may shift and subsequently lessen her emotional disturbance. Cognitive focusing sometimes allows new ideas and issues to surface which are then discussed in counselling.

Indications and contraindications

The technique is indicated when the root cause of a client's unhappiness is uncertain. It is contraindicated if a client is suffering from a severe psychiatric disorder.

Constructive self-talk

Quick and Quick (1984) describe a technique which they call 'constructive self-talk' and report that it helped individuals cognitively to reappraise stressful situations. In a given situation an individual may have a 'typical mental monologue' or 'negative self-talk' which is not constructive and does not help the person deal with the problem. The counsellor or trainer first encourages the client to recognize the negative self-talk. Once it is identified, it is written down, sentence by sentence. Then opposite each sentence a constructive self-talk alternative is developed. Initially, the counsellor will probably need to help the client develop a constructive alternative statement. However, with much practice, the client will eventually be able to undertake this exercise by herself without the need to resort to writing the thoughts down. Table 3.2 illustrates a number of examples that can be shown to a client to highlight the technique.

The counsellor should initially discuss the technique with the client. A copy of Table 3.2 may help to illustrate how the technique is applied. Then the client is asked to describe a situation that she is disturbed about. The client can rate on a scale 0–100 how stressed she is about the situation. The first two columns in Table 3.2 are completed. Then the client is asked whether she can think of a constructive self-talk alternative. Only if the client is unable to achieve this task does the counsellor offer suggestions.

The counsellor needs to ensure that any alternative that may be found challenges the corresponding negative self-talk. Some individuals have spent many years of their lives perceiving situations negatively. Frequently, alternatives they offer will not reduce their stress for a given situation. To check whether the alternative may prove helpful, the counsellor can ask the client the following question: 'If you believed this alternative, would you feel less stressed about this situation?' If the answer is 'No', then it is likely that the alternative has not accurately targeted the relevant negative self-talk, and/or other thoughts need to be targeted too. It is important that the alternative is sufficiently believable otherwise the client will not find it helpful. Once the task is completed, the client can also be asked to re-rate on the scale of 0–100 how stressed she feels about the situation. If the technique has been successful, the client's score should be lower than the initial rating.

Regularly, a table similar to Table 3.2 is completed and the client is asked to read it before the feared event occurs. If a practical solution has also been suggested, such as writing key points on cards to jog the client's memory (see Table 3.2), then the client will

Table 3.2   *Constructive self-talk*

Situation	Negative self-talk	Constructive self-talk alternative
Anticipation of arriving late for an important meeting	This is going to look so awful	I may be late but it's not the end of the world
	I'll never get that promotion	It's unlikely I'll be judged by one event
	I'm going to appear so nervous	I can take this opportunity to use my relaxation exercise and breathe slowly
Fear of giving a wedding speech	Will they laugh at my jokes and stories?	They will probably laugh at some of them
	My mouth always goes dry when I speak publicly	This time I'll ensure that I've got a glass of water on the table before I speak
	I might forget what I want to say again	This time I'll prepare the speech and write key points on cards to jog my memory
	I always get nervous when people look at me	These are only my friends and relatives; I'll focus on the far corners of the room
Returning an item to a shop	This is going to be so embarrassing	I'll choose a quiet moment. If it does become busy, I'll try to ignore the others behind me
	What if they don't believe it's faulty?	I'll ask them to try it out in the shop
	What if they don't believe I bought it there?	Before I go, I'll find the receipt. That's more than enough proof
	What if they refuse to take it back?	Right is on my side. I can always contact the manufacturer and claim on the guarantee
Going to a job interview	I really must get this job	If I carry on thinking this way I'm really going to become nervous and then I am less likely to get it!
	What if I foul up?	Although there is a chance I'll make a number of mistakes it's unlikely I'll completely foul up
	I know that I'm just wasting their and my time	I may be the person they are looking for. If I'm not they may think I have other strengths they could use. Anyway, this interview will be good practice. My performance is improving each time

need to set aside time to achieve this goal. In some cases the counsellor may need to help plan and prepare for the situation; for example encouraging the client to write down key points on speech cue cards, or to learn relaxation or breathing techniques.

Constructive self-talk is not just positive thinking, but a form of guided self-dialogue (Meichenbaum, 1985). It encourages the client to become more active in her own problem-solving and enhances cognitive self-control.

Indications

This technique is indicated when a client's attitude towards a stressor is contributing to her level of distress. Unlike some cognitive interventions, such as disputation of irrational beliefs, the constructive self-talk technique is less confrontational. Therefore, many clients find it relatively straightforward. Unfortunately, as the technique is not always targeted at irrational beliefs, cognitive distortions or underlying assumptions, it will not necessarily be so effective. However, in crisis intervention or with clients with low cognitive abilities, constructive self-talk can be very helpful. One of the technique's advantages is that clients can easily learn and apply it to many situations. The technique can also be taught in group stress counselling or stress management workshops. The participants can be divided into groups of three and they can help each other complete a similar form to Table 3.2.

Correcting misconceptions

It is possible for clients to hold misconceptions regarding health and other related issues. If misconceptions are expressed by the client during counselling, the counsellor should use his or her understanding of the topic to explain the facts clearly in a simple but non-patronizing manner.

For example, after receiving the results of a smear test, a number of our female clients have confused the term 'abnormal cells' with cancer. Understandably, a client may be extremely anxious when her doctor has informed her that she has abnormal cells, but has neglected to discuss the exact nature of the condition and the implications for treatment. The counsellor can tell the client that abnormal cells are not necessarily cancer cells and suggest educational leaflets or booklets on the subject for the client to read. The counsellor can also encourage the client to act assertively and ask her doctor questions that she wants answered.

The requirements placed upon a counsellor to be able to help clients correct misconceptions are great. A good all-round general knowledge of many topics is useful. The ability to realize that a client has a misconception about a certain topic is important, as the issue may not be raised by the client. One of the questions a counsellor can ask him or herself is 'Would I be as anxious as my client if I understood all the facts?' If the answer is 'no', then this may be a rough indicator that the client is holding a misconception. However, the client may also hold dysfunctional or irrational beliefs (see below) that are also contributing to her level of distress. We agree with Lazarus (1971) who stated 'the bulk of psychotherapeutic endeavours may be said to center around the correction of misconceptions' (p. 165).

Indications
This intervention can be used with all clients. However, it is important that the counsellor has an accurate understanding of the topic being discussed otherwise unintentional misinformation can be given which may result in the client, in some circumstances, experiencing further distress. Counsellor misinformation can also negatively affect the therapeutic alliance. Sometimes information needs to be conveyed with great sensitivity as the client may have held misconceptions on certain issues for a long time. In some cases, the misconception may have helped to lower the client's anxiety; for example, ignoring the serious nature of an illness.

Deserted Island technique

We have already mentioned the importance of disputing irrational beliefs (see Ellis and Dryden, 1987). However, it is useful to show clients the benefits of giving up these beliefs before they are disputed. One of us (see Palmer, 1992b, 1993a) has developed the 'Deserted Island' technique to demonstrate to clients that holding on to irrational beliefs, and not necessarily the activating event or situation, can lead to unhelpful emotions or a heightened emotional disturbance. Unhelpful emotions include damning anger, anxiety, depression, guilt, morbid jealousy and shame, instead of more helpful and healthy emotions such as annoyance, concern, sadness, remorse, non-morbid jealousy and regret (see Dryden, 1987). The Deserted Island technique is not to be confused with the Deserted Island fantasy developed by Lazarus (1971, 1989a) to assess interpersonal functioning. He asks clients to envision themselves on the island with a designated companion (someone the client does not already know) and inquires how they will wile away the time. Interesting trends and insights tend to emerge from this exercise.

A typical transcript of a counselling session using the Deserted Island technique follows:

> *Counsellor*: Let's say, for example, you've been left on a deserted island. You have all your needs such as accommodation and food met, but one thing you don't have on the island is any friends. Imagine being on the island and you hold the belief: I really would prefer to have a friend with me on the island but I don't have to have one. How would you feel about your situation?
>
> *Client*: I would be concerned I didn't have anybody to share it with.
>
> *Counsellor*: Now, let's say that you're still on the island but this time your belief is: I must, I must, I really must have a friend on the island. How would you feel this time?
>
> *Client*: Pretty anxious.
>
> *Counsellor*: Let's just stay with this for the moment. Just imagine that an aeroplane flies over and a friend of yours jumps out and parachutes slowly towards the deserted island. Now imagine that you are still holding the beliefs: I must, I must, I really must have a friend on the island. Then your friend lands on the island. How do you feel now?
>
> *Client*: Very relieved.
>
> *Counsellor*: After a period of time, let's imagine that you are still holding the belief: I must, I must, I really must have a friend on the island. Don't forget, you've still got your friend on the island with you. Can you foresee anything that could happen that you could become upset about again?
>
> *Client*: The friend could be taken away.
>
> *Counsellor*: So even though you have your friend on the island, after a period of time your anxiety might return, especially if you feared that your friend could be taken away.
>
> *Client*: Yeah.
>
> *Counsellor*: Let's change it slightly again. You're still on the island and your friend is there and this time you're holding on to the belief: I really would prefer to have a friend with me on the island but I don't have to have one. Would you feel anxious this time?
>
> *Client*: No. I'd be much better.
>
> *Counsellor*: Can you see that in each example I've described similar situations? The only difference has been your beliefs and the different beliefs evoked different emotions. The 'must' belief led to you feeling 'pretty anxious', while the preference belief led you to feeling just 'concerned'.
>
> *Client*: Yeah.

With the Deserted Island technique clients will often experience the unhealthy emotions of anxiety or depression when holding 'musturbatory' beliefs and the healthier emotions of concern or sadness when holding 'preferential' beliefs. After demonstrating any model to a client, it is useful to ask the client whether they have understood it. If there is any doubt, it is usually a good idea to ask the client to explain what the example demonstrated. Once the technique has been clearly understood, then the counsellor can start to dispute irrational beliefs the client may hold (see 'Disputing irrational beliefs' below).

The Deserted Island technique has also been used in stress management workshops in industrial settings. The counsellor or trainer asks every participant in turn, at each stage of the demonstration, how they would feel in the given situation with the different beliefs. In group settings, the participants are usually surprised that they may experience different or slightly different emotions from their colleagues.

Indications and contraindications

This technique can be used with most clients. However, if a client is suffering grief after a bereavement, in the early stages of counselling demonstrating how different beliefs can lead to different emotional states could have a negative effect on the therapeutic relationship. The same may apply with clients who are depressed about a partner leaving them.

Disputing irrational beliefs

At the assessment stage in multimodal counselling irrational beliefs are noted in the Modality Profile. However, as counselling proceeds, the Modality Profile will need to be updated as more irrational beliefs are found. Before these beliefs are disputed, it is important that the counsellor shows the client how the beliefs lead to heightened emotional disturbance and unhelpful behaviour, such as procrastination or avoidance. Once this has been illustrated, then the counsellor can dispute the irrational beliefs.

Rational emotive behavioural counsellors have developed a number of different methods to highlight to clients the desirability of relinquishing 'musturbatory' beliefs and replacing them with 'preferential' beliefs. One example, the Deserted Island technique, has already been described (see above). Ellis (1977) suggests that clients are taught a simple five-stage ABCDE model to help them dispute their irrational beliefs and formulate healthier alternatives. To help the client to practise the method outside the counselling session a 'thought form' is used (see Table 3.3). In the model, A represents an Activating event that the client is disturbed about; B represents Beliefs about the event; C represents the emotional and behavioural Consequences; D represents the Disputing of the irrational beliefs; E represents Effective new beliefs, emotions and behaviours.

The counsellor demonstrates to the client in the counselling

Table 3.3 *Thought form to help clients to dispute irrational beliefs*

A Activating event/problem	B Self-defeating beliefs	C Emotional/behavioural consequences	D Disputing beliefs	E Effective new beliefs, emotions and behaviours
Giving a public lecture	'I must perform well otherwise the outcome will be awful'	Anxious; inability to concentrate	*Logical:* Just because I want to perform well, how does it logically follow that I must perform well?	Although it's strongly preferable to perform well, I don't have to
			Empirical: Where is the evidence that my demand must be granted?	There is no evidence that I will get what I demand even if it is preferable and desirable
			Am I being realistic? If I don't perform well will the outcome really be awful?	If I don't perform well, the outcome may be bad, but hardly awful and devastating!
			Pragmatic: Where is it getting me holding on to this belief?	If I continue holding on to this belief, I will remain anxious and even more likely to perform badly
				If I change my attitude I will feel concerned and *not* anxious. Also, I'll be able to concentrate and prepare for the lecture

Instructions: Write your problem or activating event in column A. Note in column C your unhealthy and unhelpful emotion(s). These are anger, depression, anxiety, guilt, shame. The healthy alternatives are annoyance, sadness, concern, remorse, regret. Irrational beliefs consist of dogmatic musts, shoulds, have tos, 'I can't stand it', 'it's awful' statements which are placed in column B. Disputes are logical (how does it follow?), empirical (where is the evidence?) and pragmatic (where is holding on to this belief going to get me?). These are written in column D. Rational alternatives consist of wishes, desires and wants and are placed in column E. Effective behaviours help you deal with the situation in a helpful manner.

session how to use the thought form. A simple problem to which the client has an unhealthy or unhelpful emotional response is chosen. This is written in column A. The unhealthy emotional and behavioural response is written in column C. The irrational beliefs are noted in column B. These beliefs are then disputed in column D using logical, empirical and pragmatic (heuristic) disputes:

Logical: How does it logically follow . . .?
Empirical: Where is the evidence for . . .?
Pragmatic: Where is holding on to this belief going to get you . . .?

New beliefs, healthy emotions and effective behaviours are written in column E. It is important that the counsellor ensures that the client appreciates that it is B that largely contributes to C and not A, otherwise they will not gain a great deal from this method. Clients will need to practise disputing their irrational beliefs regularly using this thought form. Eventually they will be able to recognize their beliefs and dispute them mentally without using the form.

Additionally, counsellors can ask their clients some of the following questions in order to dispute 'it's awful/terrible/ devastating' or 'I can't stand it' irrational beliefs:

What makes that awful/terrible/devastating?
Is it really that awful?
Just because it felt awful, how does that make it awful?
Awful. Do you really mean that it was the end of the world?
Can you think of anything worse?
Is it really as bad as your finger dropping off?
I can see that it was very bad but how does that make it awful?
If you can't stand it what will happen to you?
When you say that you 'can't stand it' what do you picture happening to you?
Where's the evidence that you can't stand it?
Surely you're living evidence that you have stood it for *x* months/ years? Of course, you may have stood it miserably.

When the client is asked these questions, it is important to leave sufficient time for the client to respond. The questions may need to be phrased differently to make them relevant.

Indications and contraindications

Assuming that the client is literate, the use of this thought form is applicable with all non-psychotic clients who wish to use it. If the client is unable to use the form, the counsellor can still use the three main disputes to help challenge the client's irrational beliefs. Often the pragmatic dispute is the most effective in encouraging the client to relinquish her strongly held irrational belief because as long as she holds on to the belief she will stay emotionally disturbed and not attain her desired goals. The pragmatic dispute is particularly useful in industrial stress management workshops and group stress counselling.

Problem-solving training

Several psychologists have developed and used problem-solving approaches to training and counselling (e.g. Hawton and Kirk, 1989; Meichenbaum, 1985; Palmer, 1994). Problem-solving is a method of dealing with problems that require a practical solution and also with problems that the client is emotionally disturbed about.

One of the common factors of problem-solving training is a step-by-step approach. According to Wasik (1984), clients can reduce the problem-solving steps down to the following questions:

	Steps	*Questions/actions*
1	Problem identification	What is the concern?
2	Goal selection	What do I want?
3	Generation of alternatives	What can I do?
4	Consideration of consequences	What might happen?
5	Decision-making	What is my decision?
6	Implementation	Now do it!
7	Evaluation	Did it work?

If the problem-solving approach seems suitable for use with the client (see Indications, below), steps 1–7 are briefly explained. At step 1 the client is asked for a problem or concern that he wishes to resolve. The client's response or reaction to a stressor can be defined as a problem that needs solving; for example, depression or anxiety about a forthcoming event. Very stressful events may need to be reduced to smaller, more manageable stressors. (The identification of the client's personal assets, strengths and supports may prove to be useful if this was previously undertaken in counselling.)

Step 2 involves the setting of realistic goals. It is useful if the goals are stated in behavioural and emotional terms. The counsellor needs to challenge unrealistic goals to avoid later disappointment.

At step 3 the counsellor encourages the client to think of many possible ways to reach his goals. Brain-storming, whereby all possible solutions are written down on a large sheet of paper without criticism by the counsellor, can be a helpful technique. Some of the most ridiculous ideas may be the embryo of a good solution. One of the other methods of encouraging a variety of options at this stage is to ask the client to imagine what his friend or somebody he admires would do in a similar situation.

At step 4 the advantages and disadvantages of the different solutions are considered. It is useful at this stage to assess the possible consequences of undertaking the more desirable options. For example, if one option involves acting in an assertive manner, how would the other person react? Would the person become violent? Would the client lose their job? In this example it cannot be assumed that assertive behaviour would always lead to the client attaining his desired goal. These issues are discussed at this stage.

At step 5 the client finally decides which solution is the most feasible and most likely to succeed, with the least negative consequences.

At step 6 the counsellor or trainer helps the client to break down the chosen solution into manageable steps. The client can be asked to practise or rehearse the agreed client behaviour in the counselling session. For example, a client who decided to be assertive with her demanding boss practised saying 'I'm taking 45 minutes for lunch now. I'll be back at two. I'll finish the letter for you on my return.' In the counselling session, the counsellor acted the role of her boss and tried to persuade her not to take her lunch break. At this stage the client can be taught coping imagery to help her deal with the predicted stressful situation. Contingency plans can be drawn up (Meichenbaum, 1985), and enacted in imagery to help the client not only deal with the situation but also reduce her anxiety prior to the situation. In addition to the behaviour and imagery modalities, clients often find techniques taken from the other modalities useful such as breathing exercises (sensory modality) to control anxiety.

The counsellor may find it clinically helpful to undertake a second-order Modality Profile (see Chapter 2) to see if any other techniques could be applied. For example, the Modality Profile may highlight that the client has a number of irrational beliefs or cognitive distortions that would need to be disputed before the client undertakes the agreed solution. A common belief that a client may hold is that if he does not achieve his desired goal, then 'I would be a complete failure'. If the client holds on to this particular belief then there is a strong likelihood that he will not attempt the agreed task due to his fear of failing.

The final stage of the process is step 7 where the counsellor and the client evaluate the outcome of the chosen solution. This normally happens at the next counselling session, although it is sometimes undertaken in a telephone counselling session when necessary. If the client did not attain his goals then the counsellor will discuss with the client what has actually been learnt from the exercise. Not achieving goals is not seen as failure as useful information can often be gleaned from most situations. This can be used later to aid decision-making when examining other problems.

In the next counselling session, the homework assignment can be reviewed. Then the problem-solving method is repeated from steps 1–6. A new problem can be tackled or the earlier problem can be examined again if it was not resolved. This particular approach to problem-solving training, where clients are encouraged to ask themselves specific questions at each step, eventually helps them to apply the method without the counsellor's help. To help the learning process clients can keep diaries of their stressful problems and record their answers to the relevant questions that relate to steps 1–7.

Indications and contraindications
A problem-solving approach is normally very helpful in stress counselling, stress and crisis management. Additionally, once the method has been taught, the client can use it to prevent future situations or life-events becoming overwhelming. Hawton and Kirk (1989: 407) list a range of problems where the problem-solving approach may be relevant and effective:

- threatened loss
- actual loss
- conflicts in which a person is faced by a major choice
- marital and other relationship problems
- work difficulties
- study problems
- coping with boredom
- difficulties concerning child care
- dealing with handicaps resulting from either physical or psychiatric illness

There are several possible contraindications and reasons for failure that Hawton and Kirk (1989) refer to:

- client's problems cannot be specified
- client's goals seem unrealistic
- severe acute psychiatric illness
- low self-esteem and lack of confidence
- client's problems reflect long-standing personal difficulties

The approach is contraindicated with very deluded clients with schizophrenia, or very retarded or agitated depressed clients who will not necessarily be able to focus on the tasks. However, it has been used with less disturbed clients with schizophrenia (Falloon et al., 1984, 1987, 1993), other depressed clients (Hawton and Kirk, 1989), and suicidal clients who are not high-risk cases (Hawton and Catalan, 1987). It has also been used with clients with substance abuse, e.g. alcohol.

Rational proselytizing

In 'Rational proselytizing' (see Bard, 1973) clients are encouraged to teach rational emotive behavioural principles to their relatives and friends. Clients receiving multimodal stress counselling can also use this technique. It is hypothesized that clients teaching others rational thinking and behaviour will become more convinced of the underlying philosophy. As clients explain the concept to their friends, they will often need to think quickly to counter objections and this helps them to confront their own irrational beliefs. If they experience any difficulty disputing their friends' irrational beliefs then these are discussed in the counselling session.

Indications and contraindications

Although clients find this technique useful, they need to be warned against becoming an unwanted counsellor to their relations and friends. If this could occur then the technique is contraindicated. The technique is indicated when the client has some intellectual but not necessarily emotional or behavioural insight.

Self-acceptance training

In rational emotive behaviour therapy (REBT) clients are generally discouraged from undertaking tasks or procedures solely to improve their self-esteem as they may also dis-esteem themselves when they do not succeed at valued tasks or if they receive others' disapproval (see Dryden, 1991a). To avoid defining themselves as incompetent or worthless if they fail, REBT counsellors encourage their clients not to give themselves global ratings but to accept themselves as fallible, complex, ever-changing human beings. The rating of 'their traits, aspects and behaviour but not their selves' (Dryden, 1991a: 276; Lazarus, 1977) is acceptable. Dryden (1987: 107–8) provides an example of a 'The "self" is too complex' intervention which helps to promote intellectual rational insight for clients who 'feel worthless'.

Counsellor: OK, so you say that you're worthless for cheating on your wife, is that right?

Client: Yes that's what I believe.

Counsellor: OK, but let's test that out. Are you saying that you are worthless, or what you've done is worthless?

Client: I'm saying that I'm worthless, not just what I did.

Counsellor: OK, but let's see if that is logical. You know when you say 'I'm worthless' you are giving you, your personhood or your essence, a single rating. Can you see that?

Client: Yes.

Counsellor: But let's see if you warrant that. You're 35. How many thoughts have you had from the day you were born till now?

Client: Countless, I guess.

Counsellor: Add to that all your actions and throw in all your traits for good measure. From that time till now how many aspects of you are there?

Client: Millions, I guess.

Counsellor: At least now when you say that Y-O-U ARE WORTH-LESS you can see that you're implying that you are about as complex as a single cell amoeba, and that this cell is worthless. Now is that true from what we've just been discussing?

Client: No, of course not.

Counsellor: So do you, in all your complexity, merit a single rating?

Client: No, but I did do a pretty worthless thing and it was serious.

Counsellor: Agreed, but what has greater validity, the belief, 'I'm worthless in all my essence' or the belief 'I am too complex to be rated, but I did do something lousy which I regret'?

Client: The second.

Counsellor: Right and if you really worked on believing that would you still feel suicidal as you do now?

Client: No I wouldn't. I see what you mean.

Multimodal stress counsellors may actively encourage clients to undertake a task that they may either fail at or receive others' disapproval. The client's relevant irrational beliefs are disputed in the counselling session, e.g. 'If I fail I am a complete failure and a worthless individual.' Then the client undertakes a task at which she fails and has vigorously to dispute her irrational beliefs during and after the event. The counsellor reviews the exercise at the next counselling session.

Indications and contraindications

This philosophy is generally indicated for all clients. However, the techniques involving intentional failing or receiving others' disapproval may need to be used with some care. Clients who are severely depressed, have very low self-esteem or have suicidal ideation may find the techniques overwhelming. In all cases the counsellor should ensure that he or she has adequately challenged the client's beliefs before the exercise and that the client has a clear understanding of why she is undertaking the task. Rational-emotive imagery (see Chapter 4) can be used to help clients practise challenging their irrational beliefs before they attempt exposure in real-life situations.

Thought blocking/stopping

Several different techniques come under the category of thought stopping. Each method helps the client to dismiss or stop thinking about obsessional thoughts that he becomes disturbed about. It can be used instead of habituation training where the client is encouraged to concentrate on the unwanted thought and not avoid it until the anxiety subsides.

In the counselling session the client is asked to think about the intrusive or obsessional thought or image (Salkovskis and Kirk, 1989). (The client may need to think or visualize a triggering scene to provoke the intrusive thought.) Then the counsellor makes a loud noise: claps hands or shouts 'STOP'. The client is then asked what happened to the obsessive thought. Assuming that the thought disappeared, the counsellor informs the client that the same technique can be used in public situations except additional training will be required so that a loud external noise will be unnecessary. The process is repeated a number of times with the counsellor gradually reducing the volume of the 'STOP' or the handclap. Finally, the client is asked to think about the thought and to say 'STOP' mentally to himself. The procedure is practised in the next three counselling sessions to ensure that the client is able to stop the unwanted thoughts. In between the sessions the client is asked to practise the technique for 20 minutes a day when he is not disturbed by the thoughts. It is preferable that the client does not practise when his mood is too low or when his attention can be diverted elsewhere.

Initially it is important that the client does not practise with very disturbing thoughts. Only when the less disturbing thoughts have been effectively stopped does the client start dealing with more disturbing thoughts. After a couple of weeks' practice, the client is encouraged to re-enter situations which triggered the obsessional thoughts that had previously been avoided. The client is informed that this may not be an easy procedure to undertake and that the thought stopping may not be totally effective. As the client gradually increases control over the stopping of the thoughts, he will find them less disturbing. If the client is not undertaking regular practice, is neutralizing the disturbing thought (or image) or is obtaining reassurance from a significant other, then the technique is unlikely to be successful. These issues will need to be discussed if the technique does not appear to be working. In some cases it may be necessary for the counsellor to explain to the significant other the importance of not reassuring the client when he is using this technique.

Lazarus (1981) described a number of thought-blocking techniques. For example, clients can picture 'huge neon signs flashing the letters "STOP" on and off' when unwanted thoughts intrude. With some clients other images that have a personal meaning may prove more useful. A number of clients find positive imagery (see Chapter 4) particularly useful to block distressing images.

An alternative method that can be effective involves the client putting an elastic band around his wrist and, when an intrusive thought occurs, flicking the band. The pain distracts the person from his negative train of thought. This has proved useful with individuals who are suffering from panic attacks.

Indications and contraindications

Thought-stopping techniques for intrusive or obsessional cognitions or images can be simple and effective. They are suitable for all clients. They are generally used when the client does not wish to undertake an exposure programme to the thought or image. In the early stages regular practice is required and many clients find this very anxiety-provoking. Care is needed if the client is depressed and experiencing suicidal ideation as asking the client deliberately to invoke the thoughts may increase emotional disturbance.

Conclusion

In this chapter we have surveyed a range of cognitive interventions and techniques that multimodal stress counsellors will find useful on many occasions. Their application needs regular practice and supervision if the counsellor is to attain a reasonable level of competence. Some of the techniques may appear easy, such as constructive self-talk or teaching self-acceptance, but in fact need considerable skill to undertake properly. Counsellors may first need to apply the techniques to themselves as their own cognitive distortions or low level of self-acceptance can interfere with their effectiveness as counsellors. In addition, this process can help counsellors understand how anxious their clients may feel about undertaking similar therapeutic tasks.

In Chapter 4 we will consider imagery interventions which are particularly useful in helping clients increase their coping skills and reduce their levels of depression and anxiety. They can easily be used in conjunction with many of the cognitive techniques contained in this chapter.

4

Imagery Interventions

In this chapter we explore the nature of imagery and also discuss the 'stimulus-imagery-response' model that illustrates how images and not necessarily events can lead to negative emotions such as anxiety. We have included a number of exercises that may help clients (and counsellors) to improve their visual imagination. The last section of the chapter features a variety of imagery techniques and interventions that produce good short- and long-term gains.

What is imagery?

Some researchers believe that images are sets of symbols that correspond to natural language. Therefore, if we ask you now to picture what is on the floor of your bathroom you will first of all think in the cognitive modality about it. Then you will conjure up a mental picture from the cognitively stored knowledge you have about the room. If you have no cognitively stored information about it then you may guess and subsequently produce a mental picture which may be accurate or inaccurate. However, we do not necessarily agree with this as on many occasions the image appears to be instantaneous. For example, if we now ask you to picture a significant other, such as a parent, a lover or close friend, most individuals would be able to create a picture within a fraction of a second.

Imagery often has subtle uses in our daily lives. If we asked you to decide what is the largest in size: a house or a mouse, you may answer immediately from information stored in the cognitive modality that a house is the largest. Yet, if we asked you to decide which was the largest in size between a mouse and a gerbil, then this would probably involve a closer investigation and the majority of individuals would resort to imagery. If we asked you to consider the difference between a sphere and a cube then it is likely that you would visualize both objects in your 'mind's eye' to help you make the comparison.

When we try to consider the nature of images as mental

representations we come to a major problem: how can they exist as images in the mind? If they do exist then we would need a homunculus to see them. At present we do not believe that this minor controversy is resolvable. However, as most people report that they do have mental pictures in their mind's eye then we are happy to accept this as fact even if we are not precisely sure of the exact nature of such images.

The SIR model

For a long time cognitive therapists have not agreed with the simple model that stimulus-response (S-R) theorists have held, which can be illustrated as follows.

Stimulus ⟶ Response

Basically, a stimulus occurs and an organism has a response. If a real example is used we can show how the S-R theory applies. Helen walks into a crowded room and then feels anxious:

Stimulus ⟶ Response
Crowded   Anxiety
room

When the clinical assessment was undertaken it was found that Helen had an image of herself vomiting whenever she found herself in a crowded environment. Therefore, the correct representation of exactly what happens to Helen is as follows (see Lazarus, 1984).

Stimulus ⟶ Image ⟶ Response
Crowded   Picture of   Anxiety
room   self vomiting

It is the image of herself vomiting in public that triggers Helen's anxiety, not the crowded room *per se*. Ten years previously she had suffered a bout of food poisoning and had vomited at a social event. She had never forgotten this event nor the image she had of herself with others looking at her vomiting.

In Helen's case her negative image led to her feeling anxious. However, specific images can also be used to help clients 'shift from irrational perceptions to rational ones' (McMullin, 1986: 273). McMullin suggests that as 'images do not involve language, clients can shift their perceptions more rapidly and completely using visual images rather than semantics' (1986: 273). By encouraging Helen to visualize herself attending a forthcoming social event without vomiting helped her to realize that she might be able to cope in the situation. This perceptual shift was sufficient to help her overcome her usual avoidance behaviour and attend the event without vomiting.

Exercises to improve imagery

Lazarus (1982, 1984) suggests a number of exercises to help individuals improve their powers of imagery. Often this is necessary as many individuals have difficulty in creating images. In our experience, if clients cannot see themselves coping with stressful situations, then they are less able to deal with these situations in reality, and will frequently avoid such situations. This then has a knock-on effect with a lowering of their self-confidence and self-image. This can lead to negative emotions in the affect modality, such as depression.

The following exercises are based on the image-building techniques described by Lazarus (1982, 1984). Clients can be asked to attempt these exercises at home or counsellors can instruct them in the counselling session. If the exercise involves visualizing a location, it is useful to ask clients if they or a significant other has ever suffered a negative life-event in a similar situation. For example, if they have been physically assaulted while walking in the countryside it may be preferable not to use the related imagery exercise as it could trigger unhelpful emotions. At this stage the goal of the exercise is to increase imagery skills and not evoke negative emotions; therefore, non-threatening visualizations are chosen. If clients suffer from asthma then breathing exercises may be contra-indicated; do not instruct an asthmatic to breathe deeply while doing the imagery exercises. Also, at this stage, if a client has a specific phobia which is encountered in the imagery exercise then use a different location. For example, a client who is agoraphobic may become anxious if asked to imagine walking in the countryside.

Before clients try the different exercises they need to make themselves comfortable in a quiet place. We will present the exercises as if we are talking to a client.

Exercise 1: The white board
Concentrate on your breathing for the moment and relax. Close your eyes and picture a white board. Imagine yourself writing the number 1 on the board. Now add the number 2. Keep putting numbers on the board. See how many numbers you can write on the board. As you put more on, what happens to the previous

numbers on your board? Do they become unclear or fade away? Repeat the exercise. Try to increase the clarity and the total of numbers you can write on your board. Practise this exercise for five minutes.

Exercise 2: The candle
Relax and close your eyes. Imagine a dimly lit candle flickering at the other end of a dark room. Just imagine the small flame. Perhaps you can see the colours. Can you make it grow brighter and then dimmer in your mind's eye? Try this a number of times. Now picture the candle light becoming brighter and lighting up everything in the room. Then very, very slowly, imagine the candle becoming dimmer again until you can just see it. Practise this exercise for five minutes.

Exercise 3: An object
Find any common real object. It could be an item from your pocket or wallet. Perhaps some item from your home such as a tin of food, a pen, a coin etc. Examine it carefully until you feel that you really know it in detail. Now close your eyes. Imagine that you are still studying it. See it as clearly as you can. Study the image in an identical way to how you examined the real object. Do this for a couple of minutes. Open your eyes and re-examine the real object. Does it differ from your picture of the object? Did you forget any aspect of the object? Repeat the whole exercise again. Then repeat the exercise with a different object.

Exercise 4: The countryside
Relax and close your eyes. Imagine walking through a field in the countryside. See the hills in the distance and a forest starting at the edge of the field. It's a sunny day and you can feel the warm breeze on your face. You take a deep breath and can smell the fresh country air. You can see a stream in the distance with a weeping willow tree hanging over it, slowly moving in the breeze. You walk towards the tree and sit down next to it. You can hear the water running over some rocks and you feel relaxed. The sunlight is reflected in the stream. Can you feel any pleasant sensations that are possibly associated with this imagery?

Some clients will not need to use any practice exercises to produce images. The MLHI (see p. 7 of the inventory) may suggest whether the client has particular images that trigger the affect modality. The Structural Profile section of the MLHI (see p. 14 of the inventory) may also indicate if clients are likely to need to undertake imagery practice exercises. If they have a low imagery score than practice is usually necessary. We will now describe a method that helps clients to use their imagery potential.

Vivid, connotive counsellor language

We have found that clients can be helped to imagine events by the counsellor using colourful and evocative language to set the scene. This is particularly useful if the counsellor is uncertain about which stimuli in the activating event are directly related to the client's problem. In these cases it is a good idea to give the client many possible options. Dryden (1990: 51, adapted) found that he was unable to help a socially anxious client, Andy, to reach his potential for imagery. The following dialogue shows Dryden using evocative language such as 'smirks', 'mocking', 'blows' and 'seethe' to stimulate Andy's visual imagination.

> *Counsellor*: So at the moment we are unclear about what you are anxious about. What I'd like to suggest is that we use your imagination to help us. I will help you set the scene based on what we have already discussed. However, since we have yet to discover detailed factors, some of the things I say might not be relevant. Will you bear with me and let me know when what I say touches a nerve in you?
>
> *Andy*: OK.
>
> *Counsellor*: Fine. Just close your eyes and imagine you are about to walk into the dance. You walk in and some of the guys there glance at you. You can see the smirks on their mocking faces and one of them blows you a kiss. [*The counsellor is testing out a hypothesis based on previously gained information.*] You start to seethe inside and . . .
>
> *Andy*: OK, when you said I was starting to seethe, that struck a chord. I thought I can't let them get away with that but if I let go I'll just go berserk. I started feeling anxious.
>
> *Counsellor*: And if you went berserk?
>
> *Andy*: I couldn't show my face in there again.
>
> *Counsellor*: What would happen then?
>
> *Andy*: I don't know. I . . . It's funny – the way I see it, I would never go out again . . . .

In this example, Dryden's use of language helped the client to imagine the scene without any difficulty. It is important for the counsellor to vary his or her tone so that it matches the language employed.

In the rest of the chapter we will concentrate on various imaginal techniques. We have only included techniques that have consistently proved helpful. The techniques are contraindicated for the minority of clients who are unable to create mental images. These clients would need to practise the imagery exercises described in the previous section before attempting imaginal techniques, otherwise the counsellor and client may waste valuable therapeutic time. This contraindication applies to each of the following techniques.

Anti-future shock imagery

Generally, in stress counselling, clients are concerned about problems in the present or immediate future. Sometimes they are disturbed about personal issues and life-events from their past. However, in multimodal stress counselling and stress management, counsellors are also concerned about helping their clients deal with future life-events and changes (Lazarus, 1984). Classic examples are children leaving the home, death of parents, redundancy and retirement. (Some events such as death cannot be avoided.) Often the so-called 'male menopause' occurs when the individual realizes that he is not likely to achieve the high goals he set himself when he was young. He may have a negative picture of becoming 'old', 'useless' and 'unwanted' in his retirement. This picture can lead to low self-esteem, depression and anxiety. Anti-future shock imagery can help individuals to overcome this and similar problems.

The client is asked to visualize herself coping with future changes. For some clients this may be difficult, so before the exercise is attempted the counsellor may need to discuss the life-change and brain-storm the possible coping strategies the client could use. The counsellor can make a list of the coping strategies and then guide the client through the visualization. For many clients, if counsellor-guided imagery is used, then it is more effective than allowing the individual to create her own imagery unaided. However, one of the long-term goals of imagery methods is to enable the client to apply the techniques whenever necessary without external assistance, therefore becoming her own 'anti-future shock expert'. Literally, 'seeing' that there are possibly different ways of dealing with future major problems can help the individual to 'de-awfulize' them and cope with them in a more constructive manner.

Indications and contraindications
This technique is indicated for clients who either have not considered the impact of possible future events and changes or are concerned about them. Anti-future shock imagery is particularly indicated as a relapse prevention technique used in the last stages of counselling as it prepares clients to deal with future unexpected

problems. Although this technique may be contraindicated for severely depressed clients or those with suicidal ideation, on many occasions it can help them to get the future problems into perspective and thereby improve their emotional state. In these cases, however, the technique should only be used by experienced counsellors.

Associated imagery

Individuals often experience negative emotions and sensations, the origin of which is unclear. The 'associated imagery' technique helps to track down the source of the problem. Lazarus (1984: 18) gives self-help instructions on how to use the technique, which can be given to the client for use at home or adapted by the counsellor for use in the counselling session. We have adapted the instructions for general use. Clients may find it easier to undertake the exercise if they close their eyes. The technique sometimes evokes useful insights which can be discussed later in counselling. It is similar to the free association technique used by Sigmund Freud earlier this century.

Instructions

1 Focus on the negative feelings and try to increase them. Thus, if you feel anxious then make yourself feel more anxious; if you feel depressed then allow your depression to grow.
2 Focus on any image or picture that enters your mind. Whatever the picture happens to be then see it as vividly as possible.
3 Concentrate on any new image that may occur. See each one as vividly as possible.
4 If different images do not appear then continue to concentrate on the original image in close detail. Imagine using a zoom lens and getting very close to it. Look at it from different angles. This may help you to understand the meaning of the image in more depth or it may evoke new images for you to follow.
5 As you track different images, return to some of the earlier ones and notice if now they evoke new images. Try to see the images as vividly as possible.

Indications and contraindications

This technique is indicated for clients in whom the origin of their negative emotions and sensations is unclear. It is contraindicated for clients who would feel overwhelmed by focusing on their negative feelings.

Aversive imagery (avoidance conditioning)

A stimulus that may trigger an unwanted or undesirable response or behaviour can often be linked together with an unpleasant image (Cautela, 1967). For example, if a diabetic client with a 'sweet tooth' is having difficulty keeping to a nutrition programme, the counsellor elicits from the client what specific image would help to stop him eating unsuitable food. Often the image of somebody he dislikes vomiting over the food he is just about to eat may be sufficient to stop him from eating it. The counsellor would need to train the client in the session to picture the negative image as vividly as possible. Then the counsellor could bring a sample of the food into the session and the client could practise seeing the food and then focus on the visualization.

There is one possible drawback with this technique. If the client visualizes the negative image for a long period of time, he can then habituate to it and his revulsion may subside. In our experience we have found it useful for the client not to use the visualization for longer than 5 minutes at a time to ensure that it still remains effective.

The technique has also been used with paedophiles (Marks, 1986). If they imagine touching a child in a sexual manner they are conditioned to visualize being arrested or that their hands are becoming ulcerous etc. Their worst fear is used to help them desist from touching children.

Indications and contraindications

Although this technique is indicated for many clients to help them reduce or stop undesired behaviour, with some individuals it needs to be applied with care as it can lead to extreme anxiety. Clients may find the image so repugnant that they may vomit. The technique may be contraindicated in clients who suffer from blood, injury or medical phobia because they may faint when imagining situations that relate to these specific fears.

Coping imagery

In 'coping imagery', the individual can picture herself coping in a feared or difficult situation (Meichenbaum, 1977). This is not to be confused with 'mastery imagery' in which the client imagines herself completing tasks *perfectly* (see McMullin, 1986). In mastery imagery clients are often unable to complete the imagery exercise as they have little faith in the 'perfect picture'. For this reason, we have not included mastery imagery as a section in this chapter, although Beck et al. (1993: 163) have found that mastery imagery can help clients who are attempting to stop abusing drugs deal with the very strong cravings that they experience. Mastery imagery includes 'seeing themselves as a very strong and powerful person who is overcoming cravings and urges' (1993: 163).

In our clinical experience, however, clients find coping imagery more helpful than mastery imagery. With coping imagery, the client pictures herself dealing adequately and not perfectly with her problem. The imagery is therefore more realistic and within the capabilities of the client. We have found that if a client can hold coping images in her mind's eye then she is more likely to cope successfully with a behavioural exposure programme.

Case study

Emma was 18 years old when she came for counselling at her teacher's suggestion. She was going to sit her exams in two months and was afraid that she would have to leave the examination hall and vomit as she had done on previous occasions. However, this time these were important exams and she needed to pass them if she was to go to university. Within the first 15 minutes of being in an examination hall she would have a panic attack. At this point she would leave the hall and vomit in the lavatory. This would take up valuable time and often she would not be able to return to finish the exam. The counsellor obtained details from her about what she would normally do the night before and on the day of the examination. The disadvantages of undertaking specific behaviours that contributed to her state of anxiety, such as speaking to unconfident friends, were discussed. Then she was asked to close her eyes and to picture the following coping imagery:

Imagine yourself the evening before your examination coming home from school. See yourself sitting down at the kitchen table as usual, drinking a mug of tea with your mother. Then picture yourself going upstairs to your bedroom, sitting down at your desk and revising for the next day's exam. Later, you can hear your father call you for dinner. See yourself sitting with the family and enjoying your food. Afterwards you return upstairs and continue studying. About 9.30pm you collect your papers together and tidy your desk. You prepare your pens and papers ready for the morning. You put on your favourite music and relax in your armchair. See if you can hear the music now. About 10.00pm picture yourself getting ready for bedtime and, after thinking about the next day, you finally drop off to sleep. Next morning your alarm clock goes off and you wake up feeling refreshed. You get yourself ready for school and have your usual breakfast with your sister. Picture your mother giving you a lift in the car to school. On arrival you avoid friends who are usually pessimistic and have a quiet chat with your more confident friends. However, one of your less confident friends sees you and comes over for a chat. She tells you that she has been unable to revise properly because she has felt so anxious about failing. You feel your own anxiety rising and that familiar churning in your stomach has returned. You tell your friend that you need to go to the toilet and you leave her with your friends. In the toilet you use the breathing exercise you have learnt and manage to calm yourself back down. Now picture yourself going into the examination hall, leaving your bags at the rear, and then finding your desk. You sit down and place your pens and pencils on the desk. You familiarize yourself with the room and any instructions on the front of the examination paper. Notice the feeling of excitement and possible tension. You notice your breathing. Now picture the teacher instructing everybody to start. As your anxiety starts to return you focus on your breathing exercise again. Although this takes up a few moments of your time you begin to feel better again and you start the exam. Notice how you are breathing calmly and slowly and gradually progressing through the questions. Notice that you are so absorbed in them that you have not got time to notice what anybody else is doing. See yourself putting up your hand and asking for an additional answer book. Later, you hear the examiner give everybody a 10 minute warning that the exam is about to finish. You then read over your answers and correct any obvious mistakes. When time is called see yourself checking that answer books have your name and examination number on. Then picture yourself leaving the hall and chatting to your friends outside.

The session was recorded so that Emma was able to listen to it daily as part of a homework assignment. The outcome was a great improvement. She did not feel anxious nor did she need to leave the hall and vomit.

When a counsellor teaches coping imagery sufficient pauses should be left in-between instructions to allow the client time to visualize each scene, otherwise this technique will not be effective. The coping imagery used with Emma is easily adapted for use with other clients. However, it is important to individualize it to the surroundings and experiences of each client. The client may also need to be taught breathing exercises as a coping strategy and this can be linked to the coping imagery as illustrated in the case study.

Indications and contraindications

Unless the individual is extremely disturbed, coping imagery is indicated for all clients who have to face an event that they are feeling anxious about. It is also indicated for clients who are phobic of specific things or situations. However, care needs to be taken when used with clients who suffer from blood, injury or medical phobia as they may faint if the coping imagery is related to these specific fears; for example, visiting a hospital for a health screen. In these cases, the client may need to lie on the floor or sit in an armchair when using coping imagery to prevent her hurting herself should she faint. With practice, as habituation occurs, the client is less likely to faint (see 'Imaginal exposure' below).

Implosion (flooding in fantasy)

Implosion is prolonged exposure in fantasy to the most feared situation until the individual's anxiety subsides or habituates (see Hogan and Kirchner, 1967; Kirchner and Hogan, 1966). Although this technique can be very effective, with a minority of individuals it can actually increase their anxiety. This may result if the counsellor or client stops the exercise before the anxiety has started to subside, which reinforces the client's anxiety. The counsellor is advised to explain clearly to the client how the technique generally helps anxiety to subside. Explicit consent to use this procedure should be obtained from the client.

This technique has also proved helpful with individuals who suffer specific distressing nightmares. Individuals who have been diagnosed as having post-traumatic stress disorder frequently experience nightmares connected with a traumatic event. Repeated rehearsal of their nightmare(s) in a counselling session will reduce or stop the nightmares from occurring (see Marks, 1987). If children have specific distressing nightmares this technique can be used but, in addition, it is recommended that the child uses some form of mastery in the situation. For example, if the child sees a monster in the nightmare then when the child wakes up she tells the monster 'to go away'! This can be practised in the counselling session after repeated rehearsal of the nightmare.

Indications and contraindications
This technique should be used with care as it can cause extremely high levels of anxiety. Clients suffering from severe depression or suicidal ideation may find this technique overwhelming. It is not recommended for clients who have a history of heart complaints or other related medical problems or with pregnant women. Graded exposure, imaginal exposure, relaxation techniques or drug therapy may be the option in some of these cases. This technique may also be contraindicated in clients who suffer from asthma attacks in stressful situations.

The technique is indicated for physically healthy clients who are not suffering from any form of psychosis who wish to overcome a feared situation. Due to the possible violent reaction that can occur, it is advisable for all clients to have practised a relaxation technique before using implosion. This technique is sometimes used with clients suffering from post-traumatic stress disorder (see 'Imaginal trauma reduction techniques' below).

Imaginal exposure

Imaginal exposure is exposure in fantasy to feared situations. Unlike implosion imagery, the individual does not initially picture his worst fear. A hierarchy of fears is noted and the client chooses to visualize a fear that he does not become too anxious about. As the feared situation is imagined over a short period of time, generally under an hour, the anxiety subsides. The client then visualizes another feared situation higher up on his hierarchy of fears. The process continues until the client is able to cope with visualizing his worst feared situation and his anxiety has subsided. Imaginal graded exposure is often integrated with real exposure. When the client is going through imaginal exposure the counsellor will frequently ask him to rate how anxious he is feeling on an arbitrary scale of 0–10 where 0 represents no anxiety and 10 represents high anxiety or panic. This allows the counsellor to see if the anxiety is subsiding and can also serve as a helpful indicator to the client that he is making progress.

Case study

Sara suffered from flying phobia. She had flown once and had become anxious. Since that occasion she had always managed to avoid travelling by aeroplane. However, she was about to get married and her fiancé was keen to go abroad for their honeymoon. He had booked a holiday to Africa which would involve about three hours of flying. Sara was asked to prepare her own hierarchy of stressors related to her flying phobia. Table 4.1 shows Sara's hierarchy.

Sara started her imaginal exposure at an anxiety rating of 4.0, which felt uncomfortable but not overwhelming. Therapeutic gains are attained slowly if the exposure programme starts at a very low level of anxiety. For most clients, a subjective rating of 4.0 is a good starting place. As soon as Sara's anxiety dropped below her rating of 4.0 she then imagined the next higher feared situation on her list. Her worst fear was of the aeroplane crashing. This picture in her mind caused her great anxiety and was the main contributory factor to her avoidance of flying.

Table 4.1 *Hierarchy of fears for imaginal exposure programme*

Rank	Subjective units of distress	Event
1	10.0	Aeroplane crashing
2	9.5	Aeroplane taking off
3	9.0	Aeroplane landing
4	8.0	Aeroplane in turbulence
5	7.0	Imagining self becoming ill on the aeroplane
6	6.0	Aeroplane cruising
7	5.5	Aeroplane taxiing
8	5.0	Looking at aeroplane
9	4.5	Waiting for delayed plane in departure lounge
10	4.0	Waiting for plane in departure lounge
11	3.5	Parking the car in the airport carpark
12	2.5	Driving to the airport
13	2.0	Reading brochure about holidays abroad

Imaginal exposure is particularly useful with flying phobics as regular behavioural exposure to flying is expensive.

With an earlier and similar technique known as 'systematic desensitization' the counsellor would ensure that the client was in a state of relaxation before the feared image was introduced (see Rachman, 1968). However, in our opinion, this unwittingly taught the client that she needed to be relaxed before exposure to a feared situation with the result that the period of time that the client needed to be exposed to the image was prolonged. This proved to be an inefficient use of therapeutic time. In our view relaxation does not need to be linked to the feared image except with more extremes of anxiety.

Indication and contraindications
Graded imaginal exposure is indicated when a client wishes to overcome or reduce her anxiety about a specific situation but is not prepared to start using real-life exposure or implosion. The technique allows the client to imagine a situation that does not trigger an intolerable level of anxiety. Similar to implosion, the technique may still be contraindicated for clients who have a history of heart complaints or other related medical problems as high levels of anxiety can still be experienced by clients when they imagine a situation at the top of their hierarchy of fears. Although pregnant women should avoid experiencing high levels of anxiety, if carefully graded this technique may be indicated for those who

suffer from medical phobia to help them overcome their fears of meeting doctors, visiting hospitals or giving birth. The technique is contraindicated in individuals suffering from a severe psychiatric disorder.

Imaginal trauma reduction techniques

Essentially, imaginal trauma reduction techniques are similar or identical to implosion (see above). In this section, therefore, implosion will be discussed focusing on its application to clients who have suffered traumatic events (see Keane et al., 1989; Marks, 1987).

Traumatized individuals frequently have flashbacks to the traumatic event where they re-experience the trauma. This can provoke severe anxiety in the individual and he will generally try to avoid anything that triggers the flashback or intrusive image. The counsellor asks the client to picture the scene again and, similar to implosion, the client keeps the picture in his mind's eye until his distress subsides. Clients are also likely to experience bodily sensations and may be able to recapture sounds, smells and tastes they had at the moment of the traumatic event. This technique will help the individual to become desensitized to the negative picture and bodily sensations. Caution needs to be taken with this technique as the client may experience extremes of anxiety and fear. Some individuals may 'disassociate' and feel detached from the experience. (This is a coping strategy that helps some individuals mentally to survive a very traumatic and life-endangering event.)

Another variant of this technique encourages clients to imagine viewing the traumatic event on a cinema screen in their mind's eye as if they are a member of the cinema audience (Muss, 1991). Initially, clients can view the scene from the beginning of the traumatic event and run it through to the end. They can repeat this a number of times and then concentrate on the most traumatic part of the event. Then they can play the traumatic event backwards. As they undertake this exercise they are very likely to experience extremes of anxiety and other perceptual and sensation disturbances. This whole process is repeated until their distress eventually subsides. They may still experience negative intrusive images of the event but these images will not trigger the original levels of anxiety or fear. When using this technique, if the client remembers an earlier traumatic event, then the process is repeated for the new image.

Indications and contraindications
These techniques are indicated for clients who have been traumatized by a specific event, and particularly those experiencing flashbacks. However, as the technique can trigger high levels of anxiety, care must be taken with clients who have suicidal ideation; if there is a risk of them attempting suicide, these techniques are contraindicated. The techniques are also contraindicated if there is a high risk that the client will feel overwhelmed by the procedure and prematurely stop the intervention before habituation has occurred. If this happens, a client can remain in a disassociated state and become traumatized by the intervention itself. Similar to implosion, these techniques are contraindicated in clients with a history of heart disease or other related medical disorders, and those suffering from severe psychiatric disorders.

Positive imagery

Positive imagery literally means picturing any scene, imaginary or real, that the individual finds pleasant (Lazarus, 1981). It can be from the past, present or future. Positive imagery can reduce or inhibit anxiety and lower tension levels. It can also be used as a distraction technique and is particularly helpful in pain management. Some individuals have found this technique useful to manage boredom or mild depression.

When using this technique it is important to create an image that the client can relate to. A completed *Multimodal Life History Inventory* (MLHI) may give the counsellor some ideas of the types of images or scenes that a client finds relaxing. It is useful to discuss with the client exactly what she finds pleasant about her scene. When the exercise is first carried out, the counsellor can help the client reinforce the scene by asking her to concentrate on different aspects of it such as looking at a particular object or person. The client can be asked to use an imaginary 'zoom lens' to inspect an item in detail or to stand back from it to gain a 'wide lens' view of the whole scene.

Indications
Positive imagery is indicated for clients who need a simple technique to reduce their stress and anxiety levels. The intervention is also indicated for clients who need a basic relaxation technique. Assuming a positive image is chosen, this technique is seldom contraindicated. However, if the client has recently suffered a bereavement and feels depressed about the loss, then the counsellor

needs to ensure that the positive imagery does not necessarily involve the deceased person unless this would help to elevate the client's mood.

Rational-emotive imagery

In rational-emotive imagery (Ellis, 1979 version) a client imagines an upsetting scene; for example, being criticized at work by the managing director for making a mistake. Once the client can picture it clearly, he is asked how he feels about it. If he feels guilty, he is asked to continue picturing the scene but change his feelings from guilt to regret. If he can do this then he is asked how he did it. Usually this involves the client changing his irrational beliefs to rational beliefs (see Chapter 3). This exercise is often set as a homework assignment to help clients practise disputing their irrational beliefs (see Chapter 3). The technique is particularly useful as it shows a client that if he begins to disturb himself about something (in our example, he makes himself guilty) then there is a way of dealing with a situation even if he is already feeling distressed.

In the alternative version of rational-emotive imagery (Maultsby, 1975), the client is also asked to imagine the situation, but this time he repeats forcefully to himself a rational belief (see Chapter 3) so that he experiences a more helpful and less debilitating emotion (e.g. regret instead of guilt, concern instead of anxiety).

Indications and contraindications

Both versions of rational-emotive imagery are indicated for clients who experience unhelpful emotions in specific situations. By using imagery, the technique prepares clients to re-enter stressful situations. It is also indicated for clients who still feel disturbed about how they acted previously in a particular situation. It is contraindicated in clients with a history of heart complaints or other related medical disorders.

Step-up technique

If a client is anxious about a possible future event, such as making a wedding speech, attending a job interview, starting a relationship or going to a party, then this technique will help her determine the cause of her anticipatory apprehension. Here the client is asked to 'get comfortable, to relax, to close her eyes' (Lazarus, 1984: 25) and then to picture the possible outcomes if the situation is not avoided. Usually, the underlying cause of the anxiety soon becomes apparent. In some cases it is useful to ask the client to 'step-up' the picture by imagining the worst possible outcome and then, if necessary, imagine coping and surviving the situation. The counsellor may need to help the client identify possible solutions to her 'nightmare' scenario. Once this exercise has been done, clients usually start to realize that their worst fears are unlikely to happen and they often start to laugh at the negative pictures in their mind's eye. Lazarus (1984: 22–3) believes that:

> One of the main reasons the Step-Up technique proves so helpful is that it pushes through a barrier of natural resistance. It is human nature to back away from unpleasant thoughts, images, feelings, and events ... When we avoid thinking about and working through negative emotions we seldom conquer them. By stepping up the potential consequences, we not only face reality, but we also transcend the situation and can view it more dispassionately.

This technique is extremely useful in reducing performance anxiety, although it would seldom be used in isolation. Alongside this technique, other skills may need to be taught, such as coping imagery, diaphragmatic breathing, relaxation skills, voice projection, preparation of slides, preparing cue cards etc., to help the client perform publicly.

Indications and contraindications
This technique is indicated when the underlying cause of a client's anxiety about a forthcoming event is unclear. It is contraindicated if the client is extremely likely to find the experience overwhelming. As with other techniques that can cause high levels of anxiety, its use may be contraindicated in clients with a history of heart disease or other related medical disorders.

Time projection/time-tripping imagery

Not surprisingly, negative imagery can lead to negative emotions. If an individual only has pessimistic pictures of doom and gloom in his mind's eye then this is not going to enhance how he feels generally. If a difficult situation occurs, he is less likely to be able to see how he can cope with it. This may lead to feelings of being overwhelmed by events. Time projection imagery (also known as 'time tripping', see Lazarus, 1981: 241) guides the client either forwards or backwards in time. Re-living past events and thereby getting them into perspective, or confronting abusers from childhood in imagination, can be very liberating. Clients who are experiencing a loss, such as the ending of a relationship or job redundancy, can feel depressed or anxious about it. By asking a client to visualize for himself a period of time in the future, and by including positive pictures of the client doing things that he usually enjoys, the client's mood can change. If the counsellor knows what the client finds rewarding then this procedure poses no problem; new clients can be asked what they see themselves doing in the future. This technique helps a client to see a difficult life-event or situation as less daunting; he can begin to see 'light at the end of the tunnel'. This also helps to raise the client's level of frustration tolerance (see Chapter 3) and, in the case of depressed and despondent individuals, it may begin to instil a sense of hope. The following case study illustrates the use of this technique with a client in the first session. Multimodal stress counsellors demonstrate their flexibility in that they may sometimes use therapeutic interventions in the assessment session if it appears necessary (see also Chapter 9).

Case study
Karen's long-term relationship had just finished. Her boyfriend did not want to marry her and left her for another woman. She was feeling depressed, empty, hurt and despondent and told the counsellor tearfully that she could not go on. The counsellor asked her to picture herself in 2 months' time. The counsellor asked her what she could see? She pictured herself back at work but still living alone. The counsellor asked her how she would feel? Karen thought she would feel bad but not quite as bad as at present. The counsellor then asked Karen to imagine herself 6 months in the future. She could see herself looking a little happier. Perhaps even riding her horse. The counsellor then asked her to look forward 2 years. This time she could see herself being much happier and visiting friends. However, she still thought that she would not have a close relationship. The counsellor asked her to imagine herself in 2 years' time, looking backwards at the present event. How would she feel about it then? 'I suppose I'll be over it by then', she replied. The counsellor then asked her to go forward 5 years in time. The counsellor asked her if she could see herself with another partner by this time. She was able to have a clear picture of herself in a new relationship.

This whole process took under 10 minutes. In this time she stopped crying and smiled at the prospect of having another relationship in the future. She felt more confident as she decided that the next relationship would be on a more equal basis. She decided that there was something worth living for. This technique helped her to replace the negative images of being alone with more positive pictures and thereby improve her emotional state. In addition, she realized that she could be happy again in a short period of time.

Indications and contraindications

This technique is particularly indicated for clients experiencing anxiety or depression triggered by a life-event such as loss, especially when the more usual cognitive interventions have not proved successful. In our clinical experience we have found that 'imagery reactors' tend to respond positively to this intervention (see Chapter 2). Depending upon the visualization used, this technique is not generally contraindicated for the majority of clients unless they report during the procedure that they are feeling worse.

Trauma coping imagery

The imaginal trauma reduction technique (see above) can help many clients to re-live and subsequently reduce the influence of a traumatic event. However, this is not always successful and the individual may need to use 'trauma coping imagery' instead (see Sharpe et al., 1994). In this technique, when a client suffers a flashback, intrusive image or perceptual disturbance of a previously unpleasant experience, she is instructed to change the ending of the scene in her mind's eye. This technique has been found to be very helpful with adult clients who are incest survivors as often they have an image of being abused. Table 4.2 illustrates a number of different 'endings' that incest survivors may find reduce stress. Trusted adults are generally police officers, caring or respected relatives, or others that the client believes could have helped in the situation. The trusted adult is not always the non-abusing parent as the client may still hold that person partly responsible and may not be convinced that he or she could have been helpful in the situation.

To be effective, it is essential that the counsellor explores the nature of the flashback or image that the client wishes to deal with and discovers what replacement image could help reduce her distress. This may be very individual and Table 4.2 is only a rough guide. It is worth noting that some clients find that an image of their mother or grandmother holding or hugging them will be sufficient.

The client can practise this technique at home, first picturing the intrusive image and then changing the ending. The client may find this exercise easier if the counsellor records a description of the intrusive image onto a cassette tape and then adds the new ending. The counsellor can also add a relaxation exercise at the end of the

Table 4.2 *Trauma coping imagery: suggested endings*

Traumatic image	Suggested endings
Abuser sexually assaulting the client	Trusted adults enter the scene and remove the abuser
Abuser being violent	Trusted adults enter the scene and remove the abuser
Seeing self, siblings or non-abusing parent being injured	Ambulance arrives and takes them all to hospital for treatment. Later taken to a safe environment such as grandparents
Images of weapons used during sexual and/or physical violence	Adult or survivor removes weapon(s) from situation, e.g. throws them in a bin

coping imagery. In counselling, if new disturbing images occur, the tape can be regularly updated.

Indications and contraindications
When the client does not wish to use imaginal trauma reduction techniques (see above) to diminish the effect of flashbacks or has found them unhelpful, trauma coping imagery is usually indicated. As the client is already suffering from anxiety-provoking intrusive images, nightmares or flashbacks, practising this technique is seldom contraindicated assuming that it is being applied by an experienced counsellor.

5

Behavioural Interventions

In 1982 Arnold Lazarus stated on a training video: 'we will use techniques drawn from many disciplines without necessarily subscribing to the theories that generated them'. This attitude derived from his experience in the late 1960s when he became increasingly unhappy with the theory that underpinned behavioural interventions, which led him to develop what he called 'broad-spectrum behaviour therapy', a precursor of the multimodal approach. Lazarus discovered that strictly behavioural interventions overlooked other important maintaining factors with his clients that could not be explained easily within simple learning theory terms.

In this chapter we will consider how behavioural methods fit into the multimodal stress counselling approach, and give general guidelines for their effective application, before describing techniques that we have found helpful in our clinical practice.

Behavioural methods and multimodal counselling

In Chapter 4 we introduced the stimulus-response theory and outlined its limitations in not considering important events such as images that may be the real cause of an individual's response. The multimodal approach proposes that an individual may respond in a variety of different ways to a stimulus or event. The response may be mediated by any of the modalities:

Stimulus ⟶ Mediation ⟶ Response
or activating event   Any of the 7   Any of the 7
(real or perceived)   modalities   modalities

Therefore, if there is an initial stimulus or activating event, such as an assault, an image, a bodily sensation, a negative cognition or whatever, the individual's response is mediated by the different modalities which in turn form part of that person's response. As the modalities are intrinsically linked together and often trigger each other, the response can include the modalities firing either sequentially or in parallel.

This may help to explain why sometimes behavioural interventions are ineffective since cognitions and images need to be dealt with in the therapeutic programme. Thus, when applying the techniques mentioned later in this chapter, it is important to consider the effect of the other modalities on the individual.

General guidelines

To ensure that behavioural techniques are applied as effectively as possible, there are a number of general guidelines which we have found useful. Adhering to the following points will help to strengthen the therapeutic alliance between client and counsellor and thereby increase the chance that the client will implement the behavioural techniques.

1 Ensure that the client understands the exact nature of the proposed technique and how it will benefit her if she executes the procedure.

2 Ensure that you understand your client's problem from her own frame of reference. Take a written record of this, preferably in your client's own words.

3 Take a note of desired outcome targets and general outcome goals together with the relevant measures of anxiety which are to be rated before, during and after the intervention. Work towards the goals in a systematic manner. Refer back to measures previously taken to highlight any improvement.

4 Encourage the client to practise the technique or intervention regularly. Real-life practice is normally superior to imaginary exposure.

5 Use positive reinforcement and rewards to encourage reluctant clients to complete assignment tasks.

6 If your client is undertaking behavioural homework assignment tasks that she may become very anxious about, arrange for her in the first instance to be accompanied by an aide (sometimes known as a co-therapist) such as a partner, relative or friend. This may help her to complete the task.

7 Teach your client additional coping strategies, such as relaxation techniques, to enable her to complete some of the behavioural interventions.

8 Imagine how you would feel undertaking the proposed behavioural technique or intervention if you shared the same beliefs and fears as your client. This may help you to address

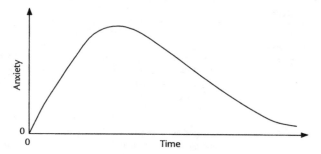

Figure 5.1 *Typical effect of habituation*

and overcome any obstacles that may exist to prevent your client from doing the relevant task.

If these general guidelines are adhered to then the effectiveness of the techniques described in this chapter will be increased.

Behavioural graded exposure

Behavioural graded exposure is exposure in real life to feared situations or stimuli, beginning first with situations that the client is less anxious about. In Chapter 4 we explained how an imaginal exposure programme is carried out, and a behavioural graded exposure programme works on the same principle. If an individual stays in contact with the feared situation or stimulus, after a period of time her anxiety starts to fall and eventually habituates (see Marks, 1969). Figure 5.1 illustrates the typical effect of habituation. (This diagram can be used to show the client how the exposure programme works.)

Habituation can occur in a short space of time, often within an hour, although sometimes it can take much longer and a client may need a number of sessions undertaking the same exposure task. It is worth noting that we have found a one-hour exposure programme more effective than four 15-minute exposures. The reason for this is that a client may not notice any substantial reduction in anxiety in the shorter exposure periods. Whenever possible, therefore, the individual should stay in the feared situation until habituation occurs. Exposure is usually graded in discrete steps and 'flooding' (real-life exposure to the most feared situation) is not used unless the client is willing to stay in the situation until habituation has occurred.

Table 5.1 *Hierarchy of fears for Margaret's behavioural exposure programme*

Rank	Subjective units of distress	Event
1	10.0	Standing in crowded underground train that has stopped in a tunnel for longer than 10 minutes
2	9.5	Standing in crowded underground train that has stopped in a tunnel for less than 10 minutes
3	9.0	Sitting in crowded underground train that has stopped in a tunnel for longer than 15 minutes
4	8.5	Sitting in crowded underground train that has stopped in a tunnel for less than 15 minutes
5	8.0	Standing in crowded train or underground train during the rush hour
6	7.5	Sitting in crowded train or underground train during the rush hour
7	7.0	Travelling a long journey on a crowded bus
8	6.5	Travelling a short journey on a crowded bus
9	6.0	Travelling on an uncrowded underground train
10	5.0	Travelling on an uncrowded train
11	4.5	Travelling on an uncrowded bus
12	4.0	Travelling in a taxi unaccompanied
13	3.0	Travelling in a taxi with a friend

A hierarchy of different fears is first constructed in a similar way to the method used with an imaginal exposure programme (see Chapter 4, Table 4.1). A typical example of a ranked hierarchy of fears is illustrated in Table 5.1. An arbitrary scale of 0–10 is used where 0 represents no anxiety and 10 represents high anxiety or panic. In this case the client, Margaret, suffered from anxiety and panic attacks when travelling on public transport.

The client first confronts the fear that she is least anxious about. However, as Margaret felt confident that the breathing exercise she had been taught by the counsellor would help her, she decided to start her exposure programme by travelling in a taxi unaccompanied. If Margaret had been too anxious or reluctant to undertake the behavioural exposure programme, the counsellor would have started with an imaginal exposure programme to reduce her anxiety to within tolerable levels (see Chapter 4).

In our experience, quicker gains are made if a client undertakes exposure to feared situations that she rates 4 or above on the anxiety scale. This also helps to raise her tolerance for frustration (see Chapter 3), otherwise she may start to believe that she is unable to tolerate facing high levels of anxiety and that she will always need to avoid highly feared situations.

Once the counsellor has assessed the hierarchy of fears and explained the rationale to the client, agreement to undertake the exposure programme is sought. Then the counsellor shows the client how to use a homework diary. An example of a completed diary for Margaret, a travel phobic, is illustrated in Box 5.1.

The goals for the week are written on the form during the counselling session. If the client is very anxious or worried about the procedure, then initially counsellor-aided exposure or the help of a therapeutic aide may be necessary. The main guideline for an aide (such as a friend or relative) is that no verbal reassurance is to be given during the performance of exposure tasks. The aide is told that if she gives reassurance then this will, in all probability, prolong the therapeutic programme as the client is not learning to cope independently. Giving reassurance is like a crutch which temporarily helps to reduce anxiety in a situation, but deprives the client of an opportunity to learn how to cope in the situation unaccompanied.

When undertaking exposure, the client's level of anxiety is rated before, during and afterwards. The time is also noted, as the length of the exposure period is a critical factor in helping to reduce the client's anxiety. The greater the length of time in a given situation the more the client's level of anxiety will fall. Comments made by the client, including coping tactics that she found helpful, can be a useful source of information for the counsellor and can be explored in the next counselling session. The client can also monitor and note in this part of the diary any thoughts, sensations or images that she had before, during or after the exposure. A multimodal stress counsellor will be interested in how the behavioural method interacts with the other modalities, as problems in these areas, such as a negative image etc., may need to be dealt with if the behavioural intervention appears not to be working (see the section on 'Tracking' in Chapter 2).

It is useful for the counsellor to keep photocopies of diaries in case the client does not believe that she is making progress. This often happens with clients who suffer from low self-esteem, especially if they have not achieved the high standards that they may have set for themselves. In such cases, the counsellor needs to challenge any 'all or nothing' perfectionist beliefs and help the client to acknowledge the progress she has made over the previous weeks. This loss of confidence often occurs as the client is about to face her worst fear.

It is a good idea to tell clients to expect days when the exposure programme will be more difficult than others, otherwise they can

Box 5.1 Homework diary for exposure programme

Week commencing: 14/3/93   Name: Margaret   Therapist: Stephen

Goals for the week
1 Travel on bus to Bromley return
2 Travel on bus to Croydon return
3 Take train to Charing Cross return

0	2.5	5	7.5	10
No anxiety	Slight anxiety	Moderate anxiety	Marked anxiety	High anxiety/ panic

Date	Session		Goal no.	Task performed	Anxiety			Comments
	Began	Ended			Before	During	After	
15/3/93	10.00	10.40	1	Travelled to Bromley on bus	3	6	2	Read panic list and used breathing exercise
15/3/93	1.30	2.10	1	Travelled home from Bromley on bus	1	5	1	Used breathing exercise and read a newspaper
16/3/93	10.15	11.20	2	Travelled to Croydon on bus	3	7	1	Used breathing exercise and read panic list. Looked at shops and counted people at bus stops
16/3/93	2.15	3.12	2	Travelled home from Croydon on bus	1	4	0	Used breathing exercise and looked at people in the streets

lose faith in the approach. This knowledge will also help to reduce the pressure they may put upon themselves to perform well.

With certain fears, such as flying, the financial cost will prohibit the client from having the opportunity of daily real-life exposure. In these cases the exposure programme will need to include imaginal exposure (see Chapter 4).

Indications and contraindications

Behavioural graded exposure is indicated when a client wishes to overcome or reduce her anxiety about a specific situation or stimulus. It is particularly effective with simple phobias, such as a fear of spiders, and with some clients habituation occurs in a few minutes. The technique is also indicated for clients who are avoiding specific situations due to the effect of post-traumatic stress disorder.

The method is contraindicated in depressed clients who are feeling suicidal as the client can become overwhelmed by the heightened levels of anxiety. The technique may also be contraindicated in clients who have a history of heart disease or other related medical problems. Clients who suffer from severe asthma may experience an asthmatic attack when their anxiety is raised. In these cases it is essential for clients to carry their medication with them during the exposure. With medically related disorders, it is advisable to obtain permission from the client's medical practitioner to use behavioural graded exposure.

The technique may also be contraindicated in pregnant women, although it may still be necessary for those women who need to confront fears about meeting doctors, visiting hospitals or giving birth. In these cases, it may be necessary for the pregnant woman to use coping imagery and relaxation techniques and for the counsellor to grade the exposure very carefully so that high levels of anxiety are not reached. This technique is contraindicated for individuals suffering from severe psychiatric disorders.

Behavioural rehearsal

If a client is unable to behave or cope in a desired manner in specific situations, he may be encouraged by the counsellor to rehearse the desired behaviour. This has many applications and is a particularly useful exercise for individuals who need to practise assertive behaviour (Lazarus, A.A., 1966; Sobel and Worden, 1981). First, the counsellor will explore the problem with the client and, together, they will decide what is the most suitable behaviour required for the given situation. The counsellor will then demonstrate the behaviour to the client and ask him to practise it in the counselling session using his own words. To help the client practise, the counsellor usually takes the role of any significant other. This may bring to light unforeseen problems or difficulties which can be discussed later in the counselling session.

Case study

Stewart was non-assertive with his work colleagues at committee meetings. If there was a disagreement he would generally back down. This would lead him to dis-esteem himself and he would become depressed. The counsellor discussed with him the benefits of being assertive at these meetings. To ensure that the behavioural rehearsal would have some validity, the counsellor asked Stewart to predict the next issue on the committee's agenda on which he would like to express his views to his colleagues in an assertive manner. There was a particular member of the committee he thought would strongly disagree with his own view. Together, Stewart and his counsellor decided what would be a good response. Stewart took the role of the 'disagreeing' committee member and the counsellor acted the role of Stewart. Stewart made the usual remarks that this other person would normally make, while the counsellor demonstrated helpful assertive skills (see Chapter 7).

Then Stewart took the role of his new assertive self and the counsellor took the role of the committee member. This was tape recorded and then analysed by Stewart and the counsellor to see if any improvements could be made in Stewart's assertive performance. This whole process was repeated a number of times until the counsellor and Stewart were satisfied with the latter's performance. Stewart then tried out his new repertoire of behaviour at the next committee meeting and was surprised to find that the particular person was more cooperative than usual once Stewart made his point and had not given up prematurely as he normally did.

Indications and contraindications

Behavioural rehearsal is indicated when clients need to learn a new method of behaving or coping in a specific situation. The technique may be contraindicated if the possible consequences of using the new behaviour or skill in real life have not been fully discussed with the client.

Empty Chair technique

In this technique, the client sits opposite an empty chair. The client imagines that she is speaking to a person sitting in the empty chair, with whom she has unfinished business. The client is encouraged by the counsellor to say exactly what she thinks and feels. The client can then sit in the 'empty chair' and become the other person. The client is instructed to respond in the manner that the other person would normally use. This conversation can go back and forth until a new insight is gained or a resolution has been attained. Sometimes the client can speak to different aspects of herself such as the 'doer' versus the 'procrastinator' and vice versa. The client can relive a previous childhood experience such as a row with a parent and use her present adult skills to convey her thoughts to the significant other. This is particularly helpful with clients who are adult survivors of child physical or sexual abuse.

The Empty Chair technique is not an established behavioural approach, but we have placed it in this chapter as the counsellor is encouraging the client in the counselling session openly to express her thoughts and feelings to a significant other or aspects of herself using her imagination. In social learning theory terms, we see it as a variant of role playing (see Dryden, 1991c). (The Empty Chair is often considered by counsellors to be an affective technique, but in this book we have incorporated techniques of the affect modality into the other six modalities.)

Case study
Barbara was socially phobic. Her problems started at a party when she was publicly ill. From that occasion, until she sought counselling, she avoided all social functions. She had undertaken a behavioural exposure programme but still experienced anxiety. Barbara had said that up until the critical event she had been 'outgoing' and 'fun loving'. Using the Empty Chair technique, the counsellor instructed Barbara to discuss with her former 'outgoing self' how to overcome her problem. Her 'outgoing self' told her not to take social mishaps so seriously and reminded her that probably everybody else at the party had completely forgotten about her vomiting and leaving early. This intervention helped Barbara to 'de-awfulize' her previous experience and take a more relaxed attitude towards future social events.

Indications and contraindications
The Empty Chair technique is indicated when clients are feeling emotionally blocked about a past event or series of events, or a current situation, thus preventing them from behaving in a desirable manner. It is contraindicated if clients have suicidal ideation and the specific intervention may exacerbate their condition. However, with this technique the therapeutic outcome may be unpredictable as catharsis can sometimes occur leading to

positive or negative results. In all cases, the counsellor needs to assess carefully the possible benefits to the client and the likely outcome before using this technique.

Environmental change

This intervention is probably the one most applied by clients without input from their counsellors and involves clients making a change in their environment. For example, if the housing conditions clients live in are bad, their general life conditions may be bettered by moving to another area. Another common example is changing employment if the person believes he cannot tolerate certain work colleagues. Unfortunately, this change may help the individual to avoid facing up to people and using skills such as assertion.

It is helpful to break down any suggested changes into discrete steps so that possible problems are not overlooked. An apparently simple task, such as visiting an employment agency to investigate different job prospects, may involve travelling on public transport. This can be difficult for people with agoraphobia. Asking the client what obstacles he thinks may prevent him from undertaking this change often reveals useful information which then needs to be explored.

Indications and contraindications

Environmental changes which lead to improvements in a client's general life-conditions are normally always indicated. However, some changes, such as repeatedly leaving close relationships, may help a client to avoid important issues. Therefore, in some instances the intervention may be contraindicated if it prevents the client achieving his long-term goals.

Fixed role therapy

This technique helps clients to construct a new attitude by incorporating new behaviours into their repertoire. It is based on the work of Kelly (1955) and encourages clients to make their constructs about life and themselves more flexible. Dryden (1987) has adapted the technique so that it does not need to be used within the framework of Kelly's Personal Construct Psychology.

The example Dryden (1987: 137) gives is when a client has intellectually agreed with the concept of unconditional self-acceptance (see Chapter 3) as opposed to the concept of conditional self-esteem. The client is asked to choose a relevant situation where she can practise the new attitude of unconditional self-acceptance. Then the client is given the following instructions (1987: 137):

> Now imagine someone with whom you can identify, who is like you in many ways apart from the fact that, at the moment, she is more self-accepting than you. What kind of thoughts will the person have about herself, others, and the situation she finds herself in? What will she say in this situation, what will she be feeling and what will she be doing?

Once this information has been collated, it can be modified to represent a realistic model for the client so that it does not lie outside her range of experience. The client is then set a homework assignment to imagine in her mind's eye, at least once a day for a week, that she is the other person. At the next counselling session, if the client has been able to do this task, then her response to the exercise is discussed. Any changes to the role that may be necessary are made and then she is set another homework assignment to imagine the modified role for another week. If no further modifications are required, the client is asked to spend a period of time, between a day and a week, acting out the new role as an experiment. The client is cautioned that she may initially feel strange acting this role but that this feeling will subside with the passage of time. At the next counselling session, the counsellor explores any difficulties or obstacles that the client may have encountered. In addition, any other beliefs she may still hold relating to conditional self-esteem are disputed.

Indications and contraindications

Fixed role therapy is indicated for clients who wish to modify their attitudes and repertoire of behaviours. It is particularly helpful with clients who experience difficulties in social situations or with specific people. It is contraindicated in severely depressed clients or individuals suffering from psychosis.

Modelling

In modelling, a client observes the counsellor demonstrate a piece of behaviour, before he practises it himself (see Meichenbaum, 1985). It is important that the counsellor performs the exercise in the manner that he or she would expect the client to be able to perform it, otherwise the client can become discouraged if the counsellor shows complete mastery without any apparent effort.

It is helpful if the new behaviour is divided into relatively easy and relevant units. For example, clients with social phobia have great difficulty writing in public. Under most circumstances they may be able to avoid writing and signing cheques in social situations such as shops. However, if they are keen to learn how to cope with the problem, the counsellor can demonstrate how to write a cheque with pen held firmly in hand, his or her wrist on the desk to steady any tremble or shakiness, and with the other hand on the cheque book to prevent it moving. The counsellor then writes the cheque out in a methodical manner, such as starting with the date first, and then finally signing it. The client then attempts the exercise. It is important for the counsellor to give the client positive feedback for attempting or completing the exercise.

The client repeats the exercise a number of times and, finally, a relevant homework assignment exercise is negotiated, preferably with graded exposure from easier situations, such as fairly empty shops, to more difficult situations, such as check-out counters in busy stores. If the client experiences high levels of anxiety, relaxation or breathing exercises can be incorporated into their behavioural repertoire and when this occurs the counsellor again models their use. (See also 'Assertiveness training', 'Communication skills training' and 'Social skills training' in Chapter 7.)

Indications and contraindications

Modelling is indicated for clients wishing to learn a new behaviour, and the technique is particularly indicated for clients with either phobic or obsessional disorders. However, as modelling can serve as a form of reassurance in exposure programmes (see above), in anxiety-related cases the use of the technique is contraindicated after the early stages of counselling.

Paradoxical intention

Paradoxical intention is a technique in which the counsellor instructs the client to engage in anxiety- or shame-provoking behaviour. This technique has been attributed to Frankl (1960) and is also known as 'paradoxical injunction'. This technique is often used when other interventions, such as relaxation, have failed to reduce the client's level of anxiety or shame in a specific situation (see 'Shame attacking' below). The rationale for paradoxical intention is that 'by bringing the feared, involuntary behaviour under voluntary control, it becomes unlikely or impossible that the person will subsequently experience such acute anxiety' (Feltham and Dryden, 1993: 129).

There are many circumstances when paradoxical intention may help the client. For example, a compulsive client is asked to increase her checking behaviour. Another example would be asking a client who fears blushing or fainting in public to try actually to blush or faint publicly. Forbidding a desired response is often used with males who have erectile difficulties. They are instructed not to engage in intercourse, although they can caress their partner. This can reduce their performance anxiety and lead to successful intercourse. Clients who are experiencing difficulties in falling asleep are requested to try their hardest not to fall asleep and to monitor their thoughts instead as this will be of assistance in the future (see Salkovskis, 1989). The technique reduces concern about sleeping problems and can also act as a cognitive distraction.

Paradoxical intention is most effective when the client is unaware of how the intervention works. In multimodal stress counselling clients are normally given an explanation of how a specific technique will help them deal with their problem and, understandably, the ethics of using this particular technique are often questioned by counsellors. In our experience, paradoxical intention needs to be used with great care and clinical acumen.

Indications and contraindications
This technique is indicated in cases which have been resistant to other interventions and is particularly useful with anxiety-related disorders such as compulsive behaviour. However, the technique is contraindicated if the client has not learnt to trust the counsellor as this intervention can have a negative effect on the therapeutic alliance, though sometimes it may still be worth the risk. The use of the technique is contraindicated in clients with personality disorders who could easily misinterpret the intervention as a hostile suggestion. As the intervention can trigger very high levels of anxiety it may be contraindicated in clients who have a history of heart disease or other related medical problems.

Risk-taking exercises

In risk-taking exercises, clients are encouraged to undertake something that they believe is 'too risky' (Dryden, 1987). Often these exercises help the client to dispute discomfort-related irrational beliefs connected to certainty. For example, a client may take a risk by acting in an unusual way without knowing how others will respond. The belief that may be disrupted in this case is 'I can't stand the uncertainty of not knowing what will happen' (Dryden, 1987: 133).

Indications and contraindications
Risk-taking exercises are indicated when clients need to deal with specific situations they find 'too risky'. However, the intervention is contraindicated if the proposed exercise will put the client in an objectively risky situation that could be life-threatening or where the law could be broken.

Response cost or penalty

This form of aversion and self-control training involves the client agreeing to a penalty if she does or does not undertake a specific behaviour or intervention (Marks, 1986). For example, whenever a client who wishes to stop smoking actually smokes, she pays an agreed amount to her least favourite political party, charity or whatever organization she would not generally give a donation to. This is also a very useful technique to use when any homework assignment exercise has been negotiated. If the assignment is not completed as agreed, the client either does not undertake a pastime pursuit such as watching her favourite television programme or she may be asked to perform an activity that she does not like doing such as cleaning the bathroom.

Case study
Mary had a problem with procrastination and did not like undertaking any homework assignment negotiated with the counsellor. Although she said that she could see the relevance of the exercise, she nearly always 'could not find the time to do them'. One homework exercise involved rational-emotive imagery which she agreed to practise daily. If she did not do this exercise she agreed (a) not to drink a glass of wine with her evening meal which was something that she always looked forward to and (b) to tidy the house which would take her a substantial amount of time. She wrote this agreement down on a homework assignment form, listed the possible obstacles and then signed the form. This demonstrated how important the counsellor believed the exercise was to reduce her anxiety about living alone. After some months of not completing any homework assignments apart from sometimes listening to a tape of the counselling session, this whole procedure cajoled her into doing the assignments. She was pleased with the outcome.

Indications and contraindications
Response cost or penalties are indicated when a client needs additional encouragement either to increase or decrease the frequency of a specific behaviour. With certain clients, such as those with personality disorders, the technique is contraindicated if its

introduction by the counsellor could have a negative effect on the therapeutic alliance.

Response prevention

This is a technique that is used with individuals suffering from obsessive-compulsive disorders (Salkovskis and Kirk, 1989). Obsessions are recurrent thoughts, images or impulses which are involuntarily produced and are senseless or repugnant; for example, I must murder my children. Compulsions are repetitive, voluntary, purposeless aspects of behaviour carried out according to set rules. Once carried out, these will usually lower the individual's level of anxiety, for example, touching the door handle a specific number of times to ensure that some feared event will not occur. Compulsive rituals with obsessions include orderliness, checking, cleaning, repeating and hoarding.

The technique involves clients being exposed to ritual evoking cues or thoughts and not carrying out the ritualistic anxiety-reducing behaviour. After a period of time has elapsed, as in a conventional exposure programme, their anxiety habituates if they do not carry out their rituals. Significant others may need to become therapeutic aides, and in extreme cases, counsellors may need to visit clients in their homes to help them undertake response prevention. The counsellor may need to take a firm but sensitive approach with clients who experience high levels of anxiety when they stop their rituals.

Figure 5.2 illustrates what normally happens without an intervention. On being exposed to the feared stimulus, the anxiety increases to a level which the individual believes he cannot stand. At this point (A on Figure 5.2) the individual will undertake the ritualistic behaviour to reduce the anxiety. The anxiety then lowers (B on Figure 5.2). However, within a short time, or after being exposed again to the feared stimulus, the anxiety returns (C on Figure 5.2). Unfortunately, the client has maladaptively learnt that repeating the ritualistic behaviour will reduce his level of anxiety. Therefore at C on Figure 5.2 the individual repeats the ritual. In some chronic cases, the individual may have forgotten the earlier associated thoughts or images that triggered the anxiety. Individuals with obsessive ruminations may neutralize them by using different thoughts or images. For example, when Ted thought 'My wife has cancer', he neutralized this belief by picturing their doctor telling both of them that she was 'absolutely fine.'

Figure 5.2 can be used to explain to the client how the disorder is maintained. Figure 5.1 can be used to show how, if he refrains from

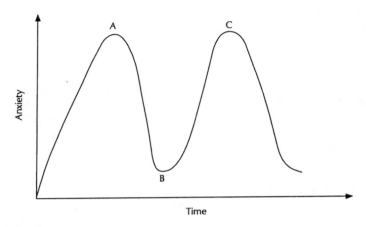

Figure 5.2 *Effect of ritualistic behaviour on levels of anxiety*

his compulsive or neutralizing behaviour, then after a period of time his anxiety will subside. As with phobias, reassurance from others such as co-therapists, aides and doctors usually acts as a neutralizer. Clients and their families need to be aware of this problem. An aide should be instructed to respond, when asked for reassurance: 'The clinic has told me not to answer such questions.'

Once the rationale for the intervention has been explained to the client, and he has agreed to undertake an exposure and response prevention programme, then diaries of the client's obsessional thoughts and/or compulsive behaviour will be necessary. It is also useful if ratings of his discomfort and the urge to neutralize are recorded. At this stage the counsellor may need to explore the client's often negative views about having this disorder. For example, Ted believed that he was going 'crazy' and thought that if he disclosed his persistent rumination about killing his wife, the counsellor may have him arrested or admitted to hospital. The counsellor had to explain to Ted that he did not believe that Ted was either 'crazy' or needed admission to hospital before a good therapeutic alliance was achieved.

It is difficult at first for most clients to stop their checking behaviour or neutralizing their thoughts. To help start the intervention, clients are encouraged to delay the neutralizing behaviour (or thought or image) for a short period of time, perhaps 5 minutes. During the course of counselling, this time period is gradually extended until the client stops neutralizing. In addition, if the client's neutralizing ritual involves a behaviour such as touching an object a specific number of times, then he is asked to reduce this frequency. With regular daily practice, the majority of clients can greatly reduce or stop their checking rituals.

Difficulties are sometimes encountered in this type of programme. It is essential not to think of the client as being 'resistant' to counselling but as reluctant to continue for other underlying reasons. By trying to understand the client's belief system the obstacles become more obvious. In some cases, even though clients are successfully completing their programmes, there may not be any improvement for two main reasons:

1 They are still obtaining reassurance in some way from a significant other during the programme.
2 They may be cognitively distracting themselves during the programme and therefore not benefiting from it.

Once again, these issues need to be explored during counselling. The counsellor will have to look closely at exactly what is happening during the programme. Sometimes, without realizing it, aides or co-therapists who are personally close to the client give reassurance just by the way they smile at the client. Also, the client will need to be asked if he is somehow secretly neutralizing or distracting himself during the programme. For example, imagining in his mind's eye that his partner is fit and well as opposed to dying of AIDS.

Indications and contraindications

This technique is indicated for clients who have obsessive-compulsive problems that involve checking behaviour or rituals. This can also include clients with bulimia or dysmorphophobia. In instances where the client experiences extreme levels of anxiety when he or she stops or delays undesired behaviour, the technique may be contraindicated, especially if the client has suicidal ideation. In these cases, the client may require residential treatment with close supervision before the technique is tentatively used. As with other techniques that can trigger high levels of anxiety, response prevention may be contraindicated in clients with heart complaints or other related medical conditions. The technique is contraindicated in individuals suffering from psychosis.

Shame-attacking exercises

In this exercise, clients are 'encouraged to act in a manner which they regard as "shameful" while disputing their shame-creating beliefs' (Dryden, 1987: 133). Clients are encouraged to act in ways that will attract the attention of others who will see them behaving in a way that the client views as 'shameful'. However, the behaviour should not harm anybody nor unnecessarily alarm others.

This exercise is not always straightforward as the client's behaviour may not elicit in others the desired response. For example, standing on a street corner next to the street name sign and asking passers-by for directions to that specific street may not induce the passers-by to laugh at the client. If the client would experience shame only if the passers-by laughed at her, then she would need to continue the exercise until enough people had laughed at her. Otherwise she would not know whether she could accept herself if she was laughed at. Assuming a passer-by actually laughed at the client, then she would be instructed to dispute vigorously her irrational beliefs (see Chapter 3) such as, 'They may think I'm stupid for acting stupidly but I can still accept myself.' This sentence can be written on a small card and the client can use it as a coping statement while undertaking the shame-attacking exercise.

Indications and contraindications

Shame-attacking exercises are indicated for clients who easily dis-esteem themselves if others think and act negatively towards them and it is particularly useful for clients who have social phobia. The technique is contraindicated if the client has not been adequately prepared for the possible response of other people to the exercise, or the client has not developed a suitable rational coping statement. It is contraindicated in clients who are depressed and have suicidal ideation.

Stability zones and routines

Adaptive routines are regular or irregular habits which help an individual to relax and unwind. They include: morning cup of tea; walking the dog; hobbies; weekend breaks; holidays; watching old films; meeting old friends; reading a book on the way to work; eating out once a week. Adaptive routines may also be absorbing, challenging or reassuring and help to lower anxiety. Stability zones are usually intrinsically linked with adaptive routines which can be thought of as 'physical areas, belongings or objects that an individual may be fond of or accustomed to, which may promote a feeling of well being' (Palmer, 1989: 4). Some examples may be an individual's favourite chair; old car; old clothes; country walk; restaurant; pub etc. They can also include the bath, the beach, the park, the holiday caravan and so on (see Handout 7).

Explaining these concepts to a client or group of clients can remind them of the particular behaviours in their repertoire that they may have neglected during a difficult and changing period. By bringing this to their attention, it allows them to have more control in their lives and to start enjoying the small pleasurable aspects of life again. Clients with obsessive-compulsive problems focus on specific unhelpful behaviours such as checking to lower their level of anxiety (see 'Response prevention' above). This concept may help give permission to these individuals to replace their unhelpful behaviours with more helpful ones as counselling proceeds, otherwise they can be left in a 'behavioural vacuum' when they reduce their checking which could lead to relapse.

One of the advantages of the concept of stability zones and routines is that clients may already possess the skill to undertake the helpful adaptive behaviour. Therefore this tends to be a proactive intervention. Stability zones and routines can involve social intercourse and this can help individuals to cope with stress.

Indications and contraindications
Discussing the concept of stability zones and routines is rarely contraindicated and is a particularly useful exercise in group stress counselling or stress management. It may be contraindicated for clients with obsessive-compulsive behaviour if they are likely to replace one compulsion with another.

Step-out-of-character exercise

This exercise is based on the work of Kelly (1955) (see 'Fixed role therapy' above) and later modified by Wessler (1984). The counsellor discusses with the client which behaviours are lacking or seldom used in her repertoire that may be worth while and beneficial. The client is asked to start practising these behaviours and concurrently tolerate any feelings such as mild anxiety that may accompany the exercise until the new behaviour becomes habitual. For example, Type A individuals may decide to walk, eat and talk more slowly and generally take life at a more leisurely pace. They may need to dispute any irrational beliefs related to this exercise such as 'I can't stand it if I work at a slow pace.'

Indications and contraindications
This technique is indicated for clients who wish to increase their repertoire of behaviour and has proved useful for clients who wish to become more assertive in a variety of social situations. The

technique may be indicated for mild to moderately depressed clients assuming that they do not have suicidal ideation.

Stimulus control

An individual may increase specific behaviours in the presence of certain stimuli. For example, smokers are more likely to increase their intake of cigarettes in situations where they are readily available. In this case, stimulus control may involve the smoker only smoking a cigarette while sitting in a certain chair, listening to a particular piece of music at a certain time of day, and only using a specific ash tray. An individual may only drink alcohol while sitting at a specific position at the dining table. Other examples include the reduction of eating snacks between meals by not permitting them to be available in the home or office; other more nutritious and healthier food, such as fruit, can be on display instead. Students who are unable to concentrate on their studies may need to clear their desk of distractions, remove their radio and record player from the room and ensure that the telephone is off the hook while studying. If they are not working then they do not remain at their desk. Clients who are experiencing difficulties in falling asleep can ensure that bedtime activities and everything in the bedroom focus on sleep; distractions such as the television or eating food are excluded.

Indications
Stimulus control is indicated for all clients wishing to reduce a specific unhelpful or unhealthy behaviour (see Lazarus, 1981). However, care may need to be taken with clients who are addicted to certain substances, such as alcohol, as a withdrawal programme may be necessary.

Time management

Clients who are suffering from occupational stress may lack time management skills. They may appear to have many demands made upon them and feel overwhelmed, but after careful analysis they may be letting others interfere with their work schedule (see stress mapping technique, in Palmer, 1990b). This may be related to non-assertive behaviour. They may also be approaching their work in a non-methodical manner and not prioritizing their daily tasks. Assuming that it is time management that is a problem, the points in Box 5.2 are worth discussing with the client for possible implementation.

Box 5.2   *Time management skills*

1 At the beginning of the working week, a list of goals is to be made and priorities set. If there is difficulty at work finding a spare moment to do this activity, then some time outside work may need to be found, perhaps on the train, in the car, at home etc. Top priority items should be highlighted. Each day add new items to the list, if necessary. Tick off items completed.

2 Group outgoing telephone calls together. Before the calls are made, make a list of items to be discussed.

3 Prepare for incoming telephone calls. If known, make a list of items to be discussed.

4 Remain brief and to the point on the telephone.

5 Prepare for meetings. List items that you wish to discuss.

6 If chairing a meeting, ensure that the agenda is adhered to and be aware of the time. Decide before the meeting how long can be spent on each item. Move the meeting on if time is being wasted on any particular item by reminding the participants that there are only so many minutes of the meeting left to cover all the items.

7 Practise saying 'No' to requests. If you want to say 'Yes' to a request that you do not have to do then ask yourself, 'Why do I want to say yes to this request? Is it just to improve my self-esteem? Will it be important in five years from now if I do not undertake this piece of work?' If in doubt, tell the other person that you are busy and will get back to them later at a specific time. Think about the request and ensure you do get back to the person with your decision.

8 Do one task at a time.

9 Ensure that you have understood instructions. Check understanding where necessary.

10 If giving instructions, check that the recipient has understood.

11 If procrastinating, imagine doing the specific job and attempt to discover what is preventing you from doing it.

12 Set aside time to deal with incoming mail. If possible, handle each piece of correspondence once.

13 Do not tax your memory by trying to remember what has to be done. Write it on the list.

Indications and contraindications
Time management is a useful skill and is indicated for all clients. On rare occasions it may be contraindicated if the client is obsessive-compulsive and takes an inordinate amount of time planning as opposed to doing.

Conclusion

We have found behavioural interventions to be very effective when used at the right time, with the right client. Many of the behavioural interventions may temporarily increase a client's anxiety levels. Do not be surprised if the client seems reluctant to undertake the exercise. We have met many counsellors who cajole their clients into doing an exposure programme that they would not do themselves. If counsellors have phobias themselves, then they could set up their own exposure programme and thereby experience the levels of anxiety that their clients suffer. This experience will help to increase empathy with clients and may also be useful for self-disclosure.

Due to the high levels of anxiety that many behavioural techniques and interventions can trigger, care must always be taken with clients who are depressed, especially those with suicidal ideation as they can easily feel overwhelmed. Extreme care should be taken with clients who have a history of heart complaints, or other related medical disorders, when using anxiety-provoking techniques. In these circumstances it is strongly recommended that the client receives permission to undertake these interventions from his or her medical practitioner. We know of cases where the client told the counsellor that he was having a heart attack during a counselling session, while the counsellor tried to reassure the client that he was only experiencing an anxiety attack due to the intervention. Needless to say, the client was correct.

Sensory interventions, such as the relaxation techniques, which we look at in the next chapter, can be helpful coping strategies which may enable clients with high levels of anxiety to undertake some of the behavioural interventions covered in this chapter.

6

Sensory Interventions

In Chapter 5 we described a wide range of behavioural techniques, the majority of which help clients to reduce their level of anxiety. This chapter concentrates on sensory interventions which are used for alleviating physical conditions. Some have a specific effect upon particular problems, for example, the prevention of rapid or premature ejaculation; whereas other techniques can reduce bodily tension and anxiety and can have the secondary benefit of lowering blood pressure, thereby reducing the incidence of headaches etc. Subsequently, as anxiety is reduced, the non-specific intervention can also have a positive effect on a client's sexual performance. Some techniques therefore work directly on the problem while others may work indirectly. Generally, teaching clients non-specific techniques such as relaxation can be of great benefit as their level of stress and anxiety may reduce sufficiently to allow them to deal with important issues inside and outside the counselling session.

Relaxation techniques included in this chapter work by decreasing the activity of the sympathetic nervous system and subsequently increasing the activity of the parasympathetic nervous system (see Chapter 1). As such, these techniques are the antithesis of the stress response. Researchers have found that relaxation techniques can help individuals exhibiting Type A behaviour (i.e. high achievers, very competitive, quick talkers, generally impatient and hostile) to lower their cholesterol levels and systolic blood pressure. General improvements such as these help to decrease the likelihood of Type A individuals experiencing coronary heart disease (see Friedman and Ulmer, 1985).

As with other techniques across the different modalities, sensory techniques may be used beyond the sensation modality. For example, Table 2.1 illustrated one client's Modality Profile on which the sensory technique of relaxation appeared in three sections as following:

Behaviour – Sleep disturbance – Benson relaxation response
Sensation – Tension – Relaxation training
Drugs/biology – Aspirin for headaches – Relaxation training

As with this particular client, if relaxation is a favoured intervention for a number of different problems, it would be advantageous to start teaching the technique in the second or third session of counselling. In some cases it may be apparent that clients would gain immediate benefit from learning a relaxation technique in the first session or being given a relaxation tape to listen to for their first homework assignment. A multimodal stress counsellor would possibly prefer such an intervention assuming more pressing issues had not arisen. This approach may lead to early therapeutic gains which allow clients to feel more in control. Early gains can also increase a client's confidence and trust in the counsellor.

This chapter includes sensory techniques and interventions that we have consistently found to be helpful to our clients receiving stress counselling or stress management. Clients who have been prescribed medication to control hypertension, anxiety, diabetes, thyroid regulation, hormonal and other related disorders may be able to reduce their medication once they become more relaxed. It is advisable to inform a client's medical practitioner that relaxation interventions are being undertaken and could result in a reduction in their patient's medication. Generally, relaxation techniques are indicated for individuals who suffer from asthma and epilepsy. However, care should be taken as in rare cases relaxation techniques may trigger an asthmatic attack or a seizure. Some research indicates that meditation techniques may precipitate a psychotic episode with individuals who have an adverse psychiatric history (for example, Glueck and Stroebel, 1975; Lazarus, 1976). Although these problems seldom arise, the counsellor is advised to supervise these clients closely in a suitable clinical setting to reduce the likelihood of complications.

Interestingly, both Jacobson (1938) and McGuigan (1993) believe that there are no contraindications for progressive relaxation. However, we prefer to err on the side of caution with all interventions.

Autogenic training

Johann Schultz developed autogenic training (AT) after first experimenting with hypnosis. His first AT presentation to his medical colleagues was in 1926. He wanted to transfer the control from the hypnotist to the client. He discovered that individuals could produce similar sensations to hypnosis, such as hand warmth and limb heaviness, by what he termed 'mental concentration'. He devised 'formulas' which were instructions that clients could give themselves relating to specific parts of their bodies. For example: 'My right (left) arm is very heavy' (see Kermani, 1992; Linden, 1990). This formula would be repeated six times in one minute while the client was in a state of relaxation. The other formulas are:

'My right (left) arm is very warm'
'My heart beat is calm and strong'
'It breathes me'
'Warmth is radiating over my stomach'
'The forehead is cool'

The client starts with the 'arm heavy' formula in the first session and, over a period of about ten weeks, gradually adds the other formulas. After daily training for about six months, the average client will be able to produce pronounced sensations. AT can help clients physically and mentally to relax and, in some cases, lower their blood pressure. Also, when clients are stressed about specific life-events, AT acts as a useful cognitive distraction technique. AT can be used with biofeedback instruments to accelerate a client's self-regulation and enhance relaxation.

Indications and contraindications

AT and autogenic biofeedback training are indicated for a wide range of different disorders such as anxiety, cardiac arrhythmias, diabetic ulcer, irritable bowel syndrome, tension headache, mixed tension-vascular headache, idiopathic essential hypertension, insomnia, classic and common migraine, primary idiopathic Raynaud's disease, tension and stress (see Norris and Fahrion, 1993). It is also indicated for clients who wish to learn a skill that may help them relax. However, care needs to be taken if used by clients suffering from glaucoma, epilepsy, gastrointestinal bleeding, peptic ulcer, irritable colon and ulcerative colitis (Luthe and Schultz, 1969; Kermani, 1992). Some blood/injury/medical phobics may feel anxious and faint when initially attempting AT. In addition, clients suffering from severe anxiety may find that AT can trigger panic attacks as they start to use the formulas and focus on their bodies. It is contraindicated in individuals suffering from severe psychiatric disorders.

Biofeedback

Certain physiological functions, such as blood pressure, heart rate, skin conductivity and temperature, can be monitored by the use of instruments or measuring devices (White and Tursky, 1982). As these instruments give feedback to the observer on biological responses, they are known as 'biofeedback' instruments. The feedback to the client can be via any of the senses, though auditory or visual feedback is most commonly used. In recent years the cost of the instruments has dropped and galvanic skin response (GSR) monitors can cost as little as £10 in Britain. These are used to measure skin conductivity. As the person's autonomic nervous system is aroused, he or she starts to sweat which increases the skin conductivity. The GSR normally responds by a change of audio tone or a movement on a meter. Other biofeedback devices such as biodots, which are only 4mm in diameter, are stuck to the client's skin and they change colour according to skin temperature. If a client is in a relaxed state, his or her surface body temperature rises due to the vasodilation of the blood capillaries. Biodots are usually available at a cost of about £12 per 100 in Britain and are reusable.

The GSR is used to illustrate to clients how different bodily sensations, cognitions and images can trigger the stress response within seconds. This is good evidence for the client that panic attacks do not generally occur spontaneously. They are also used in conjunction with relaxation exercises to confirm that the client has learnt how to relax. As the instruments give almost immediate feedback to the client, they can have the effect of positive reinforcement.

Indications and contraindications

The use of biofeedback devices is indicated in all clients who would benefit from understanding how their thoughts, sensations or negative images can trigger the stress response and subsequently panic attacks (Palmer, 1990c). Biofeedback is a useful aid when teaching clients relaxation skills. However, the use of biofeedback may be contraindicated in clients who are phobic of technology. Fortunately, these clients are rare and gradual exposure to biofeedback devices should help them overcome this particular problem. It is generally indicated for anxiety, cardiac rehabilitation, colitis, common and classical migraine, hyperarousal disorders (e.g. PTSD), certain pain disorders, irritable bowel syndrome, insomnia, premature ventricular contractions, Raynaud's disease, sinus tachycardia, tension headache and temporomandibular problems (see Blanchard and Abel, 1976; Budzynski et al., 1973; Bush et al., 1985; Freedman et al., 1985; Phillips, 1979; Weiss and Engel, 1971). Stoyva and Budzynski (1993) do not recommend biofeedback for hysterical and conversion reaction symptoms unless the client is also receiving psychotherapy to resolve any underlying conflicts.

They suggest that clients with moderate to severe depression may benefit from other interventions instead of biofeedback training.

Hypnosis

As multimodal stress counsellors tend to use hypnosis to reduce the physical effects of stress such as tension, we consider it a sensory intervention. However, it is worth noting that the technique described later in this section focuses on deep relaxation and also cognitive restructuring.

In counselling, some clients believe that hypnosis will help them cope with stress or overcome somatic problems. We have found that if we use hypnosis with these specific clients then in many cases it does seem to aid their recovery (see also Lazarus, 1973a). It is useful for counsellors to learn a number of trance induction and 'ego strengthening' techniques (see Hartland, 1987). Trance induction methods usually include eye fixation on specific points on the ceiling or a pencil tip. The client is also told simultaneously that he is feeling 'relaxed' and his 'eyes are feeling sleepy and you want to close them'. However, some clients can be reluctant to give in to these suggestions. To overcome this reluctance we have found that it is easier to ask the client to close his eyes at the beginning of this stage and to ask him to 'look upwards, your eyes closed, just look upwards . . . notice the feeling of tiredness . . . .' This usually overcomes this problem as the counsellor is not trying to 'will' the client to close his eyes and take a combative stance.

The 'ego strengthening' stage involves making positive statements designed to improve the client's physical and mental condition usually related to stress, anxiety and tension. Then suggestions can be directed towards symptom removal. The suggestions made at this point depend upon what specific complaint the client is suffering from; for example, allergies, phobias, asthma, insomnia, migraine, tics, speech disorders, dermatological disorders, smoking and over-eating (see Barber, 1993; Hartland, 1987). It can also be used for pain management and, surprisingly, in the removal of warts! However, in the context of multimodal stress counselling, we recommend that the counsellor restricts the use of hypnosis to stress management and stress-related conditions. We suggest that it is used as an adjunct to the other multimodal interventions.

The session can be recorded and the client can listen to the tape at home. Eventually, after sufficient practice, most clients will be able to induce a state of self-hypnosis and will not need the assistance of a tape or a counsellor.

Method of hypnosis

There will be an introduction to each section of the hypnosis technique described in the following script (taken from Palmer, 1993b; 33–44).

Preparation and preliminary induction
Before hypnosis is undertaken, it is helpful to discuss with the client her thoughts and fears regarding hypnosis as the client may hold unrealistic beliefs about what may happen. For example, she may be anxious that the counsellor will be able to control her totally or she may be concerned that she will not be capable of coming out of the trance. These issues need to be resolved. It is helpful to give the client an idea of the type of words and phrases that the counsellor is likely to use, and explain that hypnosis is similar to, but not quite the same as, relaxation. It is a good idea to tell the client that she may feel a warm, heavy or tingling feeling in her hands and limbs during hypnosis, and that this is quite normal and may indicate that she is becoming hypnotized.

The client should be seated in a comfortable chair, preferably with a headrest; otherwise, if the client becomes very relaxed, she may drop her head forward and this will later result in neck ache. She needs to sit with her legs and hands uncrossed to avoid possible cramp. If clients wear contact lenses or glasses, it is advisable for these to be removed before the start of hypnosis.

When reading the hypnosis script, emphasize the word 'down' by saying it slightly louder and by making it last twice as long as usual as this seems to help the client to relax. Note that a 'pause' is about 1–3 seconds long and a 'long pause' is about 5–15 seconds.

Preliminary induction (Palmer, 1993b: 33–6)

> Can you make yourself as comfortable as possible in your chair
> *Pause*
> And if you would just like to close your eyes
> *Pause*
> If you would like to listen to the noises outside the room
> *Pause*
> And now listen to the noises inside the room.
> *Pause*
> These noises will come and go probably throughout this session and you can choose to let them just drift over your mind and choose to ignore them if you so wish
> *Pause*
> You will probably notice how these noises and the sound of my voice will become softer and louder and softer again during this session. This is quite normal and will indicate that you are in a state of hypnosis

Pause
Let your whole body go limp and slack
Pause
Now keeping your eyelids closed and without moving your head, I would like you to look upwards, your eyes closed, just look upwards
Pause
Notice the feeling of tiredness, sleepiness
Pause
And relaxation
Pause
In your eye muscles
Pause
And when your eyes feel so tired, so very, very, tired, just let your eyes drop back DOWN
Pause
Notice the feeling of tiredness, sleepiness and relaxation in your eyes
Pause
Let this feeling now travel DOWN your face to your jaw
Pause
Now just relax your jaw
Pause
If your teeth are clenched, then unclench them
Pause
Now relax your tongue
Pause
Let the feeling of relaxation slowly travel up over your face to your forehead
Pause
To the top of your head
Pause
To the back of your head
Long pause
Then slowly DOWN through the neck muscles
Pause
and DOWN to your shoulders
Long pause
Now concentrate on relaxing your shoulders, just let them drop DOWN
Pause
Now let that feeling of relaxation now in your shoulders slowly travel DOWN your right arm, DOWN through the muscles, DOWN through your elbow, DOWN through your wrist, DOWN to your hand, right DOWN to your finger tips
Long pause
Now let that feeling of relaxation now in your shoulders slowly travel DOWN your left arm, DOWN through the muscles, DOWN through your elbow, DOWN through your wrist, DOWN to your hand, right DOWN to your finger tips
Long pause

And let that feeling of relaxation now in your shoulders slowly travel DOWN your chest right DOWN to your stomach
Long pause
Let that feeling of relaxation and tiredness travel DOWN from your shoulders right DOWN your back
Long pause
Right DOWN your right leg, DOWN through the muscles, DOWN through your knee, DOWN through your ankle
Pause
To your foot, right DOWN to your toes
Long pause
Let the feeling of relaxation and tiredness now travel DOWN your left leg
Pause
DOWN through the muscles, DOWN through your knee, DOWN through your ankle
Pause
To your foot, right DOWN to your toes
Long pause
I'll give you a few moments now
Pause
To allow you to concentrate on any part of your body that you would like to relax even further
15-second pause or longer if necessary

Deepening

At this stage it is helpful to deepen the client's state of relaxation. In traditional hypnosis, this may be done by arm-levitation or by arm-heaviness techniques. We have found it more useful to use either breathing or imagery techniques. If imagery techniques are to be used, before starting hypnosis the counsellor will need to elicit from the client if she has a relaxing scene which she can imagine that involves her travelling or walking down something such as a hill, flight of stairs, a beach, a country lane or whatever. The essential part is that she can see herself walking 'down' it. At the deepening stage of hypnosis it is advisable to avoid imagery that may trigger anxiety as this will not help the relaxation process; for example, instructing a client who is phobic of enclosed spaces to imagine travelling down in a lift. The example of deepening that will be illustrated is a breathing and counting technique that is normally effective. The word 'now' acts as a trigger word which helps the client to fall into a deeper state of relaxation.

If the client suffers from smokers' cough, panic attacks or asthma then this technique may not always be indicated.

Deepening (Palmer, 1993b: 36–8)

I want you now to concentrate on your breathing

Pause

Notice how every time you breathe out, you feel more, and more, relaxed

Pause

With each breath you take you feel so relaxed, so very, very relaxed

Pause

Breathe in slowly through your nose and slowly out through your mouth

Pause

With each breath you take

Pause

Every time you take a new breath of air

Pause

You are becoming more and more relaxed

Pause

Gradually you are drifting away as you become more, and more, relaxed

Pause

On every out-breath you are becoming more, and more, sleepy

Pause

More and more deeply relaxed

Pause

Notice how, as you relax, you are breathing more, and more, slowly

Pause

And more, and more, steadily, as you become more, and more, deeply, very deeply, relaxed

Pause

You are drifting DOWN into a deep state of relaxation

Pause

Your whole body is becoming more, and more, relaxed, every time, you breathe out

Pause

I'm slowly going to count to five, and as I do, you will feel even more relaxed than you do now

Pause

One

Pause

NOW you are feeling more and more relaxed than you did a few minutes ago. More and more relaxed than you did a few seconds ago

Pause

Two

Pause

Notice how you are feeling so relaxed, that you are finding it difficult to concentrate on my voice all the time

Pause

Three

Pause

Every time I say a number, every time you breathe out, you feel more and more deeply, very, very deeply relaxed. An overwhelming feeling of tiredness is descending upon you as you listen to my voice

Pause
Four
Pause
You are feeling even more relaxed now than you did a few minutes, a few seconds ago. In a moment when I say the number five, but not quite yet, you are going to feel so very deeply relaxed . . .
Pause
Five
NOW you feel even more relaxed than you did a moment ago, more relaxed than a few seconds ago, much more relaxed than you did a few minutes ago, and very much more than you did a few hours ago

Ego-strengthening
Ego-strengthening involves the counsellor at this stage of the procedure making suggestions that are related to the client's general physical and mental condition. Certain key words are stressed and frequently repeated to drive home the positive effects of hypnosis outside the counselling session in the behavioural, affective, sensory and cognitive modalities. This may have a post-hypnotic effect which is an important ingredient of hypnosis. The 'pauses' help to emphasize the ego-strengthening suggestions and enhance their effect.

Ego-strengthening (Palmer, 1993b: 38–41)
You are now so relaxed, so very relaxed, that you are becoming very aware of what I am saying to you
Pause
You are so aware that your mind is open to any suggestions I may make for your benefit
Pause
You are feeling so relaxed that when I make positive suggestions about your health, you will accept these suggestions, and gradually over a period of time you will feel better and better, even though you will not be here with me
Pause
My suggestions will just drift over your mind and you will be able to remember all the relevant ones that will influence your feelings
Pause
Your behaviour
Pause
And your thoughts
Pause
As you feel more and more deeply relaxed during this session, you will find new energy to help you cope with any problems you may have had recently
Pause
New energy to lessen any fatigue
Pause

New energy to help you concentrate on your goals
Pause
A new strength of mind and body to deal with internal and external pressures
Pause
Gradually, you will become absorbed in life again, looking forward to every day
Pause
And as every day goes by, you will become more relaxed, and much calmer than you have been for some time
Pause
And each day, you will feel far less tense, and far less concerned with unimportant matters
Pause
And as this happens, your confidence will grow as your old fears become a distant memory
Pause
Day by day, hour by hour, minute by minute, second by second, your independence will grow
Pause
Any depression or anxiety or guilt or stress will fade away as you learn to cope with life
[*NB Target relevant emotion or physical state according to the client's presenting problem.*]
Pause
You will be able to stand difficult situations much more easily
Pause
You will no longer hear yourself saying 'I can't stand it', but instead you will realistically say to yourself, 'It's unpleasant but I can stand it'
Pause
You will see situations in perspective and not blow them up out of proportion
Pause
You will question whether things are really that bad
Pause
You will no longer wish to catastrophize events beyond reality
Pause
As you learn that you can stand situations, you will procrastinate less often and you will be able to start and continue your tasks more easily
Pause
And face your fears
Pause
If you fail at a task, you will not condemn yourself as a failure or stupid
Pause
All it all means is that you did not achieve your target
Pause
No more, no less
Pause

You will learn to accept yourself more for the person you are and not just for your achievements
Pause
Your internal demands, many of those unnecessary musts and shoulds
Pause
Will change to coulds and preferences and subsequently your anxieties will lessen
Pause
Gradually, as time goes by, you will feel better and better and your life will improve
Pause
And your recent worries will be a thing of the past
Pause
And you will be able to put them behind you

Symptom removal

At this stage there are several options for the counsellor. Either the termination script can be used or a symptom removal script can be inserted. One symptom removal script will be described. It can be adapted for different symptoms or other scripts can be used (for example, Hartland, 1987). Coping imagery (see Chapter 4) could also be used to help clients overcome phobias and fear of coming events.

Any symptom-specific suggestion made should preferably be of a rational, logical and positive nature. It is useful to add a section that includes how to deal with the problem when the client is faced with it outside the counselling setting.

The following symptom removal script is to help with the alleviation of tension headaches and migraine. It is important to ensure that the client does not have an underlying organic problem and, if in doubt, a suitable referral to a medical practitioner will be necessary.

Symptom removal (Palmer, 1993b: 42–3)
    Day by day, week by week, month by month
    Pause
    As you become much more relaxed
    Pause
    And far less tense
    Pause
    Gradually, the tension in your shoulders
    Pause
    And in your neck will fade
    Pause
    You will stand and sit in very relaxed manner
    Pause

And as you do, you will feel so comfortable that any pain will become a distant memory
Pause
If you concentrate now on your face, on your head, and on your neck, notice how, as you relax even further, gradually your head and face, are starting to feel warm
Pause
As this feeling of warmth increases, you are starting to feel even more relaxed than you did a few minutes ago
Pause
And day by day
Pause
As you feel less tense, in your body and mind, this state of relaxation will help to prevent headaches occurring
Pause
And as the pain is normally related to stress and tension
Pause
Day by day, as you become more relaxed
Pause
And less tense, the pain will diminish
Pause
And if you ever feel the headache returning
Pause
You will be able to sit down, relax your shoulders
Pause
Relax your neck muscles
Pause
Relax your face and head
Pause
And the pain will just drift away

Termination

A termination is a necessary part of the hypnosis procedure. It reminds the client that they are in full control of their body and mind and brings them back to full consciousness. If the client prematurely opens her eyes during the hypnosis session, she is asked to close them and the termination stage is still used.

Termination (Palmer, 1993b: 43–4)

In a few moments' time, but not quite yet, I am going to count to three, and when I do, you will open your eyes and wake up, and feel relaxed and refreshed
Pause
You will be able to remember or forget whatever you want to of this session
Pause
And you will be in full control of your body and mind
Pause
And wake up today on [*insert here: day, time, location*]

Pause
As I count to three, you will wake up
Pause
One
Pause
Two
Pause
Three, open your eyes in your own time

When the client has opened her eyes, the counsellor can enquire how she felt during hypnosis, if there were any problems, and answer any queries that may have arisen during the session. It is worth asking the client whether she would like any part of the script altered especially if any imagery has been used. With practice, the client may be able to use a shorter, adapted version of the script to induce a state of self-hypnosis, thereby reducing her dependence upon the counsellor.

Indications and contraindications

Assuming that the client wishes to use hypnosis, it is indicated for a wide range of stress-related and psychosomatic disorders, including allergies, anxiety, asthma, unwanted behaviours (e.g. over-eating, smoking, tics), blushing, depression, tension headache, hypertension, insomnia, irritable bowel syndrome, common and classic migraine, pain, phobias, skin disorders (e.g. eczema), stress, tension and speech disorders (Hartland, 1987). However, before hypnosis is used to alleviate a physical condition it is essential that the client receives a medical check-up to ensure the problem is not of an organic nature requiring a medical intervention.

Hypnosis is contraindicated if the client is under the influence of alcohol or drugs. Care needs to be taken when using hypnosis with clients who suffer from asthma, epilepsy or narcolepsy as hypnosis (or any other form of relaxation) may in rare cases exacerbate the condition. If this occurs then hypnosis is contraindicated. Hypnosis is not recommended for hysterical and conversion reaction symptoms unless the client is also receiving counselling to resolve any underlying conflicts. Hypnosis is contraindicated if the client is very reluctant to use it. Often the client has fears about the procedure, being controlled and dominated, or becoming unconscious and out of control. However, the multimodal stress counsellor can usually overcome these obstacles by taking a modelling approach whereby the counsellor demonstrates self-hypnosis on himself and suggests that the client may wish mutually to experience the positive effects of the technique. Hypnosis is also contraindicated in clients suffering from severe psychiatric disorders.

Multimodal relaxation method

Even when running groups, it is useful to attempt to match the intervention to each individual within that group. As each participant may be more receptive to interventions directed at specific modalities, when teaching relaxation exercises it is useful to use a method that includes a number of different modalities. This will help to cater to the needs of the majority of the participants. It will also give them experience of techniques directed at specific modalities so that they can later choose which modality intervention they have found most effective. They can then concentrate their efforts on regular practice with their favoured technique. In group work, after the participants have tried the method, they can then use biofeedback instruments to discover which particular modality intervention is useful.

The multimodal relaxation method (see Palmer, 1993b: 17–23) was developed to introduce stress management, anxiety management and relaxation group participants to a combination of different modality relaxation techniques. It has also been safely used at conferences and public health lectures. It includes the affect, sensory, imagery and cognitive modalities.

Techniques such as progressive relaxation have been omitted as they are contraindicated in certain circumstances (Palmer, 1992c, 1993b) and are therefore unsuitable when working with participants whose medical history is unknown. The choice of imagery used has been left to the participant to prevent the counsellor or trainer choosing a specific image that may evoke a negative emotion with some individuals. Deep breathing techniques have been excluded in case there are participants suffering from asthma, anxiety attacks or smoker's cough.

The multimodal relaxation method takes a minimum of about 8 minutes. This can be extended up to about 30 minutes if necessary. The method was designed to take a short period of time usually to encourage group participants and clients in counselling to start to include it within their repertoire of behaviour. This is important with individuals who believe that they are too busy to incorporate relaxation techniques into their daily life. The exercise is normally taught while the participants are sitting in chairs and not lying on the floor. This is to encourage them to use the method while at work, travelling or at home. If it is used when travelling or at work, they are reminded that with practice they will not need to close their eyes to relax. When working with clients individually in counselling, the session can be recorded so that the client can use the recording at convenient times. If they are having sleeping difficulties then the end of the recording is modified (see script below) and the client can use it at bedtime.

Assuming that the usual preparation for hypnosis is undertaken, the script is as follows:

Multimodal relaxation method (Palmer, 1993b: 17–23)
   If you could make yourself as comfortable as possible on your chair
   Pause
   And if you would just like to close your eyes
   Pause
   As you do this exercise, if you feel any odd feelings such as tingling sensations, light-headedness, or whatever, then this is quite normal. If you open your eyes then these feelings will go away. If you carry on with the relaxation exercise usually the feelings will disappear anyway
   Pause
   If you would like to listen to the noises outside the room first of all
   Long pause
   And now listen to any noises inside the room
   Pause
   You may be aware of yourself breathing
   These noises will come and go probably throughout this session and you can choose to let them just drift over your mind and choose to ignore them if you so wish
   Pause
   Now keeping your eyelids closed and without moving your head, I would like you to look upwards, your eyes closed, just look upwards
   Long pause [*NB If participants wear contact lenses then they can remove them before the exercise or not look upwards*]
   Notice the feeling of tiredness
   Pause
   And relaxation
   Pause
   In your eye muscles
   Pause
   Now let your eyes drop back down
   Pause
   Notice the tiredness and relaxation in those muscles of your eyes
   Pause
   Let the feeling now travel down your face to your jaw, just relax your jaw
   Long pause
   Now relax your tongue
   Pause
   Let the feeling of relaxation slowly travel up over your face to the top of your head
   Pause
   To the back of your head
   Long pause
   Then slowly down through the neck muscles

Pause
And down to your shoulders
Long pause
Now concentrate on relaxing your shoulders, just let them drop down
Pause
Now let that feeling of relaxation now in your shoulders slowly travel down your right arm, down through the muscles, down through your elbow, down through your wrist, to your hand, right down to your finger tips
Long pause
Let the feeling of relaxation now in your shoulders slowly travel down your left arm, down through your muscles, down through your elbow, through your wrist, down to your hand, right down to your finger tips
Long pause
And let that feeling of relaxation now in your shoulders slowly travel down your chest right down to your stomach
Pause
Just concentrate now on your breathing
Pause
Notice that every time as you breathe out you feel more
Pause
And more relaxed
Long pause
Let the feeling of relaxation travel down from your shoulders right down your back
Long pause
Right down your right leg, down through the muscles, through your knee, down through your ankle
Pause
To your foot, right down to your toes
Long pause
Let the feeling of relaxation now travel down your left leg
Pause
Down through the muscles, down through your knee, down through your ankle
Pause
To your foot, right down to your toes
Long pause
I'll give you a few moments now
Pause
To allow you to concentrate on any part of your body that you would like to relax even further
15-second pause minimum
I want you to concentrate on your breathing again
Pause
Notice as you breathe
Pause
On each out-breath you feel more and more relaxed
Long pause
I would like you in your mind to say the number one

Pause [NB If the number one evokes an emotion then participants are asked to choose another number]
And say it every time you breathe out
Long pause
This will help you to push away any unwanted thoughts you may have
Pause
Each time you breathe out just say the number in your mind
30-second pause [NB Up to 20 minutes pause here if an extended session is required. If extended, then regular input from the trainer is needed to remind the participants to repeat the mantra 'one' or whatever number they have chosen]
I want you now
Pause
To think of your favourite relaxing place
Pause
I want you to concentrate
Pause
On your favourite relaxing place
Long pause
Try and see it in your mind's eye
Long pause
Look at the colours
Pause
Perhaps concentrate on one of the colours now
Pause
Maybe one of your favourite colours if it's there
Long pause
Now concentrate on any sounds or noises in your favourite relaxing place
Long pause
Now concentrate on any smells or aromas in your favourite
Pause
Relaxing place
Long pause
Now just imagine touching something
Pause
In your favourite relaxing place
Long pause
Just imagine how it feels
Long pause
I want you now to concentrate on your breathing again
Pause
Notice once again that every time you breathe out
Pause
You feel more
Pause
And more relaxed
Long pause
Whenever you want to in the future you will be able to remember your favourite relaxing place or the breathing exercise and it will help you to

relax quickly
Long pause
In a few moments' time, but not quite yet, I'm going to count to three
Pause
And you will be able to open your eyes in your own time
Pause [NB Or go off to sleep if you so wish]
One
Pause
Two
Pause
Three
Pause
Open your eyes in your own time

Indications and contraindications

The multimodal relaxation method is indicated for all individuals wishing to learn a relaxation technique. It is particularly indicated for clients with anxiety, colitis, tension headache, hyperarousal disorders (e.g. PTSD), mixed tension-vascular headache, high blood pressure, essential hypertension, insomnia, irritable bowel syndrome, classic and common migraine, stress, Type A behaviour, physical tension, and psychosomatic disorders. The method helps clients to control their general irritability if they are on a stop smoking programme. Care needs to be taken when the technique is used with clients who suffer from asthma, epilepsy, hysteria, narcolepsy or panic attacks as relaxation can exacerbate the condition in some cases. If this occurs then the method is usually contraindicated (see Lehrer et al., 1986; Lazarus and Mayne, 1990). (The main exception to this rule is when an individual is in counselling and would benefit from learning a relaxation technique to control panic attacks. However, individuals having panic attacks during a group training event may disturb other participants.) The method is also contraindicated in clients suffering from psychosis or those under the influence of alcohol or illegal drugs.

Progressive relaxation

Jacobson (1938) developed a method that he called 'progressive relaxation'. In its time it was a breakthrough and gave practitioners a powerful technique to help clients relax. It consisted of teaching clients to tense different muscle groups for approximately 6 seconds and then relax them for a longer period. The entire procedure took many training sessions and was very time-consuming. It was later refined (see Wolpe and Lazarus, 1966) and the whole process shortened. The example we give is taken from Wolpe and Lazarus

(1966). It is in four sections: relaxation of arms; facial area with neck, shoulders and upper back; chest, stomach and lower back; hips, thighs and calves followed by complete body relaxation. We will describe part of the relaxation of the arms.

> Settle back as comfortably as you can. Let yourself relax to the best of your ability . . . Now, as you relax like that, clench your right fist, just clench your fist tighter and tighter, and study the tension as you do so. Keep it clenched and feel the tension in your right fist, hand, forearm . . . and now relax. Let the fingers of your right hand become loose, and observe the contrast in your feelings . . . Now, let yourself go and try to become more relaxed all over . . . Once more, clench your right fist really tight . . . hold it, and notice the tension again . . . Now let go, relax; your fingers straighten out, and you notice the difference once more . . . [and so on].

This procedure is continued for the entire arm and takes between 4 and 5 minutes. Other parts of the body are relaxed in the same manner. In some clients the state of relaxation can be induced more quickly and many of the instructions can be omitted.

Indications and contraindications

Progressive relaxation is indicated for clients wishing to learn to relax and is particularly useful for physically tense individuals (Jacobson, 1938). It is indicated for clients suffering from generalized and specific anxiety/stress, asthma, chronic pain, chronic tinnitus, convulsive tic, depression, esophageal spasm, high blood pressure, insomnia, hypertension, phobias, spasmodic dysmenorrhoea, and tension headache (see McGuigan, 1993). However, care does need to be taken with clients suffering from high blood pressure and hypertension to ensure that their blood pressure is not raised to dangerously high levels. In these cases, clients should not tense each group of muscles for longer than 2 seconds, and the total duration of the exercise is initially limited to 10 minutes. As a precaution, the client can at first be restricted to tensing only one part of the body during each period of training.

As progressive relaxation involves physical activity, care needs to be taken with clients who suffer from cardiac disorders (e.g. angina pectoris, myocardial infarction or undiagnosed chest pains), diabetes mellitus, hormonal disorders (e.g. thyroid) and hypoglycaemia. As with other relaxation techniques, care should also be taken with clients suffering from asthma, depression, epilepsy, glaucoma, hysteria or narcolepsy (see Lazarus, 1990; Lehrer et al., 1986; Palmer, 1992c, 1993b). It has been suggested that relaxation techniques may cause internal bleeding and acidity for some individuals who have gastrointestinal tract disorders, e.g. peptic ulcer, ulcerative colitis etc. (see Luthe and Schultz, 1969). Depending upon their medical condition, in some cases it is better for clients to focus on strengthening specific muscle groups (e.g. lower back) instead of relaxing them. In these instances the multimodal stress counsellor should liaise with the client's medical practitioner to ascertain which muscle groups must not be relaxed during training. For clients who experience pain in specific muscle groups or joints, the tensing of these particular areas may be contraindicated.

Benson relaxation response

This technique is a modified version of meditation. It was western-ized by Benson (1976) when he removed any cultural influence and replaced the mantra with the number 'one'. It has an advantage over many forms of relaxation as the repetition of the number 'one' helps the client to ignore any distracting or negative thoughts that he may have as he relaxes. Through our experience, we have modified the original text:

1 Find a comfortable position and sit quietly.
2 Close your eyes.
3 Relax your muscles, starting at your face and progress down to your toes.
4 Now concentrate on your breathing. Breathe naturally through your nose. In your mind say the number 'one' as you breathe out.
5 Continue this exercise for a further 10–20 minutes.
6 When you finish, keep your eyes closed for a couple of minutes and sit quietly.

If distracting or negative thoughts occur, let them just pass over your mind and return to repeating the number 'one'. Do not try to force relaxation. Just let it occur in its own time.

Indications and contraindications
The relaxation response shares the general indications and contraindications for its use with those of the multimodal relax-ation method (see above). However, Carrington (1993: 150–1) has suggested a number of additional primary indications for modern forms of meditation:

- chronic fatigue states
- hypersomnias
- abuse of 'soft' drugs, alcohol or tobacco

- excessive self-blame
- chronic low-grade depressions
- subacute reaction depressions
- irritability, low frustration tolerance
- strong submissive trends
- poorly developed psychological differentiation
- difficulties with self-assertion
- pathological bereavement reactions, separation anxiety
- blocks to productivity or creativity
- inadequate contact with affective life
- a need to shift emphasis from client's reliance on therapist to reliance on self (of particular use when terminating psychotherapy)

Carrington (1993: 153) asserts that some individuals may be 'hypersensitive to meditation' and unable to tolerate the usual 20-minute sessions. In these cases, the technique can be adapted to the needs of the client by reducing the meditation time. 'Over-meditation' is contraindicated in all clients and a maximum of two 20-minute sessions a day is recommended.

Sensate focus training

Sensate focus training is an intervention used with sexually dysfunctional couples. Sensate focus (Masters and Johnson, 1970) consists of tactile stimulation such as touching, fondling and massaging any part of the body which the recipient gains pleasure from being stimulated. However, it is not sexual stimulation and therefore female breasts and the genitals are not touched in any manner whatsoever. This technique encourages intimacy without any pressure on either partner to engage in sex. Quite often this approach has a paradoxical element where the couple may achieve sexual intercourse even though they may have been experiencing great difficulty for some time.

Indications and contraindications

Hawton (1989: 381) offers a number of indications for sex therapy:

1 Sexual problems of long duration (at least a few months).
2 Efforts by the couple themselves to solve the problem have proved unsuccessful.
3 The problem is likely to be caused or maintained by psychological factors (e.g. aversive previous sexual experience, performance anxiety, poor self-esteem).

4 The problem is threatening the overall relationship between the partners.

Assuming the above are in accord, then sensate focus training is indicated for couples who are experiencing difficulty having a sexual relationship.

The technique is contraindicated if one of the partners is not interested in continuing the relationship or has unresolved marital or partnership issues. In these cases, the unresolved issues can first be discussed in couples counselling before any decision is made to use sensate focus training. Major psychiatric disorders are usually a contraindication of sex therapy and of this particular technique until the client's condition has improved. If either partner has a major current alcohol problem then sex therapy should not be offered because of poor compliance.

Threshold training

This sensory intervention is used when a male client suffers from rapid or premature ejaculation. At an interpersonal level, premature ejaculation can lead to relationship difficulties and a great deal of distress as the client's partner may not find this a satisfying experience. A couple may come to counselling with other declared problems and this issue may not be openly raised until later.

The technique involves the partner manually stimulating the client's penis. As soon as the client feels that he is about to reach orgasm, he will instruct his partner to stop or to remove her hand. This is usually done verbally. Once the sensation has diminished the partner then starts manual stimulation again until the pre-orgasmic sensation returns. Then the client instructs the partner to stop again. This process is repeated a number of times. At the next stage, a suitable cream can be used to lubricate the penis and the process is repeated. This whole exercise is usually undertaken three times a week for about three weeks. By this time many clients will be able to have vaginal entry and withdraw when they have a pre-orgasmic sensation. Once again, the client practises this exercise until he is able to delay ejaculation without withdrawal (see stop-start technique in Hawton, 1989).

Indications and contraindications

Threshold training is indicated when both partners wish to overcome the client's problem of rapid or premature ejaculation. The general indications and contraindications are the same as for sensate focus training (see above).

Transcendental meditation

This technique involves the trainer giving the meditator a secret sound or mantra. This is chosen by the trainer to suit the individual. The meditator is supposed to repeat the mantra in his mind, over and over again while seated in a comfortable position. This technique helps to control distracting thoughts. The meditator takes a passive attitude and if thoughts return he goes back to the mantra. Meditators repeat this exercise twice a day for 20 minutes per session. It is recommended that they do this before breakfast and evening meal.

Meditation is not a form of sleep; it seems to cause a drop in oxygen consumption, decreased carbon dioxide elimination, reduced breathing rate and alters the output of alpha-waves. There is also a decrease in blood lactate, a substance that can lead to anxiety attacks if injected into clients suffering from an anxiety disorder (see Benson, 1976). Meditation also appears to aid the reduction of blood pressure (see Benson, 1976).

Benson westernized meditation and replaced the mantra with the number 'one'. We have included in this chapter the Benson relaxation response (see above) which we have found to be just as effective as meditation; it also produces the same physiological changes as transcendental meditation.

Indications and contraindications
The indications and contraindications are the same as those for the multimodal relaxation method and the Benson relaxation response.

7

Interpersonal Interventions

In this chapter we will concentrate on interventions and skills used in the 'interpersonal modality'. These interventions usually require the counsellor to take an educational or coaching approach with the client. One task for the counsellor is to explain and clearly demonstrate the relevant skills to the client. This may require a reasonable level of competence on the part of the counsellor. As people generally learn behaviours from role models, such as significant others, it is important for counsellors to incorporate good interpersonal skills into their behavioural repertoire. Counsellors should therefore normally demonstrate these skills with their clients on a day-to-day basis, even when they are not overtly teaching them these skills.

There is an overlap between a number of the important interpersonal interventions such as assertiveness, communication, friendship/intimacy, and social skills training. In this chapter we will only describe the specific skills in depth once to avoid unnecessary repetition. Some of the skills are easier for the client to learn in group training rather than in individual counselling. We suggest that multimodal stress counsellors maintain a referral list of different agencies and organizations that regularly run group training or therapy in the specific interpersonal skills such as assertiveness. If this is not available in the locality, then training groups could be set up by the counsellor. However, unless the counsellor is experienced in group work, we strongly recommend that he or she receives further relevant training before doing so.

Assertiveness training

Assertiveness training has been described as 'a system of techniques taught to enable people to ask for what they want, complain appropriately, give positive feedback to others, stand up for themselves and, when necessary, defend themselves' (Feltham and Dryden, 1993: 12). A major part of the training involves 'identifying unhelpful messages and replacing them with clearer, well projected ones, through rehearsal, modelling and experimentation' (Feltham and Dryden, 1993: 12). Its use enables people to avoid exploitation, submission, resentment, negative consequences and misunderstanding. Clients are taught assertive techniques in groups, counselling or a combination of both (Lazarus and Nieves, 1980).

The counsellor should first explain the different concepts, such as 'assertive' or 'aggressive' behaviour, to the client. The following lists give examples of assertive, aggressive and passive/non-assertive behaviour (Palmer, 1990a). They can be given to the client as a handout so that the client understands the different behaviours.

Assertive

Behaviour
Smiles when pleased
Relaxed
No slouching/fidgeting
Good eye contact
Not hostile
Collaborative

Words/phrases used
'I' statements: I want, I think, I fear
Cooperative: we could, let's
Open questions: how do you feel;
    what do you want/think

Aggressive

Behaviour
Leans forward
Points finger
Thumps fist(s)
Sharp, firm, sarcastic voice
Dominating
Loud/shouts
Violates rights of others

Words/phrases used
Your fault
You'd better
Don't be stupid
You're joking
You should, ought, must

Some individuals exhibit aggressive body behaviour but use passive language instead. They tend to be cynical, manipulative and sarcastic but the overall intention is to avoid conflict.

Passive/non-assertive

Behaviour
Hunched shoulders
Shrugs
Shifts bodyweight
Whining, giggly, quiet voice
Hand wringing
Downcast eyes
Steps backwards

Words/phrases used

Perhaps
Maybe
I wonder if you could
Just
Only
I can't
I'm hopeless
It's not important
Never mind
Well, uh
I mean

At this stage, it is important to assess the client's needs correctly. In particular, the problem areas and lack of assertiveness skills are identified. Some of the assessment questions that the counsellor can ask are:

Are you able to express negative feelings?
Are you able to express positive feelings?
Can you express personal opinions?
Can you refuse invitations and requests?
Are you able to express justified anger or annoyance?
Are there any particular situations in which you experience problems with asserting yourself (for example, work, home, extended family, shops, neighbours, visitors to the home, restaurants, pubs, church, dealing with professionals etc.)?

The client can then complete an Assertiveness Problem Hierarchy (APH) form by ranking each problem in order of importance. A

Box 7.1   *Assertiveness Problem Hierarchy form*

Name: Bob
Date: 27/8/93

1	Relationship with father
2	Taking criticism
3	Difficulty expressing justified anger
4	Feeling unnecessarily guilty if I upset others
5	Problems with my partner
6	Avoiding being honest with friends
7	Accepting compliments
8	Dealing with situations where I feel vulnerable
9	Being sarcastic
10	Publicly putting myself down at sport
11	
12	

Continue if necessary

completed form highlighting ten specific problems that a client wanted to manage is shown in Box 7.1.

The client is asked which problem she would like to attempt first. It is advisable not to start on the most difficult problem in the early stages of assertiveness training. In order to build up the client's confidence, it is important to encourage her to practise and apply some of the basic assertiveness skills in easier and less threatening situations. Only then should a problem higher up the hierarchy be tackled, otherwise the client may not have attained the necessary competence and may fail to achieve her short-term and long-term goals.

Assertiveness skills can be taught and practised in the counselling or training session by using behavioural rehearsal, modelling (see Chapter 5) and role play (see below). Also suitable training videos can be used to demonstrate the skills. The homework assignments can include relevant reading, such as Lindenfield (1987) or Back

Box 7.2   *Assertiveness rights*

The right to say no
The right to make mistakes
The right to consider my needs important
The right to express my feelings in an appropriate manner without
   violating anybody else's rights
The right to take responsibility for my actions
The right not to be understood
The right to set my own priorities
The right to respect myself
The right to be me
The right to be assertive without feeling guilty

Source: Palmer, 1990a

et al. (1991). Although assertiveness training can be undertaken successfully in individual counselling, greater gains may be made by clients who attend assertiveness group training. The advantage of group work is that the individual has more opportunity to practise the skills in role play with a variety of different people. In addition, with the help of a qualified facilitator, the participants can share their experiences and also give each other encouragement, especially through difficult periods. It is helpful if counsellors can keep a referral list of local agencies or adult education institutes which regularly run assertiveness groups or classes. In counselling, specific problems related to assertion can be covered, while the external training can teach the general skills and provide the practice.

Before assertiveness skills are taught, clients can be given a 'Bill of assertiveness rights' (see Box 7.2; Palmer, 1990a) to read and discuss with their trainer and other trainees. This list of rights attempts to give the person permission to become assertive without any associated guilt and also provides broad social guidelines for ethical behaviour; for example, not violating anybody else's rights.

Useful assertiveness skills (see Box 7.3) can be discussed and practised in the counselling session or during group training. The client can then start to use the skills in role play and then real-life situations. For example, a common role play will be refusing requests and practising saying 'No'. In group training, trainees can be put into groups of three (triads), with one person trying to persuade another member of the group to accept an invitation,

Box 7.3   *Assertiveness skills*

Negative enquiry: Encourages the other person to express their negative feelings and criticisms of your behaviour in a constructive manner by asking for more specific information:

e.g. 'You're a hopeless secretary!'
'In what ways am I "hopeless"?'

Fogging: This skill helps you to deal with manipulative criticism and 'put-downs' and helps to protect your self-esteem by only acknowledging your mistakes.

e.g. 'You never meet your deadlines. You're stressing the whole office.'
'I admit that in the past three months I've missed two deadlines.'

Broken record: This skill involves re-stating in a calm manner your viewpoint while ignoring any baiting, irrelevant logic or manipulative traps.

e.g. 'I demand a rebate. I must be entitled to a rebate. I bet I'm not the first person to call you a tight bastard! Call yourself a manager!'
'Unfortunately you have returned the product in a damaged state. Therefore you are not entitled to any rebate.'
'You're really winding me up. Are you going to give me that rebate?'
'As the product is damaged, unfortunately I am not in a position to give you a rebate.'

Workable compromise: Assuming your self-worth or self-respect is not being challenged, then you offer the other person(s) a workable compromise.

e.g. 'You must stay tonight and ensure the work is finished.'
'As I said previously, I have already made an arrangement tonight that I am unable to change. However, as it is very important, on this occasion I am prepared to come in early tomorrow. The job will probably be finished by 10.00am. We've already missed today's post. Is that OK?'

Negative assertion: This skill involves you calmly agreeing and accepting your errors and negative qualities without apologizing or being defensive. However, you decide what you intend to do about it, if anything.

e.g. 'You're hopeless! You've made a complete mess of this diary.'
'Yes, I think I've made a couple of errors again.'

while that person attempts to refuse the invitation. The third trainee observes the role play. At the end of the exercise the three 'debrief', give each other constructive feedback, discuss the use of the skills applied and any difficulties that may have been encountered. The problems envisaged in the application of the skill to real-life situations can also be explored and possible solutions developed.

To keep a record of her application of the various skills to real-life situations, the client regularly completes an Assertiveness Behaviour diary (see Box 7.4). This is used in counselling or training sessions to monitor progress and discuss any difficulties that may have arisen. To keep to the client's goals it is important to refer to the APH regularly. Depending upon the client's progress, it may be useful to produce a new APH, especially if she is attaining her goals and wishes to include new, more difficult, targets.

Assertiveness training can also include other skills training such as communication training, social skills training, and friendship training (see below).

Indications and contraindications

Assuming that the individual is not very depressed, assertiveness training is usually beneficial for the majority of people. It can also be of help to clients with personality disorders, in particular, passive/aggressive personality disorder, as it can help to reduce interpersonal conflict. However, in group work, the individuals need to be able to cooperate with the trainer and with each other. If this is not possible, then assertiveness training may be contraindicated.

Clients or trainees should be warned when not to use assertiveness skills. For example, in relationships where their partner may resort to violence, or when their employer may use it as an excuse to dismiss them. Clients also need to be reminded that just because they have learnt assertiveness skills, they do not have to use them in all situations, especially when it may have negative consequences. They may need to consider alternative courses of action.

Communication skills training

Communication skills training is similar to basic counselling skills training and it overlaps with assertiveness training, friendship/intimacy training and social skills training (see the relevant sections of this chapter). Essentially, communication skills comprise sending and receiving skills. These skills can be taught in a variety of settings, such as clinical and educational settings. They can be taught to families which have a member who suffers from

Box 7.4 *Assertiveness Behaviour diary*

Name: Maggie

Date	Situation	Person/people involved	Assertiveness skills used	Evaluation of skills	Areas for improvement
16/8/94	Making a mistake at work. The manager over-reacted	My manager	Negative assertion	Manager realized he had been unreasonable once I used negative assertion	I need to use assertion skills as soon as problems arise. Initially, I felt overwhelmed and acted passively

schizophrenic episodes (Falloon et al., 1993). The skills and a general training format will be discussed in the next section.

Sending skills include:
Eye contact and gaze
Voice projection, volume and tone
Posture, gestures, appearance and body language (see Pease, 1984)
Maintaining suitable physical distance from another person
Maintaining suitable level of bodily contact
Personal space and bodily contact
Talking in specific terms
Probing skills e.g. open and closed questioning, making statements
Verbally accepting responsibility without blaming others
Making requests

Receiving skills include:
Active listening e.g. restating phrase or word, reflecting feelings, paraphrasing, summarizing, looking at the other person
Verification of what has been spoken (using skills of active listening)
Showing an interest in the other person e.g. 'Hmmm', 'yeah', 'go on', 'sure', 'and', 'then', nod of head in agreement
Rewarding the sender e.g. praise, agreement, smile

The skills are taught step by step. If a client has a large number of skill deficits, care is needed to break the learning down into small manageable chunks. Falloon et al. (1993: 80) use a basic seven-step procedure:

1 Assessment of participants' interpersonal communication skills
2 Providing a rationale for the use of skills
3 Outlining the steps of a skill
4 Rehearsing the skill
5 Constructive feedback
6 Repeated rehearsal with coaching
7 Real-life practice and review

To ensure maximum effectiveness, we suggest that multimodal counsellors adhere to this outline. The initial assessment of a client's interpersonal communication skills is important as it will highlight any skill deficits that need attention. The client's goals will indicate which specific skills need to be covered in a training programme. It is important for the counsellor to provide participants with a clear rationale for practising specific communication skills. For example, one of the advantages of learning to make specific behavioural requests of another person is to ensure that no misunderstanding or mind-reading occurs. This can help promote good social and work relationships and avoid unnecessary resentment.

Once the rationale for learning a specific communication skill has been understood, the counsellor can review the client's current ability to use the skill. Then the counsellor can demonstrate the use of the skill. If the counsellor is running a group, the participants can then practise the specific skill with each other in a role play situation. However, if the counsellor is teaching a client these skills within a counselling session, the client practises using the skill with the counsellor. Skill rehearsal, constructive feedback and coaching is then undertaken. If the counsellor 'models' the desired skill, it is important that the demonstration is not greatly superior to that expected of the client. Also, the person should have the opportunity to practise the skill immediately after the demonstration.

After sufficient practice, the counsellor or trainer discusses with the client or participants the application of the skill to real-life situations. A homework assignment to apply the skill in real life is then negotiated. In the next session, the client or participants review the homework exercise, and any difficulty encountered in the application of the skill is discussed. At this stage, when the client is attempting to use the skill in real life, praise by the counsellor can encourage the client to continue with difficult assignments.

It is essential that clients realize that using a skill only occasionally is seldom sufficient to help them become proficient in its application. Regular practice in different real-life situations needs to be encouraged by the counsellor or trainer. It is too easy to learn new skills and then let them fall into disuse.

Family settings

Communications skills are usually taught within a family setting as part of a problem-solving stress management approach to help alleviate high stress levels and thereby reduce the incidence of schizophrenic episodes with sufferers. The problem-solving approach involves teaching members of the family to hold regular meetings together where they discuss the main problem(s) of the week and then derive possible solutions to manage it. The approach also focuses on showing clients suffering from schizophrenia a number of different methods of remembering when to take their medication. Falloon et al. (1993: 78) suggest that the core curriculum for an intervention in a family setting includes:

- expressing pleasant feelings
- making constructive requests

- expressing unpleasant feelings
- active listening

These skills are still taught in the previous seven-step format. Within this setting, if a family member has a disorder such as schizophrenia it is vital that the rest of the family is aware of the nature and implications of the illness. An understanding of the medication that the person is taking is also useful. The counsellor needs to ensure that any misconceptions or misunderstandings about the illness are resolved.

Indications and contraindications

Communication skills training can normally be taught to any individual with communication skill deficits in the work, home or social setting. Individuals with social phobia or passive/aggressive personality disorder may find it particularly helpful. In couples or marital counselling it can help to reduce tension and bring partners closer together emotionally (see Schmaling et al., 1989). In some relationships, the expression of positive feelings may be low and a habit has formed whereby only negative feelings are expressed. Communication skills training can help to redress the balance. As it can be taught to groups, the approach can be financially economical and relatively easy to set up.

Assuming that they are not suffering from a psychotic episode, individuals with major disorders such as schizophrenia may benefit from communication skills training while they are living in a family setting, particularly as it helps to reduce high 'expressed emotion', a factor related to relapse in individuals with schizophrenia.

Communication skills training is contraindicated in individuals suffering from a current psychotic episode, high levels of depression or anxiety. If medication alleviates an individual's conditions then communication skills training may prove useful.

Contracting

In contracting, the client makes a formal agreement with a third party, for example a friend, work colleague or partner, to make certain changes in his behaviour (Marks, 1986). Both agree to alter their behaviour to those desired by the other person. The target behaviours should not be complex and it is important that the behaviours can be frequently repeated and also be perceived by the two parties as positive. This is often a useful intervention in couples or family counselling. It is helpful if the two parties write down the agreed behaviours in terms that are clear and specific. They can sign and date the form in a manner similar to a legal contract. This helps to formalize the agreement.

Indications and contraindications

If points 1–7 below apply for both parties, then the technique will generally be indicated. Otherwise, another intervention may be necessary. Both parties:

1 Need to be keen to undertake the exercise
2 Find the chosen behaviour changes acceptable
3 Work together as a team
4 Do not try to prevent or sabotage the other from completing the desired behaviour
5 Are not suffering from severe depression, or personality disorders that may interfere with cooperative behaviour
6 Do not have a physical disability that would prevent either person from performing the behaviour
7 Are easily able to repeat the behaviour

Friendship and intimacy training

Friendship and intimacy training overlaps with assertiveness training, communication skills training, and social skills training. In counselling, clients may raise the issue of making friendships to overcome being lonely. However, some individuals may lack the skills necessary to develop and maintain friendships. Lazarus (1981: 234) suggests that friendship is predicated on:

- sharing
- caring
- empathy
- concern
- self-disclosure
- give and take
- positive reinforcement
- complementarity

These skills can be taught in a manner similar to social skills training (see below). The counsellor or trainer first discusses with the client the advantages and disadvantages of developing relationships. The client is asked to disclose any difficulties that she may have previously encountered in making and retaining friendships. The counsellor then assesses the client's friendship skill deficits.

After the assessment, the counsellor explains the rationale for each skill that the client may need either to learn or to improve. Take, for example, the skill of self-disclosure whereby an individual may over a period of time progressively reveal to a friend intimate information regarding how she feels about that friend. This interpersonal skill can help individuals to deepen existing relationships. The risk of possible rejection usually needs to be explored as this is often one of the anxieties a client may have about using this skill.

The important skill of caring can be difficult for some individuals to understand depending upon their childhood family experience. In addition to discussing the skill of caring with the client, the counsellor can self-disclose the types of statements he or she makes about friends that would indicate that he cared for them. Typical statements are:

I want him/her to do well
I do my best to support him/her
I want him/her to be happy
I always remember his/her birthday
I try not to hurt him/her

Nelson-Jones (1993: 203) suggests a number of skills that we have adapted for friendship and intimacy training that can also be demonstrated to clients in couples counselling:

Sender skills
- taking initiatives
- being playful
- expressing wants
- sharing fantasies
- giving feedback
- showing vulnerability
- expressing pleasure and enjoyment
- showing gentleness and tenderness

Receiver skills
- being responsive to verbal, voice, body and touch messages

The counsellor can use modelling and role play to demonstrate the skills. However, extreme caution is needed when teaching skills that involve physical contact such as touch messages. For ethical reasons, it may be ill advised for counsellors in one-to-one sessions actively to demonstrate some of these skills.

Indications and contraindications
Many clients come to counselling because they experience difficulty with relationships. Although friendship and intimacy training is generally indicated with all clients with skill deficits in these areas, in our experience individuals with certain disorders may be more difficult to help (for example, individuals suffering from personality disorders such as antisocial, avoidant, borderline, narcissistic and paranoid). However, as they may greatly benefit from learning friendship and intimacy skills it may not be contraindicated for experienced counsellors and trainers to teach the relevant skills to this group. The main problem is that skills training with clients suffering personality disorder may involve transference issues with the counsellor or trainer that interfere with the learning of skills. Friendship skills involve trust which may be elusive for some individuals in this group.

Graded sexual approaches

In graded sexual approaches couples with anxieties about sex are encouraged to engage in sexual and sensual play only while they experience pleasurable feelings (Lazarus, 1981). As soon as one partner experiences negative or anxious feelings the couple stop their activity. Initially, to enable the couple to continue the activity for as long as possible, they are encouraged to use sensual techniques such as massage, caressing, touching and are generally discouraged from using sexual foreplay which may heighten their anxiety. Gradually, with longer periods of exposure to this programme, the couple should be able to engage in sexual and sensual play with lowered levels of anxiety. Finally, as they reach a closer level of intimacy, they will be able to have sex.

Indications and contraindications
This approach is indicated for couples who are experiencing anxiety about having sex with each other. It is important to ascertain why they are anxious about sex. This sometimes occurs for a number of reasons for example:

A partner may feel let down by the other.
They have not had sex for a long time due to physical illness.
One partner has been working away from home.
One or both partners believe that the other has been unfaithful.
One or both partners have misconceptions about sex.
One or both partners are concerned about pregnancy.

It is always useful to discuss these or other relevant issues with both partners before they engage in this method, otherwise the graded sexual approach may not work. If their levels of anxiety are high, they may need to learn and apply relaxation techniques first.

This technique is contraindicated if either partner does not wish to overcome the problem. In addition, if one partner blames the other partner for the problem then the counsellor needs to ensure that this issue has been dealt with before the method is used (see sensate focus training in Chapter 6, for the full indications for sex therapy).

Paradoxical intentions

Paradoxical intentions were covered in Chapter 5 on behavioural interventions. However, the technique can also be applied to interpersonal problems. Here, the client undertakes a behavioural task to try to trigger the feared consequence. For example, John feared fainting in social situations with his work colleagues and he was instructed to try to faint at the next opportunity. This technique sometimes overlaps with shame-attacking exercises (see Chapter 5) as there is often an element of shame experienced by the person in the feared situation.

Indications and contraindications

The client needs to be adequately prepared for the exposure to the social situation since this may contribute to his feared consequence; otherwise he may avoid undertaking the agreed task. The client also needs to have previously discussed with the counsellor how to deal with the situation should the feared consequence actually occur. The counsellor can teach coping imagery (see Chapter 4) and relaxation techniques (see Chapter 6) to help the client to deal with different feared consequences.

This technique is contraindicated if the client has been inadequately prepared, suffers from very high levels of anxiety or may be physically harmed should the feared consequence actually occur.

Role play

Role play is a method of learning based on role theory. Clients or participants adopt roles based on possible real-life situations and monitor the interactions with each other (see 'Empty Chair technique', Chapter 5). It can be used to help individuals to practise assertiveness and social life skills. It can also help clients in counselling to explore and express their feelings about significant others such as the person's parents or partner. Milroy (1982: 8) gives eight common purposes for the use of role play:

1 To put theoretical knowledge into practice
2 To consider the responsibilities and obligations of specific roles
3 To give practice in the playing of roles
4 To promote greater awareness of the behaviour of pair-roles
5 To promote more effective decision-making
6 To stimulate discussion
7 To clarify particular issues
8 To study specific problems

Role play is organized into three stages: briefing; interaction; de-brief. During the *briefing* stage, the role play is set up. A relevant simulated situation is chosen and the roles are explained to the participants. If role play is being used in group assertiveness training, a triad is formed with two role players and one neutral observer. The roles are then allocated. However, during individual counselling sessions, both the counsellor and client take roles. If a specific skill is to be practised during the role play, then the counsellor or trainer needs to ensure that the participants have been adequately instructed in its application.

The second stage is the *interaction* where the role players act out the simulated situation. The observer (if any) notes what happens in the interaction and is instructed to refrain from intervening. The counsellor or trainer stops the interaction when the client has attained sufficient competency in the skill being practised or when other relevant points have been learnt. The interaction may be stopped earlier if the role players are not keeping to the training objectives or if a participant becomes very disturbed by the experience.

The third stage is the *de-brief*. In group work, the role players and the observer discuss the simulated role play and give each other constructive feedback about the skills or roles they were practising. Then the trainer de-briefs the whole group. Topics for the counsellor or trainer to raise are:

1 What was learnt by the exercise?
2 How did they feel about undertaking the exercise?
3 Was it easy?
4 What problems were encountered?
5 How could these problems (if any) be overcome next time?

6 What problems could they face applying the skill or role play to a real-life situation?
7 What was rewarding or unrewarding about the exercise?

In counselling if the client has expressed her feelings to a 'significant other' during a simulated role play then the client may feel quite emotional. It is important that the counsellor is sensitive to how the client is feeling and leaves sufficient time for the de-brief. In addition, the counsellor stresses the need for the client to assume her own identity and to leave the role behind.

Case study

Frances wanted to express her feelings to her father about their deteriorating relationship. However, she was unsure what to say and how to say it. It was agreed that a role play may help Frances to practise telling her father how she felt and also explore her feelings about talking to her father in a frank manner. The counsellor took the role of her father. During the simulated role play Frances tried different approaches to raising the issue of the relationship difficulties and discussing her feelings. During the de-brief Frances stated how easy she found the exercise. The counsellor discussed the different possible outcomes should Frances go ahead and express her feelings to her father. A suitable approach was devised. This enabled Frances sensitively to inform her father about her concerns. This was the first time in their relationship that they were both open with their feelings towards each other. Her father took the opportunity to explain some of his past behaviour and apologize.

Indications and contraindications

Role play is an excellent method to help clients practise assertiveness skills and social skills before their use in real-life situations (Butler, 1989; Liberman et al., 1975). In group work, it is important to ensure that only role play occurs. When the multimodal stress counsellor or trainer works in an organizational setting and runs a group for staff who know each other, extra care must be given to this issue. We have heard of cases when inexperienced trainers have allowed employees to practise 'role play' with their managers. The simulated role play can soon become 'real play' as the two role players assume their real roles.

Role play can also help clients in counselling explore their feelings towards significant others (see 'Empty Chair technique' Chapter 5). However, the method may sometimes be contraindicated for very disturbed clients as it may evoke a high level of emotion which is difficult for the counsellor to contain.

Social skills training

Social skills training endeavours to teach clients how to improve existing skills or learn new skills that enhance their ability to relate to other people in a variety of settings, including the workplace, the home etc. Social skills training overlaps with assertiveness, communication, role play, friendship and intimacy training. As the skills involved are mentioned elsewhere in this chapter, this section will concentrate mainly on assessment procedures and the types of training programmes.

For the best results, social skills training needs to be undertaken in groups. This gives the participants the opportunity to learn and apply new skills in a social setting. However, if it is not possible to run a group or refer the client to a suitable group, the counsellor may need to consider teaching the client social skills without other participants. Although this is still possible, the gains may be limited as the client may lack sufficient practice with a variety of people before applying the skills in real-life social situations. However, clients who suffer from extreme social phobia may benefit from a period of individual social skills training before any group work. This helps to stop them feeling overwhelmed in the training group and prevents early withdrawal.

Assessment

Wilkinson and Canter (1983: 30) give eight reasons why the client's social skills need to be assessed accurately:

1 To specify the social skills assets and deficits of the prospective client
2 To assess the client's motivation for change
3 To decide whether social skills training is the most suitable form of training/therapy
4 To give information about social skills training
5 To identify and set training goals
6 To design the programme
7 To monitor the progress of the client
8 To evaluate the effectiveness of the programme

At the assessment stage, the counsellor will need to obtain information about the client's relationships, perceived interpersonal difficulties and how the client relates to others. The client's interpersonal goals are discussed and noted. The goals of social interaction are clearly defined; for example, purchasing an item of food from a supermarket. In social skills training it is important for clients to have explicit goals with specific behavioural targets. Vague goals are difficult to achieve and the client may need to be encouraged to be specific. For example:

Vague	*Specific*
To get out more.	To visit my friend weekly. Go to the club on Friday nights. Have lunch with my parents every Sunday. Go to the football club on home games.
Meeting members of the opposite sex.	Join the local singles club that meets fortnightly on Thursday evenings in the Hare and Billet pub. Join an adult education French class.

The Assertiveness Problem Hierarchy (see Box 7.1) can be used to list the client's goals in order of difficulty. The client starts by learning skills that can be used in situations which she feels less anxious about. The goals need to be realistic and attainable.

Self-report questionnaires (e.g. the Social Situations Questionnaire, Marks, 1986: 58; Bryant and Trower, 1974) can be completed by clients to aid the assessment process. These questionnaires help the counsellor to monitor and evaluate the effectiveness of the social skills training programme. Although self-report questionnaires may help with the evaluation, they can sometimes be of limited use as they only reflect the client's subjective views. This needs to be taken into consideration if the counsellor is not in a position to verify the client's interactions in real-life situations.

Programmes
Standardized programmes are frequently used in group training settings. For the trainer, this is easier to run and may help clients who are not able to verbalize specific requirements and goals. In a standardized programme the optimum number of participants is between eight and twelve. Depending upon the client group, the course could include modules on non-verbal behaviour, such as eye contact, proximity, gesture and vocal cues (i.e. volume/tone); listening and talking skills, such as paraphrasing and summarizing; opening and closing conversation skills; making apologies; making/refusing a request; and using assertiveness skills, such as fogging, workable compromise and broken record (see Box 7.3).

Individualized programmes are especially recommended for use within one-to-one counselling, although they can also be applied to group training. Individualized one-to-one programmes can concentrate specifically on the client's behavioural deficits and goals. This can aid monitoring of the client's progress. Sessions can also concentrate on the immediate needs of a client, for example the skills required to deal with a job interview.

Some care is needed when deciding the mix of participants for group training, especially in a psychiatric setting. Between four and six members is the ideal number in an individualized social skills training group. The psychiatric problems of the clients may make it necessary to have two trainers to help deal with any difficult situations that may arise.

The rationale for including any skill or exercise in a programme needs to be given to the participants. In particular, the use of warm up exercises before role play should be explained. In our experience, whether with group or individual training, it is preferable that the skills to be included in any programme should be negotiated with the participants. This will encourage the participants to ask questions they may have regarding the specific skill and thereby increase their level of active engagement in the exercise. If the counsellor is not convinced that the participants understand the rationale behind an exercise or skill, we have found it useful to ask the group the following questions: 'I'm not sure whether I've explained the rationale for this exercise too well. Would somebody like to explain the rationale to the group?' If there are any misunderstandings, the counsellor can either ask another member of the group to explain the rationale or the counsellor can give a clearer explanation him or herself.

In group contexts, it is recommended that programmes are for a fixed number of sessions. However, as each group is comprised of different individuals, there is no ideal number of sessions. The duration is often influenced by time and the financial restraints of the institution offering the training. Between six and twelve sessions, each of one and a half hours' length, may be sufficient to enable many individuals to make considerable progress. A follow-up session after the training programme has finished can also be helpful. This can be held between 1 and 2 months later.

Indications and contraindications

Social skills training has been used in a variety of settings: college and adult education institutes, family therapy units, counselling, the prison service, and psychiatric hospitals. Assuming the participants are not suffering from psychotic episodes, or experiencing high levels of depression or anxiety, social skills training can be beneficial to anybody who has social skills deficits.

Time-limited intercommunication

There are many other interpersonal techniques that can usefully be used within couples or family counselling that fall outside the scope of this book. We include 'time-limited intercommunication' as this has proved a useful technique to lower stress levels in a variety of settings.

Time-limited intercommunication is usually used in couples or marital counselling where there is discord (see Lazarus, 1981). The counsellor negotiates with the couple a set time every day when both partners can talk and listen to each other. A coin is flipped and the winner of the toss starts the dialogue while the other partner just listens. The listener can take notes if necessary. The talking partner can discuss anything whatsoever. Every 5 minutes the partners swap roles. This continues for 30 to 60 minutes depending upon the tolerance levels of the couple. Each partner is given an equal length of time to speak. At the end of each session the couple hug each other and then cease discussion on any topic raised. However, if they so wish, they can return to any topic in the next agreed session.

This technique allows couples to talk and listen to each other with equal parity if they adhere to the guidelines. Within a month of its use the level of mutual understanding can increase and the relationship can improve.

In a family setting where children and teenagers are included, the members can sit around a table and pass an item such as a stone to each other. The stone is passed round the group in one direction, i.e. clockwise. Only the person holding the stone is allowed to speak. The other family members do not interrupt and await their turn to hold the stone. Once again, a time limit is imposed upon each speaker. This can also be used in industrial settings as a conflict resolution intervention.

Indications and contraindications

This technique is indicated where all parties wish to improve their relationship. However, it may be contraindicated if there is a history of violence in the relationship.

8

Health and Lifestyle Interventions

In this chapter we focus on interventions used in the drugs and biology modality. As with the interpersonal interventions, the counsellor usually adopts an educational or coaching approach when working in this modality. Health and lifestyle interventions include exercise, nutrition and stopping smoking. Multimodal stress counsellors are advised to increase their general knowledge of these and other health-related interventions by reading relevant literature (e.g. Ashton and Davies, 1986; Brownell, 1991) or attending suitable courses.

It is useful for counsellors to have some knowledge of the commonly prescribed medical and psychiatric drugs as their side-effects may be similar to the symptoms of stress. Counsellors will benefit from reading suitable literature (e.g. Lacey, 1991) and receiving relevant training. *MIMS* (*Monthly Index of Medical Specialties*) and the *British National Formulary* provide up-to-date information on existing and new drugs including their contra-indications.

This chapter looks first at two important issues that are relevant to multimodal stress counsellors working with clients who have problems in this modality: referrals and liaising with medical practitioners. Various health and lifestyle interventions are then surveyed.

Referrals

When assessing clients with stress problems, counsellors will often need to refer them to medical practitioners or specialists for a diagnosis. Counsellors are strongly advised not to make any medical diagnosis as stress-related symptoms may be confused with life-threatening organic problems that require immediate treatment; for example, chest pains can be indicative of coronary heart disease. Even if the specialist has made a diagnosis of stress as the cause of the client's problems, we recommend that the counsellor does not categorically accept the diagnosis in case an error has been made. We know of a case where a number of specialists stated that the client was physically fit and that her headaches were due to stress. Unfortunately, they had all overlooked a brain tumour. We prefer to say to our clients: 'Assuming the diagnosis is correct, I will show you how to deal with your levels of stress and your stress-related symptoms.'

In Britain, the majority of clients will be registered with a medical practice. To ensure that clients receive the best overall medical help with their problems we have found that it is useful for multimodal stress counsellors to have a good relationship with their local health centre. As the counsellor may see the client more often than the doctor, the counsellor will be aware of the client's progress and be in a better position to monitor any detrimental effects of prescribed medication. A client may become very disturbed about the side-effects of her prescribed drugs and the counsellor can suggest that she speaks to her doctor about changing the medication. Alternatively, having first obtained the client's permission, the counsellor can inform the doctor in writing about the problem.

As clients may wish to try a number of different approaches to reduce their levels of stress or stress-related symptoms, we recommend that counsellors keep a register of suitably qualified therapists. This register could include practitioners of acupuncture, Alexander technique, aromatherapy, homeopathy, massage, nutrition, osteopathy, physiotherapy, physical education, relaxation therapist/teacher, as well as physicians and medical specialists. If counsellors are qualified to practise a physical therapy such as massage, we would strongly advise against them offering a client this service in addition to counselling as it would blur the client–counsellor therapeutic boundaries and may put the client in a vulnerable position.

One of the hidden benefits of liaising with other practitioners is that it can often lead to an increase in client referrals. However, this usually only occurs if the practitioner believes that the counsellor acts in a professional manner and is suitably qualified.

In the following section, health and lifestyle interventions are examined. Generally, in addition to the usual BASIC ID Modality Profile, interventions in this modality require a second-order BASIC ID to assess the problem correctly and devise a thorough therapeutic programme for the specific health-related disorder. As problems in this modality may shorten an individual's lifespan these interventions are seldom contraindicated, although their introduction may need to be graded.

Alcohol

Alcohol is a central nervous system (CNS) depressant. It is manufactured from sugar-based fluids by a process of fermentation. As acute pharmacodynamic tolerance can occur after its consumption, drinkers may underestimate their level of intoxication. Regular drinkers may exhibit chronic pharmacodynamic tolerance and need to drink increased levels of alcohol before they become aware of its subjective effects. Regular drinkers may become alcohol dependent (Ashton, 1987).

Depending upon the amount consumed, the immediate short-term effects of alcohol can include relaxation, mild euphoria, reduced motor coordination/mental/cognitive ability, slurred speech, sleep disturbance, nausea, coma or death. It can have a disinhibiting effect which can lead to general irresponsibility, violence or dangerous driving. As alcohol may stimulate the production of adrenaline, sleep disturbances can occur. The possible long-term effects of regular drinking are liver disease, liver cancer, alcoholic hepatitis, intestinal bleeding, jaundice, hypertension, heart disease, Wernicke's encephalopathy, Korsakoff's psychosis, impaired brain function, memory loss, cirrhosis and pancreatitis. Some of these disorders can lead to death.

If a client is a regular or binge drinker, the counsellor may decide to discuss the advantages and disadvantages of alcohol consumption. It is worth noting that some research suggests that daily ingestion of a unit or two of alcohol, preferably red wine, may lower the risk of coronary heart disease. If the client wishes to lower the intake of alcohol, a number of different interventions can be used such as stimulus control, keeping a drinking diary (see Box 8.1), and drinking a low-alcohol alternative. In cases where the client is regularly drinking much higher than the recommended amounts (the generally accepted maximum recommended consumption is 21 units a week for adult males, 14 units a week for adult females, where one unit is a glass of wine or half a pint of beer) more support and encouragement is generally required. This can be obtained by support group therapy. In severe cases, detoxification may be necessary where the client completely 'dries out'. The symptoms of withdrawal may be very unpleasant in these cases.

In our experience, the multimodal stress counsellor may also need to examine any relevant core irrational beliefs such as 'I can't stand it', 'I am worthless', 'life is unbearable' and 'I must consume alcohol to make my life more bearable'. Alcohol abuse often starts during a prolonged period of pressure or after a negative life-event; for example, loss of a job or a partner. Some individuals use

Box 8.1   *Drinking diary*

Day	What was consumed	When/Where/With whom	Units	Total

Weekly total _____

Units (u): a rough guide
Ordinary strength beer, lager, cider: Half-pint = 1 u; 1 pint = 2 u.
Strong beer, lager, cider: Half-pint = 2 u; 1 pint = 4 u.
Wine (11% alcohol content):   Standard glass = 1 u.
Spirits: Standard English measure = 1 u.
Sherry: Standard small measure = 1 u.

alcohol to lessen the effects of post-traumatic stress disorder (PTSD) which can occur after a life-threatening event such as experiencing a car accident, being a victim or an observer of violence. In these cases the counsellor will need to help the client come to terms with the life-event as well as reducing the alcohol intake. We have found that it may be advantageous to refer the client to an alcohol counsellor or Alcoholics Anonymous to deal specifically with the reduction in alcohol consumption, while the primary counsellor focuses the sessions on dealing with the negative life-event. Clients suffering from severe alcohol dependency may need a gradual alcohol reduction programme as opposed to a sudden cessation.

Blood pressure

Blood pressure is caused by the heart pumping blood around the body at the rate of 5 litres per minute through the blood vessels. The diameter of the blood vessels also determines the final blood pressure. For the average young adult blood pressure is 120/80 where the first figure denotes the 'systolic' blood pressure during each heart beat (contraction of the heart) and the last lower figure denotes the 'diastolic' blood pressure as the heart relaxes between beats. Blood pressure is raised when individuals become angry, stressed, anxious, excited or during exercise, and this is quite normal. However, if an individual's blood pressure is high for a prolonged period, this can lead to serious consequences such as heart attack, strokes, arterial and renal diseases (see Kannel and Schatzkin, 1983). A number of lifestyle behaviours can lead to high blood pressure, including excessive alcohol consumption, being overweight, unsuitable diet, lack of exercise, Type A behaviour and stress (Steptoe, 1981). Unfortunately, individuals often suffer from high blood pressure for a prolonged period without any obvious symptoms and this can lead to irreversible damage occurring to vital organs. Individuals with high blood pressure may experience giddiness, fatigue and headaches but this is not always the case and should not be used as an accurate guide.

Established multimodal stress counsellors are likely to be referred clients who are suffering from high blood pressure or essential hypertension. Hypertension is a chronic disorder where there has been a prolonged elevation of blood pressure within the arterial blood system. If it has been caused by a specific physical problem such as an adrenal tumour or renal failure then it is known as secondary hypertension which involves medical treatment only. However, essential (which means 'of unknown origin') hypertension is often alleviated by changing behavioural lifestyle factors. Box 8.2 highlights the changes individuals can make to improve their condition.

It is useful to undertake a second-order BASIC ID specifically targeted at the possible causes of a client's high blood pressure or essential hypertension. A typical case is illustrated in Table 8.1. Notice how an assessment across all of the modalities is necessary to devise a comprehensive intervention strategy. Even though this is

Box 8.2   *How to reduce high blood pressure*

There are several lifestyle changes you can make to help reduce your blood pressure or maintain it at a safe level. The most beneficial changes are listed below:

1 Limit your alcohol intake. The recommended maximum for males is 21 units a week and for females 14 units a week where one unit is a glass of wine or half pint of normal strength beer.
2 Reduce your weight to the accepted amount for your height and frame. If you are very much overweight you may need to start a weight reduction programme.
3 Smoking can raise your blood pressure and may damage your blood vessels and heart. Reduce the amount you smoke or preferably stop smoking altogether.
4 Salt can increase blood pressure. Use it more sparingly and try to avoid adding to your cooking.
5 Active sports such as swimming or jogging can help reduce blood pressure. Assuming you are physically well, start a sport or an exercise programme. If in doubt about your physical health or you are over 35 years of age, first discuss any exercise programme with your doctor.
6 Stress raises blood pressure. De-stress yourself. Keep negative life-events in perspective. Ask yourself 'Is it really that awful?' 'Is it really the end of the world?' 'Am I demanding too much from myself or others?' 'Do I really need to be this angry or am I making a mountain out of a molehill?' 'Is holding on to my belief or attitude helping me to get what I want – to stay calm, de-stressed, with low blood pressure?' If you become very stressed about specific situations then consider avoiding them or better still think of a constructive way to deal with them.

a multi-level approach to dealing with the health-related problem, as high blood pressure can cause irreversible damage and possibly lead to death it is important to commence with the most useful interventions as early as possible. In the case detailed in Table 8.1, instigating a weight and alcohol reduction programme first would be clinically the preferred option, closely followed by relaxation and disputation of the client's irrational beliefs.

It is important for the counsellor to liaise with the medical practitioner responsible for the client when dealing with conditions

Table 8.1 *Second-order BASIC ID for an individual with high blood pressure*

Modality	Problem	Proposed treatment
Behaviour	Type A behaviour	Behavioural education, e.g. under-take one task at a time; leave more time to do tasks; only take on tasks within job remit; leave time for relaxation. Dispute irrational beliefs which are responsible for hostility and 'hurry up' behaviours
	Smokes 30 cigarettes a day	Stop smoking programme
Affect	Feels very angry when work targets not achieved	Anger management
Sensation	Physically tense	Relaxation exercises and biofeed-back, e.g. biodots
Imagery	Picture of self failing at tasks	Coping imagery
Cognition	I/others must perform well; if I fail to reach my targets then I am a failure and I am worthless and deserve to be punished	Disputation of irrational beliefs Coping statements on cards
Interpersonal	Aggressive with staff	Assertiveness training
	Acts impatiently with staff	Dispute belief that 'I can't stand being kept waiting'
Drugs/ biology	High blood pressure	Blood pressure reduction pro-gramme; drug treatment if neces-sary. Liaise with medical specialist and general practitioner
	Poor diet	Nutritional education, e.g. decrease intake of saturated fats, consume fish three times a week, decrease salt intake, increase fibre intake, eat lean meat
	Drinks 32 units of alcohol a week	Reduce alcohol intake to 12 units a week
	2 stone overweight	Weight reduction and graded exercise programme

Table 8.2 *Average caffeine content of beverages and chocolate*

Dietary source	Average caffeine concentration (5oz cup) (mg)
Instant coffee	70
Real coffee	100
Decaffeinated coffee	3
Tea	40
Cola drink	20
Chocolate drink	10
Small milk chocolate bar	20

such as high blood pressure to ensure that no aspect is overlooked. For example, some prescribed drugs can raise blood pressure and lifestyle changes will have no effect on reducing it. Some techniques can initially raise blood pressure (e.g. progressive relaxation) and counsellors need to ensure that they are aware of the contra-indications of all techniques they may use. If clients with high blood pressure use progressive relaxation, it is important that they do not tense their muscles for more than a couple of seconds at a time and only spend a short while undertaking the entire relaxation exercise.

Caffeine

Caffeine is a stimulant that acts on the CNS. It is found in at least 60 plant species and is commonly consumed by individuals drinking coffee (*Coffea arabica*), tea (*Thea sinensis*), cola drinks (*Cola acuminata*) or cocoa and chocolate (*Theobroma cocoa*). Its consumption can lead to feelings of anxiety, nervousness, insomnia, increased alertness, palpitations, muscle tremors, restlessness, shakiness and jitteriness. Table 8.2 (Parrott, 1991: 210) illustrates the average caffeine content of various beverages and chocolate.

When assessing clients, it is useful to ascertain their average daily intake of caffeine as high levels of caffeine consumption can cause symptoms that are similar to anxiety neurosis and stress. The average daily intake of caffeine in the United Kingdom is about 444 mg (Griffiths and Woodson, 1988). A regular high intake of caffeine (700–1000 mg/day) is known as 'caffeinism' and is often misdiagnosed. General practitioners may incorrectly treat the condition with antidepressants or benzodiazepines. After the assessment, if caffeinism appears to be the case, then the counsellor may need either to ask the client to convey this information to his or her doctor or, with the client's permission, to notify the doctor directly.

When consumed, caffeine has a half-life of about 6 hours. Therefore, if an individual drinks a cup of caffeinated coffee at 6.00pm, by midnight the person will still have 50 per cent of the caffeine in the bloodstream. If the individual regularly drinks coffee throughout the day it is very likely to cause insomnia or disturbed sleep.

Clients with a high intake of caffeine generally benefit from a reduction programme. However, gradual reduction is recommended as sudden cessation can cause nausea, fatigue, headaches, migraines and coffee craving for the first 48 hours.

In our experience, many clients have their first panic attack after drinking strong coffee and alcohol which both have an effect on the CNS.

Exercise

Why exercise? A question clients may still ask even after all the public health promotion campaigns and articles published in the popular press and health magazines on the benefits of regular exercise. Research shows that the incidence of coronary heart disease is reduced in individuals who regularly engage in physical leisure-time activities or non-sedentary work (see Brunner and Manelis, 1960; Paffenbarger and Hale, 1975). In addition, vigorous exercise can improve an individual's mental health and self-esteem. Exercise is therefore recommended as an intervention for individuals who wish to have a balanced stress management programme as it aids both physiological and psychological health. Some research (Griest et al., 1978) has even found that running is more effective than psychotherapy for individuals suffering from depression. It can help some individuals release their aggression in a safe, controlled environment and not direct it at a perceived source of aggravation, such as their employer. For many people, exercise is beneficial as it works in a manner similar to cognitive distraction.

Quick and Quick (1984: 249–50) group exercise into four main categories: aerobic exercise; recreational sports; flexibility and muscular relaxation activities; and muscle strength and endurance building. Aerobic exercise is physical activity which produces a sustained metabolic, respiration and heart rate for a prolonged duration of time. The minimum recommended period is at least 20 minutes and is preferably repeated three times a week. Aerobic exercise is the best method of achieving cardiorespiratory fitness. Examples of aerobic activities include swimming, jogging, continuous cycling, skiing cross country, and sports that involve vigorous exercise such as squash or tennis.

Recreational sports include racket games, aerobics, martial arts, football, golf and walking. Other activities may include pastimes such as dancing or gardening depending upon how hard the person works. Office workers could incorporate extra exercise into their daily regime by using the stairs instead of the lift or getting off the bus one stop earlier than necessary on their way to work. Flexibility and muscular relaxation activity includes Tai Chi Chuan, yoga and calisthenics. Muscle strength and endurance building includes weight-lifting and isometric exercises.

It is important that unfit clients have a graded exercise programme towards improving their physical well-being. Most towns and cities have physical fitness centres where there are qualified physical fitness instructors who will be able to give guidance on the correct amount and type of exercise and training available. The counsellor should have suitable books, leaflets and videos that explain the different types of exercise available and related health matters.

Indications and contraindications

People of all ages can benefit from some form of exercise, but the research shows that only continued, regular exercise reduces the likelihood of individuals suffering from coronary heart disease. Any benefits gained disappear after a lapse of two to three years of no regular exercise. Therefore, clients need to have a continuing programme of exercise which they may need to adapt according to their changing physical abilities.

Counsellors should be aware of a number of important contra-indications if their clients are seeking advice about an exercise programme. Clients who have a history of heart disease, heart conduction defects, cardiac arrhythmias, angina pectoris, stroke, diabetes, lung disease, liver/kidney disorders, hormonal disorders, or other serious medical conditions should first consult their doctor before commencing *any* exercise programme. This includes any person whose resting blood pressure is greater than 100 mmHg diastolic or 160 mmHg systolic or has received previous medical advice *not* to exercise. As a 'double-check' the multimodal stress counsellor can enquire whether clients have been prescribed any medications for blood vessels or the heart in the previous 12 months. It is important to note that clients may not have been informed by their doctors that they may have a suspected heart condition and the counsellor could use the prescribed medication as an indicator to seek further medical advice.

In addition, we recommend that if clients are overweight or are over 35 years of age, it may also be wise to seek medical advice first. Some individuals insufficiently grade their exercise programme and their first attempt to run is at a fast pace for 20 minutes instead of a slow pace for a couple of minutes. This can be a very dangerous mistake as it can lead to a cardiac arrest. Even if an individual is fit, warm-up periods are advisable before undertaking exercise. Cool-down periods are also a good idea after taking exercise.

Nicotine

Nicotine is an active drug found in tobacco (*Nicotinia tabacum*). Tobacco can be smoked or chewed, and nicotine can be absorbed through the skin by using nicotine patches or even injected intravenously. Nicotine affects the CNS by increasing the level of beta-endorphin. This increases an individual's tolerance to pain, reduces aggression, increases heart rate and blood pressure, and also heightens feelings of pleasure. The levels of arousal are also affected. The act of smoking is usually a displacement behaviour that occurs during a situation that involves social uncertainty (Parrott, 1991). Role models also provide a stimulus for a person to start smoking. However, once a person has started smoking the most likely reason for its continuance is the addiction to nicotine. This probably explains why herbal non-nicotine cigarettes are still unpopular by comparison.

The main causes of smoking-related diseases are from the tar and carbon monoxide inhaled. Tar is carcinogenic (Doll and Peto, 1976) and can lead to cancers of the lungs, lips, gum and mouth depending upon how it is absorbed. Smoking can also lead to shortness of breath or emphysema and can restrict an individual's ability to undertake hard physical activity. Carbon monoxide can bond with the haemoglobin and reduce its oxygen-carrying capacity. In addition, it can cause peripheral arterial disease, arteriosclerosis, fatal haemorrhage and tissue death. The blood supply to the heart can also deteriorate with serious consequences such as heart attack. Female clients who are pregnant should be reminded of the increased rate of spontaneous abortion and other complications, such as lighter babies and abnormal placentas.

Employers have begun to receive health-related claims from employees suffering the effects of passive smoking, and there has been a move to reduce smoking at work. This has placed pressure on many people to stop smoking and the multimodal stress counsellor needs to have a working knowledge of techniques that can help. Research indicates that the most effective interventions are multi-component programmes. We have found that if a second-order BASIC ID (see Chapter 2) is undertaken, then it is possible to focus the interventions directly on the problem areas. A typical second order BASIC ID is illustrated in Table 8.3.

The second-order BASIC ID helps the counsellor and client to examine the important problems that may arise and prevent the person from achieving his goal. We normally recommend that clients agree a 'Stop Day' when they stop smoking completely. Usually two weeks are required before the Stop Day to provide sufficient time to deal with the other problems on the BASIC ID. The night before Stop Day clients will need to clear their accommodation of ash trays and cigarettes and read their coping statements. It is important for clients to start the Stop Day differently from normal to help break the smoking habit.

For example, John started the day with a shower, had a slice of toast for breakfast instead of his usual coffee and cigarette. He drank a grapefruit juice. He read the coping statements a number of times as he could feel himself faltering. He had chosen a day to stop smoking at the beginning of the month when he was under less pressure at work. If he managed to last the day without smoking, he had arranged to reward himself by going out with his partner to their favourite restaurant in the evening. If he felt tense he would listen to a relaxation tape and use positive imagery to unwind.

In our experience, some clients ask for an easy option such as hypnosis. The hypnosis script described in Chapter 6 can be adapted for this use by including stop smoking coping skills, coping imagery and the benefits of giving up smoking. We would still undertake a BASIC ID but include an extra session on hypnosis. These sessions are recorded so that clients can listen to the tape daily at the outset to help them relax and build up their confidence.

Many clients find using nicotine patches or chewing nicotine gum useful as methods to break the smoking habit. However, they may later experience difficulty in stopping these substitutes.

Indications and contraindications

Stop smoking programmes are indicated for all clients as they can improve their health and longevity. However, when clients are suffering from high levels of stress, stopping smoking can become an additional burden especially if it is one of the few, albeit unhealthy, coping strategies or pleasures they possess. In these cases it is generally beneficial to concentrate on one of their immediate problems first. Only when their situation has improved may it be possible to return to the stop smoking programme. Social support is also an important factor in a stop smoking programme. If

Table 8.3 *Second-order BASIC ID for an individual who wished to stop smoking*

Modality	Problem	Proposed treatment
Behaviour	Increased smoking under pressure (Type A behaviour)	Relaxation techniques and positive imagery
	Smokes at all meal times; increased smoking when drinking coffee	Stimulus control, e.g. remove ash trays and cigarettes from house; drink fruit juice that does not taste pleasant when smoking. Aversive conditioning: rapid inhalation and frequent, e.g. every 5 seconds: leads to nicotine overdosing and when he feels ill he is instructed to stop
Affect	More easily angered when smoking reduced	Examine what exactly he becomes angry about
Sensation	Increased tension and fatigue when not smoking	Progressive relaxation (Benson not used due to breathing difficulties)
	Food does not taste inviting	Stop smoking
Imagery	Can only ever see himself smoking	Coping imagery, e.g. seeing self in work and social situations not smoking
	Has a childhood image of his favourite uncle smoking	Aversive imagery: picture of uncle in hospital dying of lung cancer and going to his funeral
Cognition	I must have a cigarette when I want one. I couldn't stand it without one. I can't change	Disputation of irrational beliefs; coping statements on cards
	Smoking improves my concentration	Health education, e.g. concentration only improves up to certain limit, then it decreases
	I must achieve my work targets	Belief underlying Type A behaviour: disputation of belief
Interpersonal	Smokes in social situations	Initially, avoid these if possible
	Smokes when talking on the telephone	Shorten length of calls; use hand usually used for smoking to hold telephone handset and hold pen in free hand
	Passive: won't say no	Practise saying 'No thank you, I no longer smoke' (also use coping imagery)

Continued

Table 8.3 *continued*

Modality	Problem	Proposed treatment
	Works with colleague who also wishes to stop smoking	Contract with each other to stop smoking; provide support and agree to pay a penalty of £50 to a charity of colleague's choice if he smokes more than 5 cigarettes in first month
Drugs/ biology	Smokes an average of 40 cigarettes a day	Health education about the adverse effects of smoking. Agree 'Stop Day' in 2 weeks' time. Reduce intake by 50 per cent over next fortnight. Deal with other problems on BASIC ID. Once stopped, save money that would have been spent
	Sleep disturbance when smokes over 60 a day	Reduce smoking
	Breathlessness and frequently catches colds. Smoker's cough	Medical check-up in case of undiagnosed problems
	Lack of exercise	Graded exercise programme
	Very low consumption of fruit and fresh vegetables	Health education: benefits of eating this food

co-workers or partners are non-supportive then difficulty in stopping can occur.

Stop smoking programmes often fail if clients choose to stop smoking when they are about to embark on an activity that differs from their usual routine, such as going on holiday. We recommend that the programme starts only when they are in their usual surroundings.

Whenever possible, we discourage clients from using nicotine substitutes such as gum or patches as these may become yet another addiction to stop. We know of individuals who have overdosed on nicotine by accidentally using too many patches. They describe the sensation as feeling 'high' and they tend to suffer from palpitations.

Nutrition

A poor diet can lead to a number of illnesses, including heart disease, digestive disorders and obesity. Although these disorders can start in childhood, they can take many years to develop and there may be few signs of any difficulties. Taking a health educative approach with clients on the topic of nutrition can have a number of different benefits. Not only can this prove to be a fairly easy intervention to make, once clients have started improving their diet there is a strong tendency for their health locus of control to become more internal. Their belief that they have little control over their health is challenged behaviourally as they start to take more care with their diet and notice that they feel physically better and more in control. In our experience, if they have been suffering from stress, this self-efficacy (see Bandura, 1977, 1986) can lead to an improvement in their unhealthy and unhelpful emotions (see Chapter 4) as well as their physical state.

We have developed a number of handouts that educate clients on different aspects of nutrition (see Boxes 8.3 and 8.4). These handouts are generally discussed during a counselling or training session although they can be set as a homework assignment for clients to read. To avoid over-complicating the handouts, we have not included information about the two types of cholesterol: low-density lipoproteins (LDL) and high-density lipoproteins (HDL). LDL can adhere to artery walls which may lead to arterial disease whereas research indicates that HDL can protect the individual from heart attack. Vigorous exercise tends to increase the level of HDL, while a diet low in cholesterol-rich foods and saturated fats will help to reduce LDL levels. Both LDL and triglycerides are fatty substances which are carried in the blood supply and need reducing. Triglycerides are lowered by reducing sugar and alcohol consumption. The recommended triglyceride level is under 100 mg/dl.

Indications and contraindications

Improving diet and nutrition is indicated for all clients. However, care needs to be taken if clients are prone to suffer from allergies to different foods, or have specific disorders where eating certain products can lead to negative consequences.

Weight reduction and control programmes

Research indicates that for a given height there is an approximate ideal body weight. Obesity needs to be taken seriously as it can lead to a number of health-related risks, which include heart disease, high blood pressure, stroke, bronchitis, diabetes, gallstones and arthritis (see Pitts and Phillips, 1991). There can also be a negative emotional consequence as many individuals suffer from a loss of self-esteem and become depressed if they perceive themselves as overweight and therefore unattractive.

Box 8.3   *Fats and heart disease*

People who eat a diet that contains a high proportion of fats known as saturated fats may increase their chances of suffering from heart disease as fatty deposits can stick to the arterial walls. This can lead to blocked or narrowed arteries which increases blood pressure and may result in a heart attack. The fatty deposits contain blood cholesterol which can be controlled by eating suitable foods that have low levels of saturated fat and by the reduction of high levels of stress. However, some fats do not increase the levels of blood cholesterol. It is worth knowing about the three main fats that are found in food:

Saturated fats
A high level of saturated fat in a diet can increase the level of blood cholesterol and may lead to heart disease. Saturated fats are found in dairy products such as butter, cheese and milk. Fatty portions of lamb, beef and pork also contain high levels of saturated fats.

Mono-unsaturated fats
Mono-unsaturated fats do not increase blood cholesterol levels. They are found in avocado pears and olive oil. It has been suggested that olive oil is responsible for the low rate of heart disease found in individuals living by the Mediterranean.

Polyunsaturated fats
Polyunsaturated fats can help to prevent blood forming dangerous clots. These are found in oily fish, e.g. sardines, pilchards and mackerel. Polyunsaturated fats also help to reduce levels of blood cholesterol. A different type of polyunsaturates is found in vegetable oils, e.g. corn, soya, safflower and sunflower. The consumption of margarines that are labelled 'high in polyunsaturates' is strongly preferable to eating lard or hard margarine which are saturated fats.

Body weight is increased when energy intake exceeds energy consumed. To achieve the desired weight loss overweight clients will need to reduce their calorific input (eat less food) and expend more energy by undertaking more exercise and increasing their lifestyle activity. However, this is rarely easy to achieve and maintain. Too

Box 8.4   *Foods to eat and foods to avoid*

Preferred foods

Fruit or canned fruit in natural juices. Apples, grapes, berries and oranges are good sources of pectin.

High-fibre products such as wholegrain bread, maize flours, brown rice, beans, pasta, pulses, cereals, bran and oats. These products aid efficient digestion.

Low fat cheese or cheese alternatives made with sunflower oil. Also cottage cheese.

Lean meat, fish or poultry. In particular, oily fish is very healthy.

Skimmed or semi-skimmed milk.

Salad dressings or mayonnaise alternatives which are low in fat or high in polyunsaturates.

Steamed, poached or grilled food.

Foods to avoid

Canned fruit in syrup.

White bread, biscuits, sweets and pre-sweetened breakfast cereals.

Full-fat cheeses, especially Stilton, Cheddar.

Meat with fatty portions and meat products, e.g. pâtés, sausages, burgers, including pork scratchings.

Cream, whole milk and yogurt, unless low-fat natural yogurt.

Salad dressings which are oily and are not high in polyunsaturates. Also mayonnaise.

Fried food.

Salt or products with high salt content.

Products with a high sugar content, e.g. sweetened fruit juices, chocolate, some cola drinks and instant custard.

often clients want an easy 'crash diet' which seldom leads to long-term weight loss and control. Usually one of the most difficult aspects of a weight reduction and control programme is the permanent change of lifestyle that is required from sedentary to active to maintain any weight loss. There are a number of stages through which dieters may pass when attempting to lose weight (see

Brownell, 1991). The three relevant stages are: contemplation, action and maintenance.

Contemplation

The stage of *contemplation* is when counsellors can help clients to persuade themselves that losing weight would be beneficial. To aid this process the Contemplation and Information form (Box 8.5) can be given to clients to complete at home or in the counselling session. Once completed, this questionnaire is discussed in a counselling session to help clients and their counsellors assess the existing situation, examine the possible changes that may be required and consider the advantages of losing weight. It is important for counsellors not to rush this stage as most individuals need to be psychologically prepared for the task of weight reduction otherwise success is unlikely. Assuming that clients wish to start a weight reduction programme, before commencing the *action* stage, a second-order BASIC ID should be undertaken to assess clients' problems related to weight in a comprehensive manner. Some of the problems that are often raised in a second-order BASIC ID are:

Does not eat three moderate meals a day but tends to have one
     large meal
Tends to eat snacks in-between meals
Unable to refuse desserts or second helpings – non-assertive
Strong preference for sweet food and drinks
Strong preference for fatty and fried foods and avoids salads, fresh
     vegetables and fruit
Takes little exercise and has sedentary job
Comfort eats when feeling depressed, anxious or guilty
Depression and low self-esteem associated with self-image
Feelings of 'emptiness' in stomach which 'must' be filled
No coping imagery
Dysfunctional thoughts and attitudes
     'I can't stand it'
     'Being overweight is the reason why nobody truly likes me.
       However, if people didn't like me when I looked fine then that
       would be really awful'
     Thinking in 'all-or-nothing' terms e.g. 'If I eat too much today
       then I have completely blown my diet and I may as well give up
       now. This really proves that I'm a worthless individual'
     'Dieting should be easy'
     'I shouldn't have to exercise and change my lifestyle just to lose
       weight'

Box 8.5 *Weight reduction and control: contemplation and information form*

For breakfast I usually eat _____

_____

For lunch I usually eat _____

_____

For dinner I usually eat _____

_____

In between meals I usually eat _____

_____

Circle answers that apply to you:

I regularly eat crisps/biscuits/sweets/pastries/pies/fried food

I regularly eat salads/fresh vegetables/fruit

I regularly eat fibre-rich food such as pasta/wholemeal bread/
                    jacket potatoes/high-fibre cereals

I or members of my family have suffered from stroke/diabetes/
                    heart disease/high blood pressure

My weekly consumption of alcohol is _____ units

My sugar intake is low/medium/high

My lifestyle is sedentary/active/very active

Comments_____

_____

_____

_____

I wish to reduce my weight because _____

_____

_____

_____

Source: Adapted from Palmer, 1988

'Being obese runs in my family so what is the point of trying'
Has high blood pressure or high cholesterol levels

The success of an effective weight reduction and control programme is that once the ideal body weight has been achieved, clients maintain that weight for the rest of their life except during a period of illness. Unless the majority of the problems on the second-order BASIC ID are dealt with then clients are likely to relapse. This probably explains why under 10 per cent of diets actually work. Once the assessment has been completed, then the rationale for the interventions are explained. Although most overweight clients have previously attempted to diet, in our experience few have considered that their thinking and imagery processes need to be modified. In particular, counsellors need to dispute any unhelpful beliefs that clients hold (see Chapter 3), to teach coping imagery (see Chapter 4) to deal with situations involving food, and apply aversive imagery to control intake of certain foodstuffs.

Action

The next stage is the *action* part of the programme where clients start reducing their calorific intake and begin a more active lifestyle. An action plan can be developed based upon the facts gathered from the completed Contemplation and Information form and widely available information on exercise, nutrition and, when relevant, blood pressure. There are many books, audio-tapes and leaflets (e.g. Flora Project, 1991) available on the ideal body weight, losing weight, improving nutrition and lifestyle that clients can read at home, and we recommend that counsellors have information on the calorific value of food and on energy expended during exercise. Box 8.6 summarizes the main points of a weight reduction programme. We recommend that no more than 2 lb is lost in weight a week. Clients can regularly weigh themselves and record their weight.

Maintenance

Once the 'ideal' body weight has been achieved then the last and probably the most crucial stage of the programme is *maintenance* when clients incorporate their new lifestyle changes and eating habits permanently into their repertoire of behaviour. At this stage counsellors need to ensure that relapse does not occur. A review of the second-order BASIC ID with the client and dealing with any residual problems is necessary, otherwise the client may regain weight fairly quickly. Clients often find coping statements written

Box 8.6   *Weight reduction and maintenance*

1 It is preferable to steam, grill or poach food and avoid fried foods.

2 Choose low-fat foods such as low-fat cheese, low-fat natural yogurts or cottage cheese.

3 Regularly eat fresh vegetables.

4 Consume fresh fruit daily. Avoid canned fruit in syrup.

5 Eat high-fibre wholegrain bread, oats, pasta, rice, beans and breakfast cereals.

6 Always avoid sweets, sugar, pastries, biscuits, cakes, crisps and pies.

7 Avoid whole milk and cream. Choose skimmed or semi-skimmed milk instead.

8 Use sunflower margarine or low-fat spreads sparingly. Avoid butter.

9 Reduce alcohol intake. Drink water and low-calorie diet soft drinks.

10 Take regular exercise such as brisk walking or swimming. Take up sporting activities such as badminton, golf, tennis, bowls or sailing. (If you are over 35 years ensure that your doctor approves of your exercise or sports programme.)

11 Incorporate exercise into your daily routine; for example, use the stairs at work instead of the lift, walk up escalators and/or walk to work.

12 Remember, a day's lapse of the diet does not mean that the diet has been ruined. The diet can still be continued today.

13 Like driving a new car or learning a new sport, it takes time to learn new eating and lifestyle habits. It may be difficult at times but every day with more practice it will become easier.

14 Avoid eating in-between meals.

15 Imagine yourself coping with difficult situations where you often eat too much food. Write coping statements on a card to help you deal with those situations – don't forget to read the card!

16 Think of the benefits of not being overweight.

17 Slow down your eating rate. Put your knife down in-between each bite of food, completely chew your food before you swallow it. Drink water with your meal and avoid salad dressing. Ask yourself 'Do I really need to have a dessert?'

Finally, it's not luck you need to control your weight but continued hard work. Who said it would be easy? But just think of the benefits.

on cards helpful in food 'crisis' situations where they may eat too much food; for example, at social events that they are anxious about. Rational-emotive and coping imagery (see Chapter 4) can be employed to help clients practise facing these difficult events.

Finally, we suggest at the maintenance stage that regular 'booster' or follow-up sessions are arranged during the first 12 months as clients often experience difficulties and sometimes relapse.

Indications and contraindications

Weight reduction and nutrition programmes are indicated for all overweight individuals unless instructed otherwise by a medical practitioner. The interventions used, such as exercise, may be contraindicated for individuals with certain heart complaints. If there is any doubt whatsoever the client should be referred to a medical specialist for examination. In some cases a hormonal imbalance may be exacerbating the problem and this would need medical attention.

Conclusion

This chapter has included a number of the more common health and lifestyle interventions that are encountered in stress counselling and stress management. Although there are many more possible interventions, our concern is to illustrate how a multimodal stress counsellor would assess and undertake interventions in this modality. The second-order BASIC ID is an ideal assessment system for specific health-related problems and often highlights factors overlooked by health professionals using more traditional methods. Clients are usually prevented from making lifestyle changes due to emotional, cognitive and imagery blocks and not because they are resisting help or being 'bloody minded'.

9

Case Studies

This chapter considers two case studies which focus on the application of key techniques and interventions that enabled clients to manage or resolve their difficulties. The therapeutic alliance is also examined as multimodal stress counsellors attempt to determine what type of relationship and interaction a particular client will most effectively respond to (see Lazarus 1981; Laxarus, ed., 1985). This will be demonstrated with a client who was seen for 23 sessions, in contrast to another client who was seen for one session only.

Stress counsellors will often see clients for one stress counselling session including the assessment. In such cases the counsellor needs to assess the presenting problem quickly, give the client a rationale for the approach and then apply suitable techniques or interventions. This situation generally arises when people have to face a particular situation that they feel extremely anxious about, such as flying or public speaking. The one-session case example presented in this chapter shows how the counsellor intervened successfully with a client who had panic attacks in unfamiliar work settings. When counselling began, her perceived external stressor was that her employers had asked her to work in a new location which would involve living away from home.

In their *Dictionary of Counselling*, Feltham and Dryden (1993: 183) state

> the word 'stress' has come to signify the whole subject of pressure and/ or stimulation and how people cope with it . . . stress counselling refers to any counselling addressing problems of stress, is likely to be short term, and often emphasises the benefits of talking and catharsis as well as multimodal, cognitive-behavioural and problem focused strategies.

We agree with this view of 'stress' and 'stress counselling' and this is reflected in the two case studies. We also believe that the pressures leading to stress can be *internal* (e.g. perfectionist beliefs, inaccurate inferences) or *external* (e.g. heavy workload, relationship difficulties) and more usually a combination of both.

In the following case example, to disguise the identity of the clients, alterations have been made to certain pieces of information to maintain confidentiality. However, the techniques, interventions and outcome have all been accurately described.

Multimodal stress counselling with Sue

Personal and family background

Sue was a 33-year-old woman living in a provincial town. She was a graduate and since leaving university had held a post of manager for 10 years. Her father died of cancer when she was 23. On the Multimodal Life History Inventory (MLHI) she described him and his attitude towards her when he was alive as:

> A little removed with no outward displays of affection. I had a close relationship with him, particularly after I left home. I was the person he talked to quite intimately.

Her father had always wanted a boy and when young gave Sue a train set and other male-orientated games. Since his death she had often viewed life as pointless. On the MLHI she described her mother and her mother's attitude towards herself as:

> She uses a lot of emotional blackmail when dealing with me and my sister. I don't think she is particularly fulfilled and recently this has been exacerbated as my sister and I haven't been able to live up to her expectations of us, e.g. having stable relationships and grandchildren. We have a very close relationship due to dad's death.

Although she felt loved and respected by her parents, she was not able to confide in them. On the MLHI she described her home atmosphere as:

> It was rather a 'Victorian' upbringing. Sex was a taboo subject. Nudity was frowned upon, and standards had to be met, particularly in front of friends and relatives, e.g. table manners and politeness. Sometimes my parents' relationship was strained. My sister and me got on well but I probably bullied her.

She believed that a significant point in her life was when she suffered bullying at school at the age of 12. In addition, changing her school three times between the ages of 12 and 18 meant that she had to 'uproot myself from friends at a fairly crucial time in my life'. These experiences had an effect on her attitudes as an adult; for example, the strong belief that she should be treated fairly. However, overall she believed that she had had a happy childhood.

Expectations regarding counselling
On the MLHI she thought counselling was about 'Having the opportunity to talk through problems with a non-partial listener; hopefully giving a new way of thinking about things and rationalizing problems'. This indicated that she would probably be responsive to cognitive or rational-emotive behavioural techniques and interventions. She believed that counselling should last as long as it was useful and productive.

She thought the ideal therapist should possess 'warmth and friendliness, and be non-judgemental, sincere and professional'. The counsellor made sure that he was not overly warm and friendly in case this was misinterpreted as insincere and unprofessional. A careful balance was maintained and feedback on his style was obtained by Sue periodically completing relevant questionnaires on the counsellor's skills and approach.

Multimodal assessment and counselling programme
The assessment was based on the data obtained from the MLHI, the initial assessment interview and subsequent counselling sessions. The use of the MLHI is desirable but not essential. In the first counselling session Sue was most stressed about the ending of a recent long-term relationship and a subsequent series of short-term 'hurtful' relationships. On the MLHI Sue listed her problems as:

1 Being stressed about not having a steady relationship and being alone
2 I have a low self-esteem
3 People don't treat me as I want them to
4 In addition to feeling stressed I am now depressed too, particularly at weekends and evenings
5 Poor financial management
6 Unable to handle my mother's emotional blackmail

Based on her problem list, a set of goals was noted down. Sue spent most of her free time on her own. She wanted to meet more people, enlarge her circle of friends and be generally more relaxed about herself. She wanted to stop being 'so introspective' and 'sorry' for herself. She had trouble relaxing or enjoying weekends as she wanted to share them with another person. Improving this area of her life also became a goal. If she could have two wishes (see MLHI) she would have liked to find someone to share her life with and to improve her financial budgeting (these wishes were included on her BASIC ID Modality Profile). She estimated the severity of her problems somewhere between very severe to extremely severe. On a scale of 1–7 where 1 is not at all satisfied with her life and 7 is very satisfied, she rated her level of satisfaction as 2. She was most likely to lose control of her feelings at home on her own on Sunday mornings or at 3.00am when she regularly woke up early.

Sue listed her five main fears on the MLHI as:

1 Death of my mother/sister
2 Losing my job
3 Losing my flat (through financial mismanagement)
4 Being attacked (physically)
5 Having an incurable disease

Page 14 of the MLHI helped the counsellor derive a Structural Profile for Sue. Her actual and desired Structural Profiles are represented in Figure 9.1 and 9.2. It is worth noting that the two Structural Profiles are quite similar. In stress counselling this is not uncommon as clients often only enter counselling when they are feeling stressed by a limited number of stressors or problems. However, as the Structural Profile encourages the client to talk about more general issues and goals across the entire BASIC ID its use is still recommended. Sue's progress was monitored throughout the duration of counselling by regular reassessment and completion of page 14 of the MLHI. In our experience, most clients are keen to improve their drugs/biology modality and Sue was no exception. In particular she wanted to reduce her alcohol intake, stop smoking, improve her nutrition, and stop her early morning awakening.

Table 9.1 represents Sue's BASIC ID Modality Profile, giving a complete picture of Sue's problems and possible techniques and interventions to help reduce her level of stress. As one of her presenting problems was depression, and she viewed life as 'meaningless and pointless', the counsellor negotiated with Sue that the early phase of counselling would concentrate on related issues. The counsellor was aware that clients with these types of beliefs are more likely to attempt suicide. Therefore the first seven counselling sessions concentrated heavily on her recent series of short-term stressful relationships which had triggered underlying schemata and irrational beliefs. On her MLHI she wrote that she wanted to be given a 'new way of thinking about things' and a method to 'rationalize problems'. These views were apparent in the first session and this allowed the counsellor to use cognitive interventions to dispute her irrational beliefs starting in session 2.

To give the reader an insight into how a multimodal stress counsellor may structure a counselling session and not lose sight of the overall picture, the next section focuses on key issues, and the interventions and techniques applied during each interview from the beginning to the end of counselling. The first four counselling

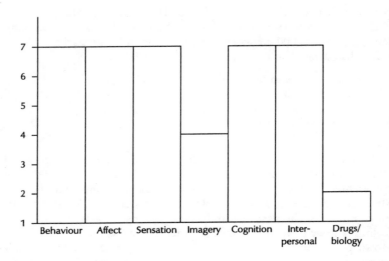

Figure 9.1   *Sue's Structural Profile*

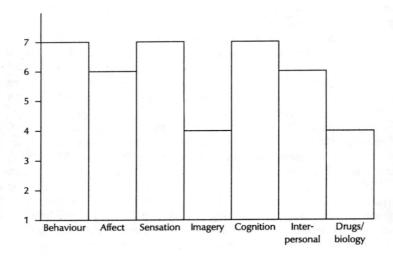

Figure 9.2   *Sue's desired Structural Profile*

Table 9.1   *BASIC ID Modality Profile for Sue*

Modality	Problem	Proposed treatment
Behaviour	Spends too much money	Discuss financial management techniques
	Drinks at least 56 units of alcohol weekly	Reduce alcohol intake to 14 units: behavioural programme
	Smokes daily	Stop/reduction programme
	Impulsive behaviour often leading to risk taking	Examine underlying reasons for behaviour and discuss strategies
	Tidies flat when not truly necessary	Response prevention; discuss pros and cons
Affect	Depression due to relationship difficulties, low self-esteem and being lonely	Discuss relationship difficulties; increase self-acceptance; rational-emotive imagery; coping statements
	Depression: life pointless since father's death	Empty Chair technique to help her express her feelings
	Anger if not always treated fairly by others	Dispute 'must' beliefs about others' behaviour; use coping statements
	Guilty due to not fulfilling mother's wishes	Disputation of irrational beliefs
	Self-pity and other-pity	Disputation of beliefs regarding the human race being horrible, everything is shitty, I'm as bad as everybody else
Sensation	Tension and unable to relax	Relaxation techniques; listen to relaxation tape
	General fatigue	Lifestyle interventions and reduce depression
	Rapid heart beat	Relaxation techniques
Imagery	Lonely images	Coping imagery and rational-emotive imagery
	'Spinster' image	Rational-emotive imagery
	Being hurt Nightmares of 'repulsive human beings, mutilated animals, birds, being attacked by dogs'	Rational-emotive imagery Discuss possible origins; implosion imagery if necessary
	Dreams of her father	Discuss; implosion if very disturbed about it or bereavement counselling

Continued overleaf

Table 9.1   *continued*

Modality	Problem	Proposed treatment
Cognition	Should not make mistakes. Should be treated fairly. Should be given a chance. My full worth should be appreciated. Partner should have been straight, honest and open. No one is bothered to help me. I need tight deadlines in order to perform well. Partners should treat me as I treat them. I must not let others down. I must not be let down. I should fulfil my mother's wishes. My contribution to life is meaningless and pointless. There must be something wrong with me. If they (partners) leave me I'm worthless. I must have a purpose to life and if I don't I can never be happy. It's all my fault. I must have somebody to be happy. I should be happily married. The human race is horrible and has buggered up the world. It's wrong to stay happy if the world stays as it is. The environment is shitty. I'm worthless if life does not have a meaning. I can't stand it. Things are awful, unbearable.	Disputation of irrational beliefs; coping statements; coping imagery; rational-emotive imagery; cognitive restructuring; challenge faulty inferences; time projection imagery; ABCDE paradigm of Ellis; bibliotherapy
Interpersonal	Has no relationships that give her any 'joy'	Discuss unrealistic expectations; discuss ways to meet new people

Continued

Table 9.1   *continued*

Modality	Problem	Proposed treatment
	Recently has had short-term relationships that have given her 'grief'	Dispute irrational beliefs
	Anxious that new partner may leave	Dispute irrational beliefs; constructive self-talk
	Easily hurt if others do not behave the way she wants them to	Dispute irrational beliefs; rational-emotive imagery
	Easily hurt if ignored	Dispute irrational beliefs; rational-emotive imagery
	Can be 'bossy', 'cruel' and 'always right'; can occur at work	Discuss pros and cons of this behaviour; assertiveness training
	'Too clinging/demanding of affection/attention'	Dispute irrational beliefs; discuss pros and cons of this behaviour; Deserted Island technique
	Thought she was 'black-mailed' and 'manipulated' by her mother	Dispute irrational beliefs that provoke guilt
	Withdraws from relationships, e.g. friends; expects friends to make an effort with her; feels lonely	Examine beliefs about 'perfect' relationships; friendship training
Drugs/ biology	Chronic asthmatic: started shortly after father's death	Physician supervised; takes Ventolin/Becotide daily; stress management programme and bereavement counselling
	Smokes 10–20 cigarettes daily	Stop/reduction programme
	Undereats frequently and eats junk food	Nutritional guidance (may reflect depression)
	Allergies	Antihistamines
	Disturbed sleep pattern	Reduce alcohol intake and dispute depression provoking beliefs
	High alcohol intake	Reduce from 56 units per week to the recommended 14 units; become less fatalistic and take more responsiblity for self; consider exercise programme

sessions including the assessment session are covered in greater depth to give the reader a feel for how the counsellor worked towards building up a good therapeutic alliance.

Session 1

Essentially, in this session, the counsellor listened to the client's story, assessed her presenting problems, considered her levels of stress and depression and ascertained whether she was likely to attempt suicide. Although she had suicidal ideation, she had not seriously considered or planned any method of killing herself. However, the counsellor believed that if Sue did not perceive any gradual improvement in her negative feelings then her suicidal ideation would possibly worsen. Normally at the end of the first session the multimodal counsellor would ask the client to take home and complete the MLHI. However, the counsellor decided in this case not to give her the MLHI as he believed that Sue could become more depressed if she completed it without seeing a way out of her predicament. Near the end of the session, the counsellor briefly explained how certain beliefs can lead to more stress. Then as a follow-up exercise the counsellor negotiated a homework assignment which involved Sue reading a book about a rational-emotive therapy approach to dealing with unhappiness (Dryden and Gordon, 1990). She was also asked to monitor her thoughts when she next felt stressed. At the end of the session the counsellor checked with Sue how she felt about her first session. Due to her previously negative experience of therapy with a psychodynamic therapist, the counsellor wanted to ensure that Sue was receiving the type of counselling she desired otherwise she may have terminated prematurely. The dialogue was as follows:

> *Counsellor*: Have you any feelings or thoughts about this session and have I said anything that you found upsetting?
> *Sue*: No! Not at all. In fact it's been quite helpful to talk about things like the alcohol problem that I've been too embarrassed to discuss with others. I've been more embarrassed about that than being stressed because of the way it is perceived in society or whatever. I don't know, it's strange. I feel quite happy.

Session 2

The session started with the counsellor asking Sue how she had been feeling in the past week and then negotiating an agenda with her. The homework assignments were discussed. Sue had monitored her thoughts and feelings in a situation involving a friend when she felt stressed. The emotion she experienced was guilt. She remembered thinking 'I should have gone there and helped her out and I didn't.' The counsellor asked her if it was possible to change that belief and thereby reduce her level of guilt. She was able to reduce her level of guilt by deciding that it was more important to do what she wanted instead of helping her friend. At this stage the counsellor believed it would be useful to show Sue how she could alter her emotion by changing the absolutist 'should' belief. Therefore the counsellor decided to use an abstract example, to demonstrate how holding 'must' beliefs (commonly known as 'musturbatory' beliefs) led to higher levels of stress compared to 'preferential' beliefs. The intervention was based on Dryden's technique (1990: 47–8). In this case, the Deserted Island technique (see Chapter 3) was *not* chosen as Sue had strong beliefs about not being alone and was therefore likely to experience difficulty in separating her musturbatory beliefs from preferential beliefs. Finally, the counsellor explained the ABC paradigm of Ellis and how the musturbatory beliefs led to the consequences of guilt etc.

Counsellor: Can you imagine just for the moment that you have this belief that you would prefer or like to have £11 in your pocket but that you don't have to have this amount. Unfortunately, there is a hole in your pocket and you've lost £1 and that's left you with only £10. How would you feel?

Sue: It wouldn't concern me too much as I'm used to being like that anyway!

Counsellor: Right. You wouldn't be very stressed about it. You would probably feel some concern. Let's suppose you are now telling yourself that you 'absolutely must have £11 in your pocket' and you still only have £10. How would you feel this time?

Sue: Anxious.

Counsellor: If I said 'here's a £1 coin' how would you feel?

Sue: Relieved!

Counsellor: Right. However with that belief 'I must at all times have £11 in my pocket' you would still be anxious. Why?

Sue: Because I would think that I could lose another £1.

Counsellor: So even when you have what you demand your anxiety could return.

Sue: Yeah.

Counsellor: Can you see now how earlier you were describing how you felt guilty about not helping a friend out and in that situation you were also placing demands upon yourself? [*Counsellor relating the abstract exercise back to the present.*]

Sue: I think that whenever I feel guilty it's because I'm telling myself that I should have done something or shouldn't have done something.

Counsellor: Maybe we could consider in counselling looking at these shoulds and musts.

Sue: Yeah.

Counsellor: However, if you've just got a preferable should, for example, I preferably should . . .

[*Sue interrupted at this point.*]

Sue: No, No! It's I should have done that; it should have been done; it shouldn't have happened; it shouldn't have occurred.

Counsellor: And that's when you get the guilt or the anxiety? [*At this stage to confirm that the client understood the model the counsellor would normally have asked her to explain it in her own words. However, in this case she clearly demonstrated her understanding of the model and the counsellor thought that it was unnecessary to check this.*]

Sue: Yeah.

Counsellor: To simplify things, we call the activating event 'A'. Thus, when you didn't help your friend this was the 'A'. We call your beliefs such as 'I should have helped my friend' the 'B', and the consequences, in this case guilt, the 'C'. If you can remember the sequence as ABC it helps to analyse what is going on in any situation. Therefore it is mainly the 'Bs' and not the 'A' that lead to 'C', the consequences.

[*The A, B and C were drawn on a whiteboard by the counsellor to demonstrate the sequence.*]

Sue: Hmmm. It wasn't just that I should have helped her but the other side of it was that I felt selfish as I wanted to carry on with what I wanted to do. I wanted to have my curry and drink my bottle of wine.

Counsellor: You're right. There are usually a number of thoughts that may be involved with an emotion.

Sue was then asked which recent incident she would like to examine during the remainder of the time available in the session. She chose to look at a recent stressful event when she was rejected by a partner and subsequently felt very depressed about it, with a goal of not becoming so disturbed if she was rejected again. The ABC model was used to analyse the situation and assess any musturbatory beliefs that she held. It became apparent that she disesteemed herself when she was rejected by a partner. The counsellor used interventions to illustrate how unconditional self-acceptance is preferable to high self-esteem when life goes well and low self-esteem when life goes badly. Logical, empirical and pragmatic disputes (see Chapter 3) were used to dispute her musturbatory beliefs. Sue was asked at the end of the session to develop her own coping statements:

If he doesn't appreciate me then tough. He doesn't have to appreciate me. There's no law of the universe that states that he should have given me a chance, it's only preferable if he had done so.

However, Sue was not prepared to relinquish her strong absolutist demands about being treated fairly and was unwilling to create a coping statement on this issue. It was agreed that the subject of being treated fairly would be discussed in the next counselling session.

The homework assignments included listening to a recording of the session; monitoring and recording thoughts about fairness and completing the MLHI. If possible, Sue was going to put herself into a position with a partner where she would be treated unfairly so that she could monitor her beliefs and emotions. This was nicknamed her 'unfairness exercise'. To help her cope with the exercise, the counsellor suggested a coping statement that she could use to help alleviate any distress she experienced.

Session 3

Due to holidays this session was one month later. After this session the meetings were usually fortnightly. She felt 'fine; not too bad'. She reported that it felt strange completing the MLHI and writing about her parents. She found listening to the tape of session 2 'interesting' and the previous discussion about how she demanded others to act 'helpful'. She managed to cope with the 'unfairness exercise' in which a friend 'should' have contacted her but didn't. She did not reach 'the depths of despair' as she predicted. The counsellor briefly demonstrated how she could use time-projection imagery to keep events in proportion (see Chapter 4).

> *Sue*: Listening to the tape made me think that I'm so desperate to want to have someone, to be loved and give out this love, that I'm happy to be indiscriminate and compromise myself. If they show an interest in me then I'm prepared to have a relationship. The issue is not the people but me thinking that I must be loved and it doesn't matter who it is. This isn't particularly useful to me. I'm not objective.
>
> *Counsellor*: Going back to what we discussed last time, if you did not have the demand what would have happened? [*Socratic pragmatic dispute*].
>
> *Sue*: I would have been less pained by it. I would not have read too much into the situation.
>
> *Counsellor*: So you would have felt less disturbed.
>
> *Sue*: Yep . . . The other thing I got from listening to the tape was that if someone comes up to you and says 'You're crap or whatever' it does not physically change you. You are still the same as you were before. Your own internal scales in which you measure people . . . .
>
> *Counsellor*: And you measure yourself.
>
> *Sue*: Yeah. And if they don't come up to those scales then why the hell should they!?

In this session the counsellor went through the MLHI which Sue had completed at home to ensure that she had understood the questions and he understood her answers. Then the counsellor showed Sue her Structural Profile (Figure 9.1) and confirmed that she still agreed with her scoring. Then a desired Structural Profile was drawn (see earlier comments in this chapter). This process of deriving the desired Structural Profile took 15 minutes approximately. As Structural Profiles are generally only used in multimodal counselling, we include a section of the dialogue to illustrate how the counsellor helped the client derive her desired Structural Profile.

> *Counsellor*: This is a visual representation of the Structural Profile you completed on p. 14 of the questionnaire. Is there any score you would like to change?
> [*Counsellor shows Sue Figure 9.1 and p. 14 of her MLHI.*]
> *Sue*: I think they are probably about right. Do you think they aren't?
> *Counsellor*: There's no right or wrong. Are there any areas you would like to work on? For example, if we look at the biological factors, are you healthy and health conscious? Do you avoid bad habits like smoking, too much alcohol? Do you notice that you scored 2 out of 7 there?
> *Sue*: Yeah.
> *Counsellor*: Would you like to change that while in counselling here?
> *Sue*: Yeah.
> *Counsellor*: Some people believe that their physical health has an effect on their mental health. They are inter-related.
> *Sue*: There's a bit of a contradiction in that I don't actually feel unhealthy and I'm reasonably fit and I have quite a lot of stamina, mainly because of the type of job I do. I used to be an athlete. Yes, I do smoke too much and drink too much, I eat reasonably well.
> *Counsellor*: Did you score it low because of your more negative habits?
> *Sue*: Yeah.
> *Counsellor*: Like too much alcohol, smoking. Would you like to change that?
> *Sue*: Yeah, I think so.
> *Counsellor*: So looking at this, what number on the scale up to 7 would you like to achieve?
> *Sue*: I'd like to get it up a bit. Like 4 or 5 or something like that.
> *Counsellor*: So I can draw it on the Profile, what would you like, 4 or 5?
> *Sue*: Let's go for 4 because I don't know if I can do it [*Laughter*].

The counsellor then elicited from Sue specific targets focusing on each modality that she wanted to change. As Sue wanted to look at the subject of being treated unfairly by her previous partner, the remaining part of the session concentrated on an occasion when he did not tell her about his other girlfriend. The goal was to change her anger to annoyance. The beliefs targeted for logical, empirical and pragmatic disputes were:

He should have been straight, honest and open
He should be fair
This is awful

The homework assignment was to use rational-emotive imagery (see Chapter 4) to challenge her irrational beliefs about her ex-partner. It was negotiated that she would close her eyes, and imagine him acting unfairly. She was then to disturb herself by repeating the irrational beliefs: 'He should have been straight, honest, open and fair.' Once she felt angry she was then asked to change the irrational beliefs to preferential statements: 'I prefer him to have acted fairly, but if he's not, that's too bad. He's just a fallible human being.' This exercise would be repeated daily. As a penalty, if she did not complete the exercise then she would not have a drink.

Session 4

When negotiating the agenda, Sue wanted to allocate time to discuss her poor financial management and a problem about being a victim. Session 3 and the homework assignment were briefly reviewed. It is usually important for the counsellor to investigate the client's impression of the previous session to see if any misunderstandings have arisen or if any setbacks have occurred since the last meeting:

Counsellor: Now you've had an opportunity to listen to the recording of the last session, have you any comments to make or have you any issues you would like to raise about what we covered?

Sue: [*Laughter*] I think I'm finding that the sessions help a lot. Sorting my brain out about things. So coming back to it (listening to the recording before the session) seemed a bit strange because I've been thinking a lot about what was said in that particular session and perhaps coming to terms with a lot of those issues in my head. I think my views have changed a lot since that session.

Counsellor: Changed in the past two weeks?

Sue: Yeah.

Counsellor: What particular views?

Sue: Just this bit about fairness. I've been thrashing it out for that length of time and now it isn't such a big issue inside my head. I've moderated the attitudes I had in that session about it. I feel more comfortable with the whole thing. I think pin-pointing the feeling down to one word and one set of beliefs makes it easier to deal with.

At this point the counsellor gave Sue a copy of a cartoon that summed up the relationship difficulties she had described in the previous sessions. Although this intervention added humour to the session, it helped Sue recognize that others also had similar demands which had led to emotional disturbances and helped her to laugh at her previous attitudes and behaviours, perhaps reinforcing a cognitive shift. A stock of cartoons on different themes that regularly arise in stress counselling, which target different beliefs, emotions and behaviours, can be a useful asset for a counsellor. This intervention should be done with sensitivity, however, to ensure that the client recognizes that the counsellor is targeting the attitudes and behaviours and not the client herself.

The client believed that if she sold her property she would overcome her financial difficulties. However, the counsellor queried whether selling property would only defer her financial problems if the real problem was poor financial management. To feel better she would drink alcohol, smoke, buy clothes or plants. The counsellor suggested that if she started to feel better emotionally then she may not need to spend so much on herself or the 'quick fix'. Fortunately, her new exercise programme was inexpensive and had started to take the place of drinking alcohol. Financial budgets were discussed to manage the existing situation.

The remaining 40 minutes focused on Sue's belief that she had been a victim and her major prediction was that 'bad things are going to happen which would be horrible'. The counsellor used a continuum of badness scale from 1 to 99.9 and demonstrated that when Sue thought an event would be awful, she invariably magnified its 'badness' beyond reality and totally out of proportion. When discussing a difficult concept with a client, it is important to check whether she has really understood it:

> *Counsellor*: I'm not too sure whether I've explained 'de-awfulizing' very well. Could you explain it in your own words?
>
> *Sue*: When I say the words awful, terrible or horrible, I should think about whether it really is and what kind of scale I'm putting it on, what level of badness it could be. And ensure I don't go off the scale to 110 per cent!
>
> *Counsellor*: Can you see its relevance to your 'victim' scenarios?
>
> *Sue*: Yeah.
>
> *Counsellor*: How?
>
> *Sue*: When I think bad things such as being a victim are really awful I make myself very upset. In reality it may feel bad but it's hardly awful.

The homework assignment was to monitor herself thinking that something was 'awful' and record her thoughts. She was to continue her exercise programme and her 'unfairness exercises'. She would also work out a suitable financial budget for survival. As usual, the counsellor asked for feedback about the session:

Counsellor: How do you feel about this session?

Sue: Good! I was actually thinking today that I'm feeling a lot better about myself and I haven't had any moments when I've felt stressed or miserable. It's been a busy couple of weeks and I want to keep things going. I feel more positive . . . I'm enjoying this sports thing and it's not an effort for me to go to the gym. I've persuaded my lodger to join me too.

Counsellor: At this rate your Biological Profile will be going up.

Sue: Yeah. And I'm starting to feel guilty about smoking as well . . . and I've started a new relationship.

After four counselling sessions the client was feeling less stressed and less emotionally disturbed. However, as Sue had started a new relationship and her life was generally improving, the counsellor was unsure at this stage whether her improvement was due to her new attitudes and beliefs or life changes. In particular, he was concerned that she might relapse if she experienced a negative life-event such as another rejection.

As the client's condition had greatly improved, the remaining counselling sessions are only briefly reviewed to give a basic overview of the remaining course of therapy.

Session 5

This session focused on two issues. Sue felt guilty about sacking an employee who had failed to comply with her organization's regulations. As Sue thought she was responsible for the outcome, the counsellor helped her explore the employee's responsibility to himself and the organization. As this work-related issue arose unexpectedly it was not on the Modality Profile. The second issue covered was her attitude towards a previous partner's behaviour.

Session 6

This session concentrated on reviewing Sue's progress with reference to her original problem list and receiving feedback about her thoughts on the previous counselling sessions. She still believed she was a 'horrible person' and that 'humans are cruel'. She wanted to look at these issues at a 'deeper level'. She re-scored her Structural Profile.

Session 7

This session dealt with the possibility of her existing partner leaving. As previously suspected by the counsellor, she predicted that she could become depressed, withdrawn, drink and smoke more. The beliefs targeted for disputing included:

My contribution to life is meaningless and pointless
There must be something wrong with me
I'm worthless if life does not have a meaning
I must have a purpose to life and if I don't I can never be happy
If they leave me I'm worthless

Sue suggested that these beliefs were triggered by her father's death and she wanted to spend the next counselling session discussing her feelings and thoughts about her father.

Session 8
This session concentrated on her relationship with her father and how she felt since his death. She thought that in her previous long-term relationship her partner had become a father substitute which had a negative effect on their relationship. The Empty Chair technique was used to help her express her feelings towards her father. In particular she felt angry towards him as he was not affectionate and she thought that he had wanted a boy. Six months after his death she became asthmatic.

Session 9
Sue could not remember how her father had become a topic to be discussed in counselling so she listened to a recording of session 7 before she arrived. This highlights the usefulness of clients having recordings of their counselling sessions. Sue began to realize that since her father's death life had become pointless and unless there was a purpose to life she could never be happy. Later, the focus of the session shifted to the relationships within her family before her father's death and of her regrets.

Sessions 10–15
Session 10 focused on her relationship with her mother in contrast to Session 11 which shifted onto her depression-invoking thoughts about the world. In Session 12 she was stressed again about the possibility of her new partner finishing the relationship. To ensure that Sue understood the homework assignment (rational-emotive imagery) she was asked to complete an Assignment Task sheet (see Box 9.1) in the session. This included discussion of how she could overcome any obstacles to undertaking the assignment. Session 13 concentrated on her image of becoming a 'spinster' which she found very depressing. Session 14 returned to her feelings and thoughts about her 'manipulative' mother and how she could improve the relationship. Her belief that she 'couldn't stand the situation' was disputed. The counsellor suggested that she was 'living proof that

Box 9.1   *Assignment task sheet*

Name <u>Sue</u>   Date <u>28/10/94</u>   Negotiated with <u>Stephen</u>

Agreed task – state the task and when, where and how frequently you have agreed to do it: Sit at my kitchen table and imagine my partner leaving me. I will concentrate on the negative thoughts which mainly cause my depression and stress. Once I feel depressed and really stressed I will challenge my negative thoughts, and then replace them with the coping statement I have prepared in this counselling session. I will then feel the new healthier emotion. I'll do this assignment every evening before dinner.

The therapeutic purpose(s) of the task: The next time I'm in a similar situation (i.e. someone leaving), I will have a more constructive attitude towards the problem, feel less stressed and only sad instead of depressed.

Obstacles to carrying out the task – what obstacles, if any, stand in your way of completing this task and how you can overcome them:

1 *Lack of time.* I'll make sure that there are no interruptions around dinner time, e.g. turn off telephone, don't answer front door.
2 *Not being alone.* If I'm unable to be alone at the kitchen table, I'll do the assignment in the bath.
3 I might be unwilling to do the exercise as it will be upsetting. I can think of the long-term benefits.

Penalty
If I don't do the assignment, I will dust the entire house before bedtime.

Reward
If I complete the assignment, I can do my favourite *Guardian* crossword.

Signed: Sue

she could stand it' to which she agreed. Session 15 returned to her fears about her existing partner leaving.

Session 16

This session reviewed her progress since the last review session (Session 6). As she had become less emotionally disturbed about her mother's 'manipulative' behaviour, her own behaviour towards her mother had started to change. This had led to her mother's behaviour improving. She was now able to picture herself beyond the age of 35. To encourage her to relinquish her strong demands about not being alone, the counsellor used the Deserted Island technique (see Chapter 3).

Sessions 17–21

In these five sessions the counsellor and client focused on any outstanding problems on the Modality Profile or problem list that had not been previously covered. This included Sue confronting her demand for a very tidy flat. The counsellor and Sue considered the advantages and disadvantages of her demands, subsequent behaviour and arising interpersonal difficulties. She had been experiencing some difficulties with her work colleagues and this reminded her of being bullied at school. Her strong emotional response was mainly due to her underlying belief that 'she must be treated fairly'. At the end of session 21 it was agreed that the next session would be in two months' time. (This helps clients to become less dependent on their counsellors and allows clients to deal with problems if they arise without the counsellor's help.)

Session 22

Sue's progress was examined again. She had continued to make improvements across the entire BASIC ID. She now believed that she had an ability to 'think things through'. In addition, she had reduced her alcohol consumption down to 14 units per week and had refrained from smoking for three months. Her financial position had improved and relationship with her partner had stabilized. In fact, she told the counsellor that she was also looking forward to getting married to her partner in a month's time. At the beginning of counselling, she had stated on the MLHI that she wished to 'share her life with somebody' and, although this issue was never directly dealt with in counselling, related obstacles such as unconstructive irrational beliefs associated with relationships were covered (see Table 9.1).

On the MLHI she now scored 6 out of 7 on the satisfied scale (previous score 2) and 2 on the relaxation scale (previous score 4).

A final follow-up counselling session was negotiated which would be three months later to see how Sue was coping with life.

Session 23: follow-up session
In this final session, problems that had arisen since the previous session were discussed. This included her demands that her husband should always pay her attention. Strategies and techniques across the entire BASIC ID to cope with anticipated problems were reviewed. She had not relapsed and was neither stressed nor depressed. Page 13 of the MLHI was completed to check improvements in the drugs/biology modality. She was still not smoking and was no longer under-eating. Both her sleep pattern and general fatigue had improved. She was pleased that on rating her drugs/biology modality on the Structural Profile she scored 6 as this was higher than she originally thought she could achieve at the beginning of counselling. It was agreed that she could contact the counsellor again if she became stressed and was unable to deal with problems after first attempting to solve them by herself.

Single-session stress counselling with Rachel

There are times when individuals request single-session stress counselling and this is usually due to unexpected crises or severe anxiety about forthcoming events. To ensure the client's time is not wasted, we recommend that the counsellor has a short telephone conversation with the potential client before confirming an appointment for the following reasons:

1 To ascertain the client's formulation (if any) of the causes of his/her stress
2 To explain briefly the rationale of multimodal stress counselling and how it could possibly help the client
3 To ascertain whether the client understands how multimodal stress counselling may help reduce his/her levels of stress and/or manage his/her problem
4 To confirm that the client is willing to try the approach
5 To ensure that multimodal stress counselling is not contraindicated (see below)
6 If counselling is indicated, to arrange an appointment and explain to the client that he/she will need to set 1–2 hours aside for single-session counselling

Assuming points 1–5 are met, then multimodal stress counselling may be indicated. In our clinical experience the major contraindications are if the client has:

1 A current severe psychiatric disorder
2 No belief in *all* of the following three points:
   (a) relaxation techniques will help reduce stress;
   (b) by moderating or changing his/her attitudes (or images if relevant) he/she may reduce stress levels;
   (c) a problem-focused approach may be beneficial
3 Been in long-term therapy elsewhere and strongly believes that catharsis alone will reduce his/her levels of stress
4 A very strong conviction that only medication will help
5 Very low self-esteem and a severe lack of confidence
6 Current problems abusing alcohol or drugs
7 Current problems which reflect long-standing personality difficulties or disorders

However, depending upon the experience and clinical acumen of the counsellor, clients with a number of the contraindications listed may still benefit from single-session multimodal stress counselling.

Single-session stress counselling sessions should be problem focused with the counsellor ensuring that little time is lost discussing facts not related to the stressor/problem or the emotional disturbance (e.g. anxiety) that the client wishes to resolve or manage. However, it is still important to build up a good therapeutic alliance and a balance does need to be maintained between listening to the client's story and making suitable interventions (for additional guidance, see Dryden and Feltham, 1992).

It is advisable to set aside up to 2 hours for single-session counselling, otherwise by the time the counsellor has grasped the salient information there may be insufficient time left to intervene. In a severe crisis, McMullin (1986) recommends 4-hour 'marathon' sessions. We have found it quite helpful if the client completes a shortened version of the MLHI in reception before the counselling session begins. This three-page version asks a few key questions relating to the drugs/biology modality and what the client is hoping to get out of counselling, as well as basic information such as name, address, age, name and address of their medical practitioner etc.

Whenever possible, if there is sufficient time for the client to read relevant literature on understanding and managing stress before the counselling session then this should be arranged (e.g. Burns, 1989; Cooper et al., 1988; Dryden and Gordon, 1990, 1992, 1993; Marks, 1980). It is helpful if the counsellor directs the client to the relevant chapters of a book, otherwise some very distressed individuals may find reading an entire book an additional burden. In the first instance, we normally suggest clients read short guides such as

Think Rationally by Dryden and Gordon (1992). We do not recommend clients with hypochondriasis to read literature about stress that could trigger further anxiety.

Rachel's personal and family background

Rachel was 25 years of age. She lived alone in her own house. She had had an abortion six months earlier and recently had become very depressed about it. She used to argue regularly with her father when she was a teenager as he was 'strict'. However, Rachel believed his respect for her grew when she left school and become employed. He had died of heart attack 2 years previously. She saw her mother as her 'best friend' who was kind, loving, caring. Rachel had an older brother and older sister.

Assessment and treatment

On the shortened MLHI she described her reasons for seeking stress counselling as:

> Soon I have to work away from home at a new location. When I stop working I lose my confidence and get panic attacks, my heart races, I sweat, I feel dizzy and think I'm going to lose control. I love my job very much, it's the one secure thing in my life so I'm very scared of failing in it. Once I know the people I'm dealing with I'm very confident but until I feel secure I panic. On top of this I am also feeling very stressed and low about the abortion, and hurt from a relationship that ended last year.

She thought her problem started 'when I was little. Spelling tests, exams, anything I can't see the other side of'. She believed that the problem was maintained by her 'being judged'. Her main aim was to improve her confidence. The counsellor briefly read the completed questionnaire before the client was invited to enter the counselling room.

> *Counsellor*: Before we start is there anything you would like to ask about myself, the counselling centre?
> *Rachel*: No. There's nothing.
> *Counsellor*: OK. It's probably a good idea if we set an agenda. We could put on it what you see your problems as being. When I spoke to you briefly on the telephone you mentioned that you are going away this weekend to work at a new location and you would like to know how to deal with the situation. You were anxious that you would experience panic attacks again.
> *Rachel*: Yeah.
> *Counsellor*: OK. I'll put that on the agenda. Is there anything you would like on the agenda?
> *Rachel*: Feeling depressed about the abortion.

Counsellor: We need to prioritize here. Today we only have a short period of time. I tend to see clients for a number of sessions regarding abortions.

Rachel: Just feeling positive about me. Giving me confidence to work away from home.

Counsellor: So that would be the immediate problem. I'm sure there's an overlap.

Rachel: Yeah. Also I had this awful split up with somebody last year. I ended up being his problem helper for six months. He'd just gone through a divorce. He was out of work and going through a real crisis. I ended up taking his problems on and I forgot about myself. He was also very possessive and in the end he just went off with someone else.

Counsellor: It may be an idea when we start talking about your problems for you to attempt to summarize them, which I realize may not be very easy, and then we can deal with the immediate problem involving you going away to work. Then we could consider any suitable homework assignments to help you manage your anxiety and finally review the session at the end. Is that OK?

Rachel: Yeah.

In brief single-session counselling, when agenda setting, the counsellor needs to ensure that the most immediate problem the client wants to manage is on the list. For Rachel, this was dealing with working away from home and not having panic attacks. She was also very disturbed about her abortion and a previous relationship, although she did not have any suicidal ideation. The counsellor decided that there was probably insufficient time to cover all three problems successfully in one session. He was also aware that Rachel would probably have been able to talk about the abortion and the previous relationship for the entire 2-hour counselling session without focusing on her immediate problem. However, he did not believe that it would help the therapeutic alliance if no time had been allocated to these less immediate problems; therefore they were placed at the top of the agenda.

Counsellor: OK, could you summarize what you believe your problem or problems are?

Rachel: Just confidence. I don't know, just taking over from someone else. If I know the people I'm working with, there's no problem. I just get excited. But when I don't know any of them I feel I'm put in the limelight. They are all going to watch every movement I make. Try and find fault. I'm just scared of getting too anxious, hyperventilating, shaking too much, and going too dizzy so I can't do anything. Mind you, it's never got that bad anyway, but what if it did?

[*Rachel was upset talking about this subject.*]

Counsellor: As far as you're concerned, it really must not get that bad even though it never has.

Rachel: Occasionally I've had it but I've managed to beat it. Because of all my problems I just haven't the energy to beat it this time.

Counsellor: And how did you beat it before?

Rachel: I actually chanted in my head. I do a bit of meditation.

Counsellor: You have a mantra?

Rachel: I use a number and it seems to make it go away or I just stop what I'm doing and go and make a cup of tea or visit the loo.

[*Rachel relaxed as she described how she had previously coped with her panic attacks.*]

Counsellor: We could come back to this subject a bit later in this session. Perhaps you would like to give me an insight into your other problems. You mentioned the relationship you had and the abortion.

Rachel then described those experiences and life-events which were adding to her current state of stress. She felt angry, sad and guilty about what had happened in recent years. After 8 minutes the counsellor asked her if there were any additional factors she thought were relevant and she said that an additional stressor was living alone and briefly talked about her relationship with her parents. Then the discussion reverted to dealing with the impending work-related problem.

While listening to the client the counsellor produced a simplified BASIC ID Modality Profile (Table 9.2) which he used to keep himself focused on the relevant issues. It was agreed that her main problem was about 'being judged'.

The Ellis ABCDE paradigm was described by the counsellor and then the irrational beliefs on the BASIC ID Modality Profile were disputed (see Chapter 3). In this extended counselling session, which lasted approximately 2 hours, other techniques used included:

The double-standard method (see Chapter 3)

Examine the evidence (see Chapter 3)

Dryden technique to demonstrate 'musts' versus preferences (see above)

Reframing bodily sensations as part of experiencing a challenging and not a 'stressful' situation

'De-awfulized' the feeling of anxiety

Humorous dispute of 'I can't stand it'

Homework assignments

Once the core irrational beliefs had been disputed, a coping statement was developed and noted down:

I would strongly prefer not to suffer from this anxiety, but if I do, it's bad but it's not awful. It's not the end of the world. I can stand it.

Table 9.2   *BASIC ID Modality Profile for Rachel: a quick formulation*

Modality	Problem	Proposed treatment
Behaviour	Avoidance	Exposure
Affect	Anxiety	Appears to be main issue that she wants resolved today
	Anxiety about her anxiety	Clarify this problem
	Depression	Not suicidal; deal with this at a later session (abortion)
	Shame	Shame about anxiety: dispute irrational beliefs
Sensation	Hyperventilation	Symptoms of anxiety and panic attacks; use 'tracking' to check which modality fires first; then decide whether to use relaxation techniques, meditation
	Feels faint	
	Sweats	
	Palpitations	
	Shakes	
Imagery	Non-coping images	Coping imagery
Cognition	If I fail I'm a total failure	Dispute beliefs; coping self-statements; panic list; cognitive restructuring; reframing; ABCDE paradigm of Ellis; demonstrate how 'musturbatory' beliefs increase stress levels; double-standard method; bibliotherapy
	I must be capable of doing this job	
	I shouldn't suffer from this anxiety	
	I should be nervous!	
	I must not lose control	
	I must be a failure because I have to take anti-depressants	
	It's awful if it happened	
	I can't stand it	
Interpersonal	Anxious in social settings when she is in the 'lime-light'	Reframe situation
Drugs/ biology	Prescribed anti-depressants	Check whether shame is present
	Smokes	

She was to read the coping statement before work and whenever she had negative thoughts about the situation. Two other home-work assignments were negotiated, including reading a 27-page booklet on challenging irrational beliefs (Dryden and Gordon, 1992) and reading a panic list which had been written on a small card and could be carried in a wallet. The counsellor was concerned that Rachel may avoid doing her assignments. So he self-disclosed how he had decided to manage his anxieties about public speaking and performing by volunteering to speak at as many conferences as possible and thereby reduce his anxiety. He hoped this would demonstrate that in the long term it was better to face fears rather than avoid them.

Outcome

Rachel did manage to work away from home and did not suffer from any panic attacks. She returned to counselling a year later to concentrate on issues related to a bereavement. Interestingly, she still kept her coping statement written on a card in her wallet just in case a problem arose.

10

The Compleat Stress Counsellor

The previous chapters have covered the theory and practice of multimodal stress counselling. In this final chapter, we cover the main organizational and occupational stressors that counsellors need to understand to enable them to help clients suffering from occupational stress. We also cover additional information that the 'Compleat Stress Counsellor' needs in order to run stress counselling groups and stress management workshops. We include sections on dealing with clients who do not complete self-help assignments and on relapse prevention. We finish this chapter by emphasizing the importance of self-care for the counsellor and thereby the prevention of counsellor 'burn-out'.

Understanding occupational and organizational stress

The 'Compleat Stress Counsellor' is very likely to work with clients in 'one-to-one' counselling or in group counselling or therapy. Other situations may include stress management workshops in counselling, clinical, educational or organizational settings. Unless the counsellor only works with clients suffering from stress emanating from outside the workplace an understanding of occupational and organizational stress is necessary.

Clients frequently point to occupational stress as the major cause of their problems, and very real stressors can exist in the workplace. We do our clients a disservice if we do not help them recognize and manage workplace stressors. Although each occupation has its own potential stressors, there are several common organizational stress factors (Cooper et al., 1988):

- factors intrinsic to the job
- organizational structure and climate
- career development
- role in the organization
- relationships at work

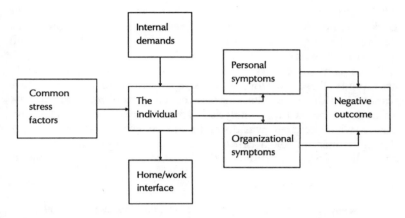

Figure 10.1 *The relationship between personal and workplace factors in occupational stress (Palmer, 1993d)*

In addition, the home/work interface and the individual's internal demands (or beliefs) can also increase the level of stress experienced (Palmer, 1993c, 1993d). Some of the organizational symptoms of stress are high staff turnover, high absenteeism, low morale, lowered efficiency, industrial relations difficulties and increased industrial accidents. Figure 10.1 (Palmer, 1993d) illustrates the relationship between all of these factors, the individual and his or her symptoms. These will now be briefly considered.

Factors intrinsic to the job

A wide range of stressors intrinsic to the job can cause stress. The more common environmental stressors are:

- air pollution
- dust/fibres
- heat
- humidity
- lighting
- noise
- noxious chemicals, including nicotine
- 'sick building' syndrome
- static electricity
- uncomfortable chairs/work stations
- VDU screen glare

These stressors can lead directly to physical ailments such as backache, headache, skin rashes, allergic reactions, chest infections, deafness and eye strain. An individual's work productivity and general morale can also be affected.

When assessing clients for occupational stress, counsellors should ask about these environmental stressors just in case they are responsible for any disclosed stress-related symptoms. Additionally, an in-depth behavioural analysis is sometimes required to ascertain exactly what the client was doing before the symptoms appeared. A typical transcript of a stress counselling session, in which the counsellor is trying to discover the cause of a recurrent headache, is as follows:

Counsellor: Is there any pattern to when your headaches occur?

Client: No. They just come out of the blue.

Counsellor: Hmm. When did the last one occur? [*The counsellor wishes to examine a specific example to assess whether the headaches do occur at random.*]

Client: Last Tuesday afternoon. It was so bad I had to take some pills.

Counsellor: What exactly were you doing beforehand?

Client: I'd just had lunch.

Counsellor: Did you eat or drink anything different from usual? [*The counsellor is checking whether there is any possibility of the client suffering from an allergic reaction.*]

Client: I've already thought of that. No, I went to the canteen and had my usual cheese sandwich and a cup of coffee.

Counsellor: Did you speak to anybody at lunchtime or have any disagreement? [*The counsellor is assessing whether the client became stressed about any conversation or event that may have occurred during her lunch break.*]

Client: I had a good chat with Jane. No rows!

Counsellor: What were you doing before lunch?

Client: There was bit of a panic. The boss wanted a report finished before the 12.30pm post. I spent the morning typing it up.

Counsellor: Did you type on a different machine from usual? [*The counsellor is still trying to ascertain whether she did anything different from her usual routine.*]

Client: No. I used my word processor.

Counsellor: Try to picture yourself back in the situation. Imagine looking around the office while you are sitting on your chair in front of the word processor. Describe what you see. [*In the counsellor's experience word processor screens can sometimes be a cause of headaches. He is now asking the client to imagine being back in the situation which may aid her recall.*]

Client: I remember now. It was the first sunny day we've had for a week. Jack said that he wanted to let the sunlight in so he adjusted the blind.

Counsellor: And . . .

Client: There was a glare of sunlight on the VDU screen most of the morning. You know, that's it! I've had headaches before when there was a glare.

It is important to ask the client to describe specific situations in detail otherwise it becomes difficult to assess the case systematically. The hypothesis as to the cause of the problem can later be tested by the client repeating the process in the real-life situation and recording any symptoms experienced. In the example given, the more usual interventions to alleviate headaches, such as relaxation exercises, would probably have been useless, while removal of the stressor – the VDU glare – would have been far more effective.

Other stressful factors intrinsic to the job that counsellors can explore with clients are:

1 Does the job involve boring repetitive tasks?
2 Is the work dangerous, requiring close concentration?
3 Does it involve working to deadlines and are they reasonable?
4 Does the job involve excess travel or isolated working conditions?
5 Are the hours long or the shift work of an unsocial nature?
6 Is the workload excessive for the individual or not within his/ her capabilities to carry out?

When examining the above factors, the counsellor also needs to assess the cognitive modality to ensure that the client is not making the situation worse by having a negative attitude towards specific or general work issues. We will look more closely at attitudes later in this chapter. It is worth noting that research has found some occupations to be more stressful than others; for example, acting, advertising, building, dentistry, journalism, mining and work in the police force are more stressful than accountancy, astronomy, biochemistry, geology, nature conservancy and horticulture (Sloan and Cooper, 1986).

Organizational structure and climate
In many companies the organizational structure and climate limit the autonomy of the individual. Staff may consider that they have no influence or control over their workload. This can contribute to job dissatisfaction, reduced self-esteem, apathy, resentment and a loss of identity. These can, in turn, lead to an increase in stress-related illness and absenteeism. Reduced self-esteem is largely dependent upon the individual's belief system and this can be explored by the counsellor in counselling or in group training/ therapy. There are several organizational interventions that may

help to alleviate some of these problems: for example, increased participation in decision-making and the introduction of teamwork can improve perceptions about control. Staff can elect their own supervisors and be involved in planning job rotation which can increase morale and commitment to the work.

The recession of the late 1980s and early 1990s meant that organizations placed redundancies firmly on their agenda and this led to increased levels of stress for many staff. Probably the only way for an organization to help alleviate this problem is to ensure that senior managers communicate quickly and effectively on all relevant issues. The recession also led to many changes in industry, such as the increased use of technology, reduced staffing levels and job relocation. Re-training, stress/change management seminars or workshops and outplacement counselling can help to reduce the negative effects of these types of change. The stress counsellor or trainer can help clients to 'de-awfulize' such changes or negative events (see Chapters 3 and 9).

Racism, sexism and ageism can be prevalent in some organiz-ations, and suitable policies and procedures may be needed to deal with them. The in-house stress counsellor may be able to take a proactive approach in dealing with these matters and encourage the personnel department to implement procedures. However, when working with clients in one-to-one counselling it is usually easier and more appropriate for them (rather than the counsellor) to raise these issues with their management or personnel department.

Career development

In many cultures people believe that career development is an important part of their work life. However, promotion prospects can become increasingly difficult to achieve at higher levels of the organization. When employees have reached their plateau, they may perceive that their only chance of improvement is to change their job. In addition, older staff may need re-training in order to use new technology or learn new management skills. All of these factors can contribute to stress and anxiety in individuals. Other concerns that older staff tend to share are a fear of redundancy, demotion, obsolescence, lack of job security and forced early retirement. This can help reduce self-worth and self-esteem. These issues can be examined in counselling and on relevant workshops and coping strategies can be taught.

Role in the organization

Different roles in an organization can lead to varying levels of stress. Research shows that individuals who are responsible for staff are more likely to suffer from coronary heart disease than those who are just responsible for machines. In our experience clients (in counselling or in group training) are often unaware of the source of their occupational stress, especially if it involves role demands. Role overload and role underload are relatively easy for clients to recognize as they may notice that they are either doing too much or too little work, whereas role conflict and role ambiguity are more insidious and clients usually fail to articulate these as causes of their stress.

Role conflict involves different expectations or sets of expectations made by the following groups on the employee:

- superiors
- superiors' superior
- peers
- clients
- subordinates
- subordinates' subordinates

In addition, the employee's own role expectations may also conflict with her work contract. Other forms of conflict may occur in a particular job if too many different roles are expected or where the expected role behaviour is too difficult to perform for the particular employee. Another form of conflict occurs when the employee's own value system conflicts with the expectations of the organization; for example, in a recession a pacifist may work in an armaments factory as there is no other job available.

Role ambiguity occurs when employees are uncertain about the role expectations that are required of them. They may have received inadequate or conflicting information about their job and have unclear role objectives. In these cases they will not know what behaviours will lead to the fulfilment of the role expectations. Sadly, we know of cases where this has led to disciplinary action or even dismissal!

The counsellor's task is to recognize the specific role demand that may be a cause of occupational stress and to brain-storm with clients various courses of action, such as obtaining clear written contracts of induction training. In some cases, clients may need to practise assertive techniques with their counsellors to ensure that they can communicate clearly to their employers the exact nature of the problem. However, care always needs to be taken to judge the likely impact of such techniques used with specific people.

Relationships at work

Interpersonal relationships can be a major source of stress in organizations, and this often highlights insufficient training in human resource skills given to managers and supervisors. Basic skills, such as being able to listen to staff or giving instructions in an assertive and not aggressive manner, are sometimes overlooked by management. Other factors that can lead to occupational stress include abrasive personalities, leadership style, peer/group pressures, social incongruence and social density (Quick and Quick, 1984).

Relationships between co-workers can be negative and are sometimes fuelled by 'office politics', yet they can also provide a social support system which helps to buffer employees from stress (Cowen, 1982). Social support is often fostered by organizations that offer employees social and sports facilities (Cox et al., 1988). A positive nurturing work environment is likely to lower the incidence of stress-related problems. We have often found that clients who tend to keep their problems to themselves and not share them with their co-workers suffer higher rates of stress-related disorders than workers who discuss their problems with each other. Counsellors working with clients suffering from occupational stress can suggest the sharing of work-related problems with co-workers as a possible adaptive coping strategy. Often clients who attend group counselling or stress management courses discover how helpful the sharing of their experiences with others is in reducing their levels of stress. This is a non-specific intervention that helps employees put work events into perspective as co-workers share, debate and discuss their experiences.

Home/work interface

High levels of stress can be caused by the interaction of problems in an employee's home life with those at work and vice versa. Thus an employee having marital difficulties may not be able to concentrate fully on his job. If his performance suffers badly then he may suffer disciplinary action by his manager. This additional burden may exacerbate an already difficult situation at home. However, if at an early stage, this problem is recognized by his manager then he could be referred to a counsellor for assistance. Some organizations may employ a stress counsellor (Allison et al., 1989), whereas others may use an Employee Assistance Programme or an external counsellor to help alleviate these types of problems.

Internal demands

In our experience it is the internal demands (irrational beliefs) that employees hold regarding the workplace which considerably increase their levels of occupational stress (see Figure 10.1). Some of the major occupational demands are (Palmer, 1993c, 1993d):

I/others must perform well at all times
I/others must always reach deadlines
I/others must be perfect
The organization must treat me fairly at all times
I should get what I want otherwise I can't stand it
Significant others must appreciate my work otherwise I am worthless

Employees, especially those holding a management grade, who have these internal demands will usually try to indoctrinate other employees in them too. They will frequently act in a non-constructive passive or aggressive manner towards other employees who do not appear to attain the over-stringent criteria such as 'others must perform well at all times'. The counsellor can use interventions described in Chapter 3 to help employees give up their unhelpful internal demands and change them to preferences. Relevant literature and self-help forms focused on these issues are very helpful.

Running multimodal stress counselling groups

The multimodal approach to counselling and training is easily adapted to stress counselling groups and stress management workshops. In our experience working in these settings has a number of distinct benefits that often outweigh one-to-one counselling sessions. First, it enables the counsellor to work with a large number of clients which can help to reduce waiting lists. Second, there can be considerable financial savings for the counsellor's organization. Lastly, participants can act as a resource for each other and this often leads to a greater understanding of stress and how to manage it. The very process of sharing experiences and listening to how different group members deal with problems reinforces the idea that stress can be managed or even eliminated. In continuing programmes, participants can discuss how effective they have found the different techniques taught and how they applied them in a variety of situations. We agree with Lazarus' claim that 'consensual validation tends to carry more weight than the views of one person, even if that person is a highly respected authority' (1981: 203); when a participant confirms the effectiveness of a technique, other group members are far more likely to use it themselves. In industrial settings the approach not only reduces stress levels but can increase performance and profitability too.

Although we have highlighted the benefits for individuals of attending stress counselling/management groups, there are some people that the counsellor may need to see in one-to-one counselling only or refer elsewhere. For example, individuals suffering from severe obsessive-compulsive rituals, severe depression, paranoia, severe hostility, delusions or psychosis may prove disruptive in stress counselling or stress management groups and will probably not benefit from attending. Multimodal groups can be run for specific groups such as children or adolescents or problems such as losing weight, phobias, stop smoking, assertion and communication difficulties, or under a more general heading of 'Stress Management' or 'Stress Control'. In our experience in industry, workshop headings such as 'Managing Pressure to Increase Performance' (Palmer, 1992d) tend to create interest with employers and employees alike and to reduce any reluctance to attend.

There are several differences between multimodal counselling groups and stress management workshops. Generally individuals attending the counselling groups have been referred by health professionals and may be suffering from specific stress-related problems such as phobias, hypertension or headaches. Alternatively, they may be having difficulty dealing with negative life-events. Therefore, in counselling groups, clients may be interested in learning how to cope or manage current problems and this will often lead to self-disclosure about personal issues to the counsellor and their peers. In stress management workshops, by contrast, the participants may be comprised of individuals who are interested in the prevention of stress but are not necessarily suffering from stress themselves. Thus the needs of the members in counselling groups and workshops may differ.

Ideally, in a clinical, counselling or educational setting, multimodal counselling groups would meet on a weekly basis, are normally time-limited (e.g. run for a set number of weeks, perhaps between 6 and 12), for one and a half to two hourly sessions. This can be for six to twelve members, led by a male and female co-counsellors. However, these guidelines are flexible; if there is only one counsellor available or the group consists of more than twelve members, then the counsellor can take an educational approach, with small group work restricted to suitable exercises that can be easily monitored. Some researchers have found that they have achieved beneficial results teaching groups of over twenty members cognitive-behavioural skills and by using an entirely educational approach with no small group work whatsoever (see White and Keenan, 1990; White et al., 1992).

In counselling groups or stress management workshops, for

maximum effectiveness, apart from tea breaks, all of the time available is focused on the subject of stress, including any introductory games or 'ice-breaker' exercises. For example, the participants may construct and compare Structural Profiles, discuss their 'stress diaries' or some other relevant exercise. We have found that asking participants to keep a 'Day in the life of "X" Stress Diary' before the start of a counselling group or stress management workshop improves the level of commitment of the participants. Multimodal counselling groups and stress management workshops are generally goal-directed and task-orientated and each participant learns techniques to help prevent, alleviate, stop or control different problems from which they currently suffer or suffer from when under stress. Participants are taught techniques and interventions from all of the different modalities.

To ensure that the participants of groups or workshops understand the nature of stress, it is crucial for the counsellor or trainer to give some indication of its psychophysiology. Most participants find relevant handouts, leaflets and audiovisual material helpful, and the counsellor or trainer is advised to obtain literature that is easily photocopied (see Cabinet Office, 1987; Clark and Palmer, 1994; Palmer, 1988).

We have found that teaching Ellis' ABCDE paradigm early on in the programme has helped participants to take responsibility for their emotions and behaviour and this can lead to passive individuals becoming willing to practise and subsequently apply assertive techniques in real life. Other useful interventions have included role play, exposure programmes, modelling, stability zones, feeling-identification, relaxation exercises, biofeedback, coping imagery, disputing irrational beliefs, constructive self-talk, problem-solving, stress mapping (see Palmer, 1990b, 1992d), bibliotherapy, assertion and communication skills training, friendship training, exercise programme, nutritional education, and moderating smoking and alcohol programmes (see Chapters 3–8).

If there is sufficient time available, participants may be taught diagnostic techniques such as 'tracking' (see Chapter 2) to aid their own choice of interventions. In multimodal counselling groups, members devise their own BASIC ID Modality Profile with the assistance of the counsellor(s). Alternatively, participants work towards devising their own stress management plan where they list a number of lifestyle changes, interventions and techniques they will undertake on a regular basis (e.g. see Box 10.1) once the group has disbanded.

Before a counsellor runs an industrial stress management workshop, it is important to assess the needs of the organization

Box 10.1   *Stress management plan*

Date 1/8/94

Action to be taken by___Alan Jones___

Stability zones:	Take long weekend break every 2 months.
	Visit favourite restaurant every Friday.
	Start day with a relaxing bath.
Time management:	Don't be side-tracked by phone calls.
Relaxation:	Practise multimodal relaxation method daily.
	Use quick relaxation when queuing.
	Use relaxation tape and biodots on Sundays.
Coping imagery:	Use coping imagery before doing presentations at work.
Thinking skills:	Watch out for twisted thinking, especially overgeneralization and 'musts'.
	Use constructive self-talk.
	See events in terms of overall perspective.
Assertion:	Become more assertive and less aggressive with work colleagues.
Diet:	Cut out night-time coffee.
	Have some fresh fruit daily.
Exercise:	Walk to station daily instead of driving.
	Help wife with gardening.

and potential client group first. If the counsellor works for the organization he or she may have a biased perspective of its needs. It is crucial initially to gather information from the organization and its staff on what they believe the problems are and what interventions they would prefer. Even if the staff are not sure what interventions could be made, the process of asking them for their opinion can help to put stress management on the agenda. A stress management workshop could increase stress levels and *not* decrease them if the staff attending believe that the organization is only 'going through the motions' and holds them totally responsible for their own levels of stress. From the trade union viewpoint, it is often the organization that needs to change rather than the staff. Therefore, the counsellor may need to liaise with their representatives as well as others from different departments of the organization; for example, personnel, training etc. (Counsellors may benefit from reading literature about organizational interventions and assessment; see Cockman et al., 1992; Evans and Reynolds, 1993; Palmer, 1992d, 1992e.)

Industrial stress management training workshops are usually held over a one or two-day period, occasionally with a follow-up day about a month or two later as it is easier for staff to take blocks of time out of the workplace as opposed to regular weekly sessions. Therefore the training tends to be more intensive and there is a greater need to structure the time available. It is useful to ask potential participants what they hope to get out of the workshop. Time should be made available for prospective participants to be interviewed or asked to complete a brief questionnaire focusing on what they hope to learn from the stress management workshop. If this is undertaken at least one month before the workshop then this will give the counsellor adequate time to prepare materials, venue and equipment.

In industry, the counsellor takes the role of a trainer and facilitator using basic counselling skills when necessary. In contrast to counselling groups, the emphasis is on 'training' skills and not 'therapeutic' skills; therefore cognitive techniques and cognitive distortions are described as 'thinking skills' and 'thinking skills deficits', respectively. This helps to overcome any prejudices participants and management may hold towards this type of psychological training. Although actual and desired Structural Profiles are used, a full BASIC ID profile is not so essential as long as the trainer has provided a selection of techniques and interventions from each modality and ensured that the participants can apply them to their own problem areas. This allows the participants to develop their own stress management plans where they list a number of lifestyle changes, interventions and techniques they will undertake once the course is finished (see Box 10.1). In a two-day stress management workshop the following can be covered:

1 Discussion of ground rules
2 Ask participants what they hope to learn and achieve over the next two days
3 Participants share their 'Stress Diaries' with the group
4 Look at cartoons illustrating stress and relate them to the participants' experiences
5 Discuss and look at an example of a completed Stress Management Plan
6 Discuss simple definition of stress, e.g. too much or too little pressure leads to stress
7 Small group work considering symptoms of stress that participants have experienced. Participants directed to put symptoms under BASIC ID headings
8 De-brief and then watch video explaining the psychophysiology of stress
9 Participants draw actual and desired Structural Profiles
10 Simple biofeedback 'biodots' used by participants to monitor vasodilation and subsequent surface skin temperature
11 Discuss cognitive distortions or 'twisted thinking'. Then small group exercise where participants share distortions they commonly have
12 De-brief
13 Discuss constructive self-talk alternatives and then small group exercise helping each other to derive constructive self-talk alternatives from negative mental monologues
14 Demonstrate the different effects people experience when holding musturbatory beliefs as opposed to preferential beliefs, e.g. use Deserted Island technique on participants (Palmer, 1993a)
15 Discuss Ellis' ABCDE paradigm. Then small group exercise helping each other to recognize and dispute irrational beliefs
16 Demonstrate effects of negative thoughts and images on the stress response. Participants use biofeedback machines to monitor change in skin conductivity when aroused or stressed
17 Participants use the multimodal relaxation method (Palmer, 1993b, see Chapter 6) and immediately afterwards use 'biodots' to monitor skin temperature
18 Participants use skin conductivity biofeedback machines to assess which part of the multimodal relaxation method (see Chapter 6) they found most useful

19 Imagery techniques taught, e.g. coping imagery, time projection imagery etc
20 Occupational and organizational stress discussed, e.g. role demands, Type A behaviour. Group to consider organizational changes that could be made and individual coping strategies, such as stability zones, assertion, time management
21 Lifestyle changes discussed, e.g. diet, exercise, environment. Referrals to specialists discussed if relevant
22 A multimodal stress management plan devised by each participant. Counsellor/trainer gives guidance if necessary
23 Discussion of 'where to go from here' and possibility of follow-up day
24 Feedback and evaluation

Often the discussion of suitable techniques reflects the order in which the participants disclose their problems and not any rigid course outline previously developed by the counsellor. The above outline reflects a typical multimodal two-day stress management workshop, but it is not set in stone. A one or half-day workshop would still include the basic psychophysiology and techniques from different modalities. A follow-up one-day or half-day would focus on how the participants fared with the application of the techniques and when possible any organizational changes they managed to introduce. The techniques would be discussed and demonstrated again, if necessary, and new techniques introduced if relevant.

Clients who do not complete self-help assignments

Effective multimodal stress counselling is underpinned by clients completing self-help assignments, such as exposure programmes, relaxation exercises and coping imagery, outside the therapeutic hour. Clients may feel anxious about completing assignments or may not understand the relevance of such exercises. It is important that the counsellor ascertains the reason why the client does not undertake the self-help assignment and then helps the client to overcome his difficulties. Dryden (1990: 94–5) has devised a questionnaire that the client completes to aid exploration of the possible reasons for not completing assignments (see Box 10.2).

Clients are often more prepared to give honest answers about their reasons for not undertaking assignments if they complete a questionnaire rather than discuss the subject face to face with the counsellor. This can be for a variety of reasons such as fear of

Box 10.2 *Possible reasons for not completing self-help assignments*

(To be completed by client)

The following is a list of reasons that various clients have given for not doing their self-help assignments during the course of counselling. Because the speed of improvement depends primarily on the amount of self-help assignments that you are willing to do, it is of great importance to pinpoint any reasons that you may have for not doing this work. It is important to look for these reasons at the time that you feel a reluctance to do your assignment or a desire to put off doing it. Hence, it is best to fill out this questionnaire at that time. If you have any difficulty filling out this form and returning it to the counsellor, it might be best to do it together during a counselling session. (Rate each statement by ringing 'T' (True) or 'F' (False). 'T' indicates that you agree with it; 'F' means the statement does not apply at this time.)

1 It seems that nothing can help me so there is no point in trying. T/F
2 It wasn't clear, I didn't understand what I had to do. T/F
3 I thought that the particular method the counsellor had suggested would not be helpful. I didn't really see the value of it. T/F
4 It seemed too hard. T/F
5 I am willing to do self-help assignments, but I keep forgetting. T/F
6 I did not have enough time. I was too busy. T/F
7 If I do something the counsellor suggests I do it's not as good as if I come up with my own ideas. T/F
8 I don't really believe I can do anything to help myself. T/F
9 I have the impression the counsellor is trying to boss me around or control me. T/F
10 I worry about the counsellor's disapproval. I believe that what I do just won't be good enough for him/her. T/F
11 I felt too bad, sad, nervous, upset (underline the appropriate word or words) to do it. T/F
12 It would have upset me to do the homework. T/F
13 It was too much to do. T/F

Continued

Box 10.2 *continued*

14 It's too much like going back to school again.   T/F
15 It seemed to be mainly for the counsellor's benefit.   T/F
16 Self-help assignments have no place in counselling.   T/F
17 Because of the progress I've made, these assignments
   are likely to be of no further benefit to me.   T/F
18 Because these assignments have not been helpful in
   the past, I couldn't see the point of doing this one.   T/F
19 I don't agree with this particular approach to
   counselling.   T/F
20 Other reasons (please write them).

_____

_____

_____

being rejected by the counsellor or concern about upsetting the counsellor. Completion of the questionnaire in reception or at home can also avoid any potential difficulties.

As the main burden of responsibility for promoting client change rests on the client carrying out homework assignments between sessions, it is important that the client is adequately prepared to execute such homework assignments. To encourage clients to undertake their homework tasks Dryden (1990: 78) advises counsellors to:

1 Provide a persuasive rationale for the importance of executing homework assignments in multimodal stress counselling.
2 Negotiate with your client suitable homework assignments rather than unilaterally suggest what these assignments should be.
3 Negotiate homework assignments which are relevant to your client achieving her goals (see Golden, 1983).
4 Negotiate assignments which follow on naturally from what has been discussed in stress counselling sessions.
5 Specify as fully as possible what these assignments will be, when your client is going to do them, and where and how she is going to execute them.
6 Elicit a firm commitment from your client that she will execute these homework assignments.

7 Encourage your client, whenever possible, to rehearse the particular homework assignment in the session. Your client is more likely to execute homework assignments successfully when she can picture herself doing so in imagery.

8 Identify and overcome potential obstacles that may prevent your client from putting into practice particular homework assignments (see completed homework Assignment Task sheet (Box 9.1).

9 Negotiate homework assignments which are not too time-consuming for your client.

10 Suggest assignments which are challenging at a particular time for your client but not overwhelming for her.

We suggest that multimodal stress counsellors stick to the motto 'challenging but not overwhelming'. When clients do undertake homework assignments, inexpert counsellors often fail to check adequately their clients' experiences in executing the tasks. When this occurs, clients are likely to start believing that homework assignments are not important and subsequently stop doing them. When checking your client's experiences of executing assignments, Dryden (1990: 79) makes a number of recommendations:

1 Ask your client to report what he learned or did not learn from carrying out the assignments.

2 Reinforce his success at executing assignments and, where necessary, reinforce his attempts at executing these assignments.

3 Identify and correct errors that your client has made in carrying out his homework assignments.

4 Identify, assess and deal with your client's reasons for not attempting or not completing his homework assignments. In particular, help him to dispute his resistance-creating irrational beliefs.

5 Encourage him to re-do the assignment.

Relapse prevention

After clients have terminated counselling, some relapse back into previous dysfunctional patterns which may include a problem from any modality of the BASIC ID. There are several methods that counsellors can employ to prevent relapse from occurring.

In our experience, it is important to reduce the frequency of counselling sessions as counselling proceeds. This can also help dependent clients, who do not wish counselling to finish, gradually to adapt to supporting themselves without the counsellor's help. Throughout the duration of counselling, the counsellor needs to identify any obstacles to change and subsequent barriers to maintenance. These problems can be discussed and creative methods of overcoming them devised. It is recommended that clients overlearn skills with a wide range of targets so the skills become incorporated into their daily repertoire of behaviour. Later in counselling, clients can be encouraged to design and undertake their own assignments in-between sessions.

Towards the end of counselling, clients can be taught how to anticipate future difficult situations and how to deal with them by planning, rehearsing and practising the techniques or using interventions that they have previously learnt during counselling. Clients can be helped to recognize the warning signs of possible relapse and develop strategies to deal with them. For example, clients who previously suffered from obsessive-compulsive disorder may relapse when they perceive that they are under severe pressure. If they are aware of their level of stress they can start using coping strategies that they learnt during counselling to reduce their day-to-day stress levels. These 'emergency strategies' are discussed with clients before the last counselling session, as they may take some time to learn and the client may need the counsellor's help. Clients can be asked to imagine their worst scenario and to picture themselves applying their 'emergency strategies' to deal with the situation. In some cases clients may need to ask for the assistance of significant others such as family members to help them.

While reducing the frequency of counselling sessions, we have found that 'booster' sessions are sometimes necessary to help clients over a difficult period. If the counsellor can anticipate a difficult period, for example the anniversary of a significant death, then a definite appointment can be made. Otherwise a 'booster' session can be arranged for some months later as a preventative measure or the client can be advised to contact the counsellor if a major problem arises. One of the aims of multimodal stress counselling is for clients to become their own effective counsellors and this is possible with adequate preparation in the majority of cases. Multimodal stress counsellors need to be their own effective counsellors too.

Counsellor self-care

We believe that continuing counsellor self-care is important for a number of different reasons. If a counsellor does not manage his or her own levels of stress, in severe cases this can lead to burn-out which is extremely debilitating and involves absence from work and possible financial difficulty. If he/she is employed, this can place an extra burden upon his organization, colleagues and clients. The situation becomes more difficult for his or her clients if the counsellor is in private practice and is not in a position to refer them elsewhere. In less extreme cases, when a counsellor is only moderately stressed, it is likely that he or she may not be able to concentrate fully on the work in hand and may become a poor role model for his or her clients, for example, arriving late for appointments or inadequately preparing for counselling sessions.

When counsellors put self-care at the top of their agenda they are more likely to be mentally and physically healthy on a day-to-day basis than counsellors who put others, including their clients, first. This does not necessarily reflect a selfish approach to life as counsellors who take this attitude are far more likely to be able to take care of their family, friends, work colleagues and clients if they have first taken care of themselves. In the long term, they will not succumb to burn-out, be generally more efficient, be able to maintain performance levels and be of more benefit to the community at large. Counsellors can develop their own stress management plans based on the BASIC ID. If they do not have any stress-related problems appearing on the Modality Profile, their stress management plan can still include preventative techniques such as time management, time-out for lunch, stability zones, relaxation exercises, self-hypnosis, biofeedback, coping imagery, constructive self-talk, assertiveness, safe aerobic sports, healthy diet, balanced lifestyle etc. Two other major factors involved in counsellor self-care are counsellor-related irrational beliefs and supervision.

Counsellor-related irrational beliefs

Ellis (1983) believes that a counsellor's most difficult client is often him- or herself. He advocates that counsellors preferably should dispute and relinquish any irrational beliefs focusing on their work. As mentioned in Chapter 3, the common disputes that can be used to challenge these beliefs are:

1 Logical (e.g. is this belief logical?)
2 Empirical (e.g. where is the evidence for the belief?)
3 Pragmatic (e.g. where is it going to get you if you continue to hold on to this belief?)

The irrational beliefs that usually apply to counsellors which can be very disabling are (Ellis, 1983):

I have to be successful with all my clients virtually all of the time.
I must be an outstanding therapist, clearly better than other therapists that I know or hear about.
I have to be greatly respected and loved by all my clients.

Since I am doing my best and working so hard as a therapist, my clients should be equally hard working and responsible, should listen to me carefully and should always push themselves to change.

Because I'm a person in my own right, I must be able to enjoy myself during therapy sessions and to use these sessions to solve my personal problems as much as to help my clients with their difficulties.

These irrational beliefs can lead to intrapsychic stress and reduce the counsellor's effectiveness in stress counselling or stress management (Palmer, 1995). For example, counsellors may 'back off from encouraging clients to change' (Dryden and Gordon, 1990: 48). If we take the example of the irrational belief: 'I have to be greatly respected and loved by all my clients', the counsellor can ask himself:

Logical: Although it may be preferable to be greatly respected and loved by my clients, does it logically follow that I *have to* be thus respected and loved? *Answer*: It does not logically follow.

Empirical: There is evidence for my strong preference to be greatly respected and loved by my clients but where is the evidence that they *have to* at all times greatly respect and love me? Where is it written that they *have* greatly to respect and love me? *Answer*: There is no evidence anywhere, nor is it written anywhere (apart from inside my own head) that my clients *have to* greatly respect and love me.

Pragmatic: If I carry on holding on to this belief that my clients *have to* greatly respect and love me, where is it going to get me or my clients? *Answer*: Whether my clients greatly respect and love me or in fact do not, either way I will remain anxious. This will reduce my therapeutic effectiveness and I may back off from encouraging my clients to change in case I lose their respect and love. This will be a no-win situation and potentially unprofessional.

Once the counsellor has disputed his or her irrational beliefs, then he/she can develop a more helpful coping statement as below.

Coping statement: Although it may be preferable to be greatly respected and loved by my clients, it is by no means essential. In fact to do the best for my clients it would be better just to concentrate on the therapeutic goals of my clients and not my own personal desires.

Counsellor self-care is also enhanced by regular supervision.

Supervision

Counselling supervision is a formal arrangement where counsellors discuss their counselling in a confidential setting on a regular basis with one or more counsellors. Supervision protects the client by ensuring the counsellor is acting in a professional and ethical manner. In multimodal stress counselling supervision by experienced counsellors ensures that the counsellor in supervision is applying the correct technique or intervention for the specific stress-related problem. Multimodal supervision places emphasis on the counsellor's therapeutic skills by monitoring the exact application of a technique by the use of audio-cassette recordings of the counselling sessions. Otherwise a counsellor may believe that he or she has used an intervention correctly, such as disputing an irrational belief, when in reality he/she has made an error and in this example disputed a rational belief. Multimodal supervision also places an emphasis on the client–counsellor relationship to ensure that the counsellor is maximizing the session and not entering into unhelpful negative transference or negative countertransference issues.

If clients appear reluctant to apply specific techniques then the possible reasons for this problem are analysed in supervision. It is *rarely* assumed that clients are being 'awkward' or 'resistant' or any other pejorative label, but more realistically that they are experiencing anxiety about the suggested intervention. Therefore a 'difficult client' is reframed as a 'client experiencing difficulties'.

The necessary frequency and duration of supervision depends upon the number of client hours the counsellor is undertaking and the experience of the counsellor. Essentially, beginning or trainee counsellors require more in-depth supervision than experienced counsellors. They will need a greater tutorial input than the more consultative requirements of experienced counsellors. Supervision may be undertaken one-to-one, with peers, in a group, or a combination of these methods. Group supervision has a number of advantages; for example, mutual support from peers and the sharing of experiences which aid learning (see Wessler and Ellis, 1980). It is also more economical (Perris, 1993).

Regular supervision aids counsellor self-care by focusing on the counsellor's work and his or her concerns about clients. In particular, beginning or trainee counsellors often view their clients' problems as overwhelming or insurmountable and as they become anxious their therapeutic effectiveness and general health suffers. Inexperienced counsellors may fail to recognize important material about their clients or know how to deal with clients with suicidal ideation, whereas experienced supervisors can advise what action to take especially when clients may wish to harm themselves or others. This aids counsellor self-care and client-care. Finally, if a counsellor is becoming generally very stressed and disturbed the supervisor may recommend that he or she temporarily (or permanently) ceases counselling and perhaps receives suitable treatment him- or herself. Counsellor burn-out is always a possibility and the supervisor should know how to recognize the early signs.

Postscript

This book has included a wide range of different techniques and interventions, some of which may be quite new for many counsellors. We therefore recommend that counsellors receive adequate supervision when using this approach. For those counsellors with insufficient experience in the application of these techniques, further training is available in Britain at the Centre for Multimodal Therapy (address below). In the United States of America training is available at a number of centres.

Although the *Multimodal Life History Inventory* is not essential for stress counselling, we have found that it helps the counsellor to develop an individual stress programme for each client. In Britain counsellors can purchase copies from the Centre for Multimodal Therapy. In America they can be purchased from Research Press. Counsellors experiencing any difficulty obtaining biofeedback instruments, biodots, client handouts or other items mentioned in this book can write to the authors for further information and advice.

The authors would be interested to hear your views and experience of multimodal stress counselling and stress management. Please write to:

Centre for Multimodal Therapy
156 Westcombe Hill
London
SE3 7DH

Appendix: Handouts and Information

Throughout this book we have included boxed information which can be used as handouts to clients in stress counselling or stress management workshops. Here we offer additional sample materials, which the multimodal stress counsellor or trainer may find useful, followed by a section on recommended manuals and audio-visual materials.

Handout 1: Definitions

The following definitions will be helpful to you as you begin to learn about how you might best cope with stress in your life.

Stress
  Bodily reaction to some stimuli in the environment.

Anxiety
  Learned. Pairing of stimuli and response.
  Emotional response to a threatening situation or object.
  Prepares body for fight or flight.
  Normal reaction to stresses of life; no one is anxiety free.
  Can be useful to us by causing increased alertness, taking important things seriously, and motivating change and development.

Distress
  Unmanaged stress and anxiety.
  Anxiety is a problem when it occurs in response to non-threatening stimuli or events and/or is an unrealistic fear of failing at tasks.

Possible consequences of distress
  Impaired health.
  Blood pressure increases in response to stress.

Increased blood pressure can increase incidence of hardening of arteries, heart attacks and strokes.

Combined with other factors, such as heredity, diet and exercise, high blood pressure and associated disorders account for almost half of all deaths in the United States and the United Kingdom.

Source: Ross and Altmaier, 1994

Handout 2: What is stress?

Too much or too little pressure leads to stress

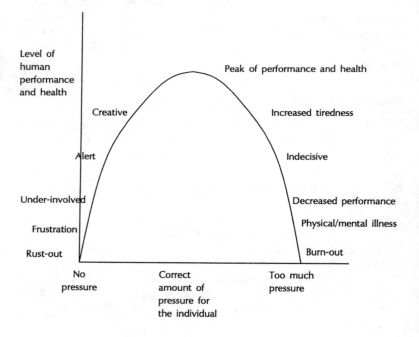

Handout 3: Daily log

Name _____   Date _____

Intensity of symptom or feeling																									
10
9
8
7
6
5
4
3
2
1

Time of Day	4am	5	6	7	8	9	10	11	Noon	1	2	3	4	5	6	7	8	9	10	11	Night	1	2	3	4am

Medications taken
Time _____
Quantity _____

Alcohol consumed
Time _____
Quantity _____

Stimulants consumed

Tea
Time _____
Quantity _____

Coffee
Time _____
Quantity _____

Other drinks
Time _____
Quantity _____

Cigarettes
No. _____

Food consumed
Type _____
Time _____
Type _____
Time _____

Relaxation
Time, type and duration _____

Physical activity
Time, type and duration _____

Accomplishments of day
Achieved _____
Not achieved _____
Avoidance strategies used and time _____

Source: Palmer, 1988

Handout 4: Distress symptoms or signals

As a way to begin to evaluate how much distress you are experiencing in your life, consider the list of symptoms below. Place a tick next to all the symptoms that describe you currently.

—— Expression of boredom with much or everything
—— Tendency to begin vacillating in decision-making
—— Tendency to become distraught with trifles
—— Inattentiveness or loss of power to concentrate
—— Irritability
—— Procrastination
—— Feelings of persecution
—— Gut-level feelings of unexplainable dissatisfaction
—— Forgetfulness
—— Tendency to misjudge people
—— Uncertain about whom to trust
—— Inability to organize self
—— Inner confusion about duties or roles
—— Physical changes such as:
　　—— Sudden, noticeable loss or gain of weight
　　—— Sudden change of appearance
　　—— Decline or improvement in dress
　　—— Sudden changes of complexion (sallow, reddened, acne)
　　—— Difficult breathing
　　—— Sudden change in smoking habits
　　—— Sudden change in use of alcohol
　　—— Allergies or new allergies
　　—— Sudden facial expression changes
　　—— Sudden changes in social habits
　　—— Not going to work or home according to past schedule
　　—— Change of life situation or style (for example, marriage, birth of baby, divorce, death of spouse)

Source: Ross and Altmaier, 1994

Handout 5: Relaxation diary

Date	Session		Time in minutes	Relaxation technique used	Tension levels Relaxed – 0 Tense – 10		Name: Feelings		Comments
	Began	Ended			Before	After	During	After	

Instructions: Note the date, time, duration and type of relaxation exercise used. On a scale of 0–10, where 0 represents a relaxed state and 10 represents a tense state, write down scores before and after a training exercise. Monitor emotions and bodily feelings in the appropriate column. Record any variations to the technique used and any other comments.

Source: Palmer, 1993b

Handout 6: Three basic musts

1 *Demands about self*
   I must do well
   And be approved by significant others
   If I'm not, then it is awful
   I can't stand it
   And I am a damnable person to some degree when I am not
   loved or when I do not do well

Leads to stress, anxiety, depression, shame and guilt

2 *Demands about others*
   You must treat me well and justly
   And it's awful and I can't bear it when you don't
   You are damnable when you don't treat me well
   And you deserve to be punished for doing what you must not do

Leads to anger, rage, passive-aggressiveness and violence.

3 *Demands about the world/life conditions*
   Life conditions under which I live absolutely must be the way I
   want them to be
   And if they are not, it's terrible
   I can't stand it, poor me

Leads to self-pity, other pity, hurt, procrastination and addictive
behaviour

Flexible beliefs, desires, wants, preferences *v.* absolute/dogmatic
musts, shoulds, oughts

Self-esteem *v.* self-acceptance (of fallibility)
Statements of toleration (it's bad but not awful)
Always and never thinking (always will fail, never succeed)

Handout 7: Stability zones

Stability zones can be considered as those physical areas where an individual may be able to relax, feel safe and be able to forget about worries. However, this is different for every individual but some examples may be:

Home with or without the family
Holiday home/caravan
Park
Room
Bath
Beach
Favourite pub, restaurant, café, chair, country walk, old car, old clothes

Rituals are enjoyable regular or irregular habits or routines that individuals may have in their repertoire of adaptive behaviour. However, these rituals are not to the point of obsession. Some examples may be:

Walking the dog
Morning cup of tea
Hobbies
Weekend breaks
Eating out on Friday nights
Reading book on the way to work
Sunday outings
Holidays
Watching old films
Talking/meeting old friends

Often stability zones and rituals are linked together, e.g. drinking a cup of tea while sitting in a favourite chair and listening to one's favourite radio programme. Stability zones and rituals are one way of coping with stress and when used in moderation they act as buffers. However, if applied inappropriately or to excess, they can inhabit creativity and change.

Source: Palmer, 1989

Handout 8: Value of various exercises

Energy range[1] (approximate calories used per hour)	Activity	Benefits
72–84	Sitting Conversing	Of no conditioning value.
120–150	Strolling, 1 mph Walking, 2 mph	Not sufficiently strenuous to promote endurance unless your exercise capacity is very low.
150–240	Cleaning windows Mopping floors Vacuuming Bowling Walking, 3 mph Cycling, 6 mph Golf, pulling cart	Adequate for conditioning if carried out continuously for 20–30 minutes. Too intermittent; not sufficiently taxing to promote endurance. Adequate dynamic exercise if your capacity is low. Useful for conditioning if you walk briskly, but if cart is heavy, isometrics may be involved.
300–360	Scrubbing floors Walking, 3.5 mph Cycling, 8 mph Table tennis Badminton	Adequate endurance exercise if carried out in at least 2-minute stints. Usually good dynamic aerobic exercise. Vigorous continuous play can have endurance benefits. Otherwise only promotes skill.

Continued

Handout 8 *continued*

	Volleyball Golf, carrying clubs	Promotes endurance if you reach and maintain target heart rate. Aids strength and skill.
	Tennis, doubles	Not very beneficial unless there is continuous play for at least 2 minutes at a time. Aids skill.
	Many calisthenics	Will promote endurance if continuous, rhythmic and repetitive.
	Ballet exercises	Promotes agility, coordination and muscle strength. Those requiring isometric effort, such as push-ups and sit-ups, not good for cardiovascular fitness.
360–420	Walking, 4 mph Cycling, 10 mph Ice or roller skating	Dynamic, aerobic and beneficial. Skating should be done continuously.
420–480	Walking, 5 mph Cycling, 11 mph Tennis, singles	Dynamic, aerobic and beneficial.
	Water skiing	Can provide benefit if played for 30 minutes or more with an attempt to keep moving. Total isometrics. Very risky for persons with high risk of heart disease or deconditioned normals.
480–600	Jogging, 5 mph Cycling, 12 mph	Dynamic, aerobic, endurance-building exercise.
	Downhill skiing	Runs are usually too short to promote endurance significantly. Mostly benefits skill. Combined stress and altitude, cold and exercise may be too great for some heart patients.

Continued

Handout 8 continued

Energy range[1] (approximate calories used per hour)	Activity	Benefits
	Paddleball	Not sufficiently continuous. Promotes skill.
600–660	Running, 5.5 mph Cycling, 13 mph	Excellent conditioner.
Above 600	Running, 6 or more mph	Excellent conditioner.
	Handball	Competitive environment in hot room is dangerous to anyone not in excellent physical condition. Can provide conditioning benefit if played 30 minutes or more with attempt to keep moving.
	Squash	
	Swimming[2]	Good conditioning exercise if continuous strokes. Especially good for persons who can't tolerate weight-bearing exercise, such as those with joint diseases.

[1] In all activities, energy used will vary depending on skill, rest patterns, environmental temperature and body size.
[2] Wide calorie range depending on skill of swimmer, stroke, temperature of water, body composition, current and other factors.

Source: Ross and Altmaier, 1994

Handout 9: Role demands

At WORK my role demands are

_____   _____
_____   _____
_____   _____
_____   _____
_____   _____
_____   _____
_____   _____
_____   _____

I experience role conflict when _____
_____
_____
_____
_____

I experience role ambiguity when _____
_____
_____
_____
_____

Comments: _____
_____
_____
_____

Possible changes: _____
_____
_____
_____
_____

Source: Palmer, 1988

Handout 10: Constructive self-talk

Situation	Negative self-talk	Constructive self-talk alternative

Handout 11: Assignment task sheet

Name _____ Date __/__/__ Negotiated with _____

Agreed task:

The therapeutic purpose(s) of the task:

Obstacles to carrying out the task — what obstacles, if any, stand in your way of completing this task and how you can overcome them:

1

2

3

Penalty:

Reward:

Signed _____

Handout 12: Homework diary for exposure programme

Name: Therapist:

Week commencing:
Goals for   1
the week   2
                3

Anxiety scale:

0	2.5	5	7.5	10
No anxiety	Slight anxiety	Moderate anxiety	Marked anxiety	High anxiety/ panic

Session		Goal no.	Task performed	Anxiety			Comments
Date	Began	Ended			Before	During	After	

Handout 13: Stress management plan

Date_____

Action to be taken by _____

_____

_____

_____

_____

_____

_____

_____

_____

_____

_____

_____

_____

_____

_____

_____

_____

_____

_____

Handout 14: Assertiveness Problem Hierarchy form

Name

Date

1 _____

2 _____

3 _____

4 _____

5 _____

6 _____

7 _____

8 _____

9 _____

10 _____

11 _____

12 _____

Continue if necessary

Handout 15: Assertiveness Behaviour diary

Name:

Date	Situation	Person/people involved	Assertiveness skills used	Evaluation of skills	Areas for improvement

Handout 16: Thought form to help clients to dispute irrational beliefs

A	B	C	D	E
Activating event/problem	Self-defeating beliefs	Emotional/behavioural consequences	Disputing beliefs	Effective new beliefs, emotions and behaviours

Instructions: Write your problem or activating event in column A. Note in column C your unhealthy and unhelpful emotion(s). These are anger, depression, anxiety, guilt, shame. The healthy alternatives are annoyance, sadness, concern, remorse, regret. Irrational beliefs consist of dogmatic musts, shoulds, have tos, 'I can't stand it', 'it's awful' statements which are placed in column B. Disputes are logical (how does it follow?), empirical (where is the evidence?) and pragmatic (where is holding on to this belief going to get me?). These are written in column D. Rational alternatives consist of wishes, desires and wants and are placed in column E. Effective behaviours help you deal with the situation in a helpful manner.

Handout 17: Stress mapping

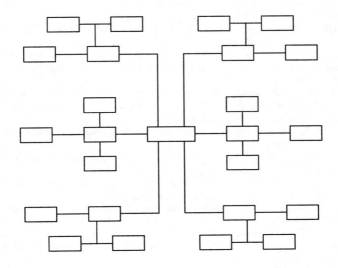

A stress map is a visual means of representing the sources of stress in your life. The central box represents yourself and the other boxes represent people you are in contact with. The other boxes can represent other potential stessors too, such as new computers or internal demands you place on yourself e.g. perfectionist beliefs.

Complete the boxes and then rate the amount of stress each other potential stressor can cause you on a scale of 1 to 10, where 10 represents high levels of stress. Place the score next to the appropriate stressor. Then ask yourself how much stress you may cause the other people on your stress map. Also note these scores down.

Once the exercise is completed, note down any insights that you may have gained from undertaking stress mapping.

Source: Palmer, 1990b

Training materials

Bailey, R. (1989) *50 Activities for Managing Stress*. Hampshire: Gower (trainer's manual).

BBC (1991) *Managing Pressure at Work*. London: BBC Training Videos (useful video for stress management workshops).

Clarke, D. and Palmer, S. (1994) *Stress Management*. Cambridge: National Extension College (a trainer's manual and self-help book for clients or course participants).

HMSO (1987) *Understanding Stress*, part 3. London: HMSO (trainer's manual).

Howell, M. and Whitehead, J. (1989) *Survive Stress: a Training Guide*. Cambridge: Cambridge Health Promotion (trainer's manual).

Lazarus, A.A. (1975) *Learning To Relax*. New York: Institute for Rational-Emotive Therapy (cassette).

Lazarus, A.A. (1995) *Personal Enrichment through Imagery*. London: Centre for Multimodal Therapy (cassette).

Lazarus, A.A. (1995) *Multimodal Training Aids: Insomnia, Tension, Headache and Smoking*. London: Centre for Multimodal Therapy (cassettes).

Palmer, S. (1988) *Personal Stress Management Programme*. London: Centre for Stress Management (handouts for completion by clients or course participants).

Ross, R.R. and Altmaier, E.M. (1994) *Intervention in Occupational Stress: a Handbook of Counselling for Stress at Work*. London: Sage (book with 25 useful sample handouts for clients).

Wycherley, R.J. (1990) *Stress at Work*. East Sussex: Outset (trainer's manual).

References

Allison, T., Cooper, C.L. and Reynolds, P. (1989) 'Stress counselling in the workplace', *The Psychologist*, 12(9): 384–8.

Ashton, D. and Davies, B. (1986) *Why Exercise*. Oxford: Basil Blackwell.

Ashton, H. (ed.) (1987) *Brain Systems, Disorders, and Psychotropic Drugs*. Oxford: Oxford University Press.

Back, K., Back, K. and Bates, T. (1991) *Assertiveness at Work: a Practical Guide to Handling Awkward Situations*. Maidenhead: McGraw-Hill.

Bandura, A. (1977) *Social Learning Theory*. Englewood Cliffs, NJ: Prentice-Hall.

Bandura, A. (1986) *Social Foundations of Thought and Action: a Social Cognitive Theory*. Englewood Cliffs, NJ: Prentice-Hall.

Barber, T.X. (1993) 'Hypnosuggestive approaches to stress reduction: data, theory, and clinical applications', in P.M. Lehrer and R.L. Woolfolk (eds), *Principles and Practice of Stress Management*, 2nd edn. New York: Guilford Press.

Bard, J.A. (1973) 'Rational proselytizing', *Rational Living*, 12(1): 2–6.

Beck, A.T. (1976) *Cognitive Therapy and the Emotional Disorders*. New York: New American Library.

Beck, A.T., Rush, A.J., Shaw, B.F. and Emery, G. (1979) *Cognitive Therapy of Depression*. New York: Guilford.

Beck, A.T., Wright, F.D., Newman, C.F. and Liese, B.S. (1993) *Cognitive Therapy of Substance Abuse*. New York: Guilford Press.

Beitman, B.D. (1990) 'Why I am an integrationist (not an eclectic)', in W. Dryden and J.C. Norcross (eds), *Eclecticism and Integration in Counselling and Psychotherapy*. Loughton: Gale Centre Publications.

Benson, H. (1976) *The Relaxation Response*. London: Collins.

Blackburn, I. and Davidson, K.M. (1990) *Cognitive Therapy for Depression and Anxiety*. Oxford: Blackwell Scientific Publications.

Blanchard, E.B. and Abel, G.C. (1976) 'An experimental case study of the biofeedback treatment of a rape-induced psychophysiological cardiovascular disorder', *Behavior Therapy*, 7: 113–19.

Brownell, K.D. (1991) *The LEARN Program for Weight Control*. Dallas: American Health Publishing Company.

Brunner, D. and Manelis, G. (1960) 'Myocardial infarction among members of communal settlements in Israel', *The Lancet*, 2: 1049.

Bryant, B. and Trower, P.E. (1974) 'Social difficulty in a student sample', *British Journal of Educational Psychology*, 44: 13–21.

Budzynski, T.H., Stoyva, J.M., Adler, C.S. and Mullaney, D.J. (1973) 'EMG biofeedback and tension headache: a controlled outcome study', *Psychosomatic Medicine*, 35: 484–96.

Burns, D.D. (1980) *Feeling Good: the New Mood Therapy*. New York: Morrow.

Burns, D.D. (1989) *The Feeling Good Handbook*. New York: William Morrow and Co.

Bush, C., Ditto, B. and Feuerstein, M. (1985) 'A controlled evaluation of paraspinal EMG biofeedback in the treatment of chronic low back pain', *Health Psychology*, 4: 307–21.

Butler, G. (1989) 'Phobic disorders', in K. Hawton, P. Salkovskis, J. Kirk and D. Clarke (eds), *Cognitive Behaviour Therapy for Psychiatric Problems: a Practical Guide*. Oxford: Oxford University Press.

Butler, G., Fennell, M., Robson, P. and Gelder, M. (1991) 'Comparison of behavior therapy and cognitive-behavior therapy in the treatment of generalized anxiety disorder', *Journal of Consulting and Clinical Psychology*, 59(1): 167–75.

Cabinet Office (1987) *Understanding Stress. Part 3: Trainer Guide*. London: HMSO.

Carrington, P. (1993) 'Modern forms of meditation', in P.M. Lehrer and R.L. Woolfolk (eds), *Principles and Practice of Stress Management*, 2nd edn. New York: Guilford Press.

Cautela, J.R. (1967) 'Covert sensitization', *Psychological Reports*, 20: 459–68.

Clarke, D. and Palmer, S. (1994) *Stress Management*. Cambridge: National Extension College.

Cockman, P., Evans, B. and Reynolds, P. (1992) *Client-Centred Consulting: a Practical Guide for Internal Advisors and Trainers*. Maidenhead: McGraw-Hill.

Cooper, C., Cooper, R. and Eaker, L. (1988) *Living with Stress*. Harmondsworth: Penguin.

Cowen, E.L. (1982) 'Help is where you find it', *American Psychologist*, 37: 385–95.

Cox, T. (1978) *Stress*. London: Macmillan.

Cox, T. (1993) *Stress Research and Stress Management: Putting Theory to Work*. London: HMSO.

Cox, T. and Mackay, C.J. (1981) 'A transactional approach to occupational stress', in E.N. Corlett and J. Richardson (eds), *Stress, Work Design and Productivity*. Chichester: Wiley.

Cox, T., Gots, G.N. and Kerr, J. (1988) 'Physical exercise, employee fitness and the management of health at work', *Work and Stress*, 2(1): 71–6.

Dewe, P., Cox, T. and Ferguson, E. (1993) 'Individual strategies for coping with stress at work: a review of progress and directions for future research', *Work and Stress*, 7: 5–15.

Doll, R. and Peto, R. (1976) 'Mortality in relation to smoking: 20 years' observations on male British doctors', *British Medical Journal*, 152: 1536.

Dryden, W. (1987) *Counselling Individuals: the Rational-Emotive Approach*. London: Taylor and Francis.

Dryden, W. (1990) *Rational-Emotive Counselling in Action*. London: Sage.

Dryden, W. (1991a) *Reason and Therapeutic Change*. London: Whurr Publishers.

Dryden, W. (1991b) *A Dialogue with Albert Ellis*. Buckingham: Open University Press.

Dryden, W. (1991c) *A Dialogue with Arnold Lazarus: 'It Depends'*. Buckingham: Open University Press.

Dryden, W. and Feltham, C. (1992) *Brief Counselling: a Practical Guide for Beginning Practitioners*. Buckingham: Open University Press.

Dryden, W. and Gordon, J. (1990) *Think your Way to Happiness*. London: Sheldon.

Dryden, W. and Gordon, J. (1992) *Think Rationally*. London: Centre for Rational-Emotive Therapy.

Dryden, W. and Gordon, J. (1993) *Peak Performance: Become More Effective at Work*. Didcot: Mercury Business Books.

Ellis, A. (1962) *Reason and Emotion in Psychotherapy*. New York: Lyle Stuart.

Ellis, A. (1977) 'The basic clinical theory of rational-emotive therapy', in A. Ellis and R. Grieger (eds), *Handbook of Rational-Emotive Therapy*. New York: Springer.

Ellis, A. (1979) 'The practice of rational-emotive therapy', in A. Ellis and J.M. Whiteley (eds), *Theoretical and Empirical Foundations of Rational-Emotive Therapy*. Monterey, CA: Brooks/Cole.

Ellis, A. (1983) 'How to deal with your most difficult client: you', *Journal of Rational-Emotive Therapy*, 1(1): 3–8.

Ellis, A. and Dryden, W. (1987) *The Practice of Rational-Emotive Therapy*. New York: Springer.

Evans, B. and Reynolds, P. (1993) 'Stress consulting: a client centred approach', *Stress News*, 5: 2–6.

Falloon, I.R.H., Boyd, J.L. and McGill, C. (1984) 'Problem-solving training', in *Family Care of Schizophrenia*, pp. 261–84. New York: Guilford Press.

Falloon, I.R.H., Boyd, J.L., O'Conner, M., Anastasiades, P. and Cooper, P.J. (1987) *Family Care of Schizophrenia*. New York: Guilford.

Falloon, I.R.H., Laporta, M., Fadden, G. and Graham-Hole, V. (1993) *Managing Stress in Families*. London: Routledge.

Feltham, C. and Dryden, W. (1993) *Dictionary of Counselling*. London: Whurr Publishers.

Fennell, M.J.V. (1989) 'Depression', in K. Hawton, P. Salkovskis, J. Kirk and D. Clark (eds), *Cognitive Behaviour Therapy for Psychiatric Problems: a Practical Guide*. Oxford: Oxford University Press.

Flora Project for Heart Disease Prevention (1991) *Eating for a Healthy Heart*. London: Flora Project.

Frankl, V.E. (1960) 'Paradoxical intention: a logotherapeutic technique', *American Journal of Psychotherapy.*, 14: 520–35.

Freedman, R., Ianni, P. and Wenig, P. (1985) 'Behavioural treatment of Raynaud's disease: long-term follow-up', *Journal of Clinical and Consulting Psychology*, 53: 136.

Friedman, M. and Ulmer, D. (1985) *Treating Type A Behaviour and Your Heart*. London: Michael Joseph.

Gendlin, E. (1981) *Focusing*. New York: Everest House.

Glueck, B.C. and Stroebel, C.F. (1975) 'Biofeedback and medication in the treatment of psychiatric illness', *Comprehensive Psychiatry*, 16: 302–21.

Golden, W.L. (1983) 'Resistance in cognitive-behaviour therapy', *British Journal of Cognitive Psychotherapy*, 1(2): 33–42.

Grayson, J.B., Foa, E.B. and Skeketee, G. (1985) 'Obsessive-compulsive disorder', in M. Hersen and A.S. Bellack (eds) *Handbook of Clinical Behavior Therapy with Adults*. New York: Plenum.

Griest, H.H., Klein, M.H., Eischens, R.R. and Faris, J.W. (1978) 'Antidepressant running', *Behavioral Medicine*, 5(6): 19–24.

Griffiths, R.R. and Woodson, P.P. (1988) 'Caffeine physical dependence: a review of human and laboratory animal studies', *Psychopharmacology*, 94: 437–51.

Hames, C. (1975) 'Most likely to succeed as a candidate for a coronary attack', in H.I. Russek (ed.), *New Horizons in Cardiovascular Practice*. New York: University Park Press.

Hartland, J. (1987) *Medical and Dental Hypnosis and its Clinical Applications.* London: Baillière Tindall.

Hawton, K. (1989) 'Sexual dysfunctions', in K. Hawton, P. Salkovskis, J. Kirk and D. Clark (eds), *Cognitive Behaviour Therapy for Psychiatric Problems: a Practical Guide.* Oxford: Oxford University Press.

Hawton, K. and Catalan, J. (1987) *Attempted Suicide: a Practical Guide to its Nature and Management*, 2nd edn. Oxford: Oxford University Press.

Hawton, K. and Kirk, J. (1989) 'Problem-solving', in K. Hawton, P. Salkovskis, J. Kirk and D. Clark (eds), *Cognitive Behaviour Therapy for Psychiatric Problems: a Practical Guide.* Oxford: Oxford University Press.

Hogan, R.A. and Kirchner, J.H. (1967) 'Preliminary report of the extinction of learned fears via short term implosive therapy', *Journal of Abnormal Psychology*, 72: 106–9.

Jacobson, E. (1938) *Progressive Relaxation.* Chicago: University of Chicago Press.

Kannel, W.B. and Schatzkin, A. (1983) 'Risk factor analysis', *Progress in Cardiovascular Diseases*, 26: 309–32.

Karasu, T.B. (1986) 'The specificity versus nonspecificity dilemma: toward identifying therapeutic change agents', *American Journal of Psychiatry*, 143: 687–95.

Keane, T., Fairbank, J., Caddell, J. et al. (1989) 'Implosive (flooding) therapy reduces symptoms of PTSD in Vietnam combat veterans', *Behaviour Therapy*, 20: 245–60.

Kelly, G.A. (1955) *The Psychology of Personal Constructs.* New York: Norton.

Kermani, K. (1992) *Autogenic Training: the Effective Way to Conquer Stress.* London: Thorsons.

Kirchner, J.H. and Hogan, R.A. (1966) 'The therapist variable in the implosion of phobias', *Psychotherapy: Theory, Research and Practice*, 3: 102–4.

Lacey, R. (1991) *The Complete Guide to Psychiatric Drugs: a Layman's Handbook.* London: Ebury Press.

Lazarus, A.A. (1966) 'Behavior rehearsal vs non-directive therapy vs advice in effecting behavior change', *Behaviour Research and Therapy*, 4: 209–12.

Lazarus, A.A. (1971) *Behavior Therapy and Beyond.* New York: McGraw-Hill.

Lazarus, A.A. (1973a) '"Hypnosis" as a facilitator in behavior therapy', *International Journal of Clinical and Experimental Hypnosis*, 21: 25–31.

Lazarus, A.A. (1973b) 'Multimodal behavior therapy: treating the BASIC ID', *Journal of Nervous and Mental Disease*, 156: 404–11.

Lazarus, A.A. (1976) 'Psychiatric problems precipitated by transcendental meditation', *Psychological Reports*, 10: 39–74.

Lazarus, A.A. (1977) 'Toward an egoless state of being', in A. Ellis and R. Grieger (eds), *Handbook of Rational-Emotive Therapy.* New York: Springer.

Lazarus, A.A. (1981) *The Practice of Multimodal Therapy.* New York: McGraw-Hill.

Lazarus, A.A. (1982) 'Personal enrichment through imagery' (cassette recording). New York: BMA Audio-Cassettes/Guilford.

Lazarus, A.A. (1984) *In the Mind's Eye.* New York: Guilford Press.

Lazarus, A.A. (1986) 'Multimodal therapy', in J.C. Norcross (ed.), *Handbook of Eclectic Psychotherapy.* New York: Brunner/Mazel.

Lazarus, A.A. (1987) 'The multimodal approach with adult outpatients', in N.S. Jacobson (ed.), *Psychotherapists in Clinical Practice.* New York: Guilford Press.

Lazarus, A.A. (1989a) *The Practice of Multimodal Therapy.* Baltimore, MD: The Johns Hopkins University Press.

Lazarus, A.A. (1989b) 'Why I am an eclectic (not an integrationist)', in W. Dryden and J.C. Norcross (eds), *Eclecticism and Integration in Counselling and Psychotherapy*. Loughton: Gale Centre Publications.

Lazarus, A.A. (1989c) 'The case of George', in D. Wedding and R.J. Corsini (eds), *Case Studies in Psychotherapy*. Itasca, IL: Peacock.

Lazarus, A.A. (1990) 'Can psychotherapists transcend the shackles of their training and superstitions?', *Journal of Clinical Psychology*, 46: 351–8.

Lazarus, A.A. (ed.) (1985) *Casebook of Multimodal Therapy*. New York: Guilford Press.

Lazarus, A.A. and Fay, A. (1982) 'Resistance or rationalization? A cognitive-behavioral perspective', in P.L. Wachtel (ed.), *Resistance: Psychodynamic and Behavioral Approaches*. New York: Plenum.

Lazarus, A.A. and Lazarus, C.N. (1990) 'Emotions: a multimodal perspective', in R. Plutchic and H. Kellerman (eds), *Emotion: Theory, Research and Experience*, vol. 5, *Emotion, Psychopathology and Psychotherapy*. New York: Academic Press.

Lazarus, A.A. and Lazarus, C.N. (1991) *Multimodal Life History Inventory*. Champaign, IL: Research Press.

Lazarus, A.A. and Mayne, J.J. (1990) 'Relaxation: some limitations, side effects, and proposed solutions', *Psychotherapy*, 27: 261–6.

Lazarus, A.A. and Nieves, L. (1980) 'Assertiveness training in the multimodal therapy framework', *Comprehensive Psychotherapy*, 1: 39–46.

Lazarus, R.S. (1966) *Psychological Stress and the Coping Process*. New York: McGraw-Hill.

Lazarus, R.S. and Folkman, S. (1984) *Stress, Appraisal and Coping*. New York: Springer.

Lehrer, P.M., Hochron, S.M., McCann, B., Swartzman, L. and Reba, P. (1986) 'Relaxation decreases large-airway but not small-airway asthma', *Journal of Psychosomatic Research* 30: 13–25.

Liberman, R.P., King, L.W., De Risi, W.J. and McCann, M. (1975) *Personal Effectiveness*. Champaign, IL: Research Press.

Linden, W. (1990) *Autogenic Training: a Clinical Guide*. New York: Guilford Press.

Lindenfield, G. (1987) *Assert Yourself: a Self-Help Assertiveness Programme for Men and Women*. Wellingborough: Thorsons.

London, P. (1964) *The Modes and Morals of Psychotherapy*. New York: Holt, Rinehart and Winston.

Luthe, W. and Schultz, J.H. (1969) *Autogenic Training: Medical Applications*. New York: Grune and Stratton.

Marks, I.M. (1969) *Fears and Phobias*. London: William Heinemann.

Marks, I.M. (1980) *Living with Fear*. New York: McGraw-Hill.

Marks, I.M. (1986) *Behavioural Psychotherapy: Maudsley Pocket Book of Clinical Management*. Bristol: Wright.

Marks, I.M. (1987) 'Nightmares', *Integr. Psychiatry*, 5: 71–81.

Masters, W.H. and Johnson, V.E. (1970) *Human Sexual Inadequacy*. Boston: Little Brown.

Maultsby, M.C., Jr (1975) *Rational Behavior Therapy*. Englewood Cliffs, NJ: Prentice-Hall.

McGuigan, F.J. (1993) 'Progressive relaxation: origins, principles, and clinical applications', in P.M. Lehrer and R.L. Woolfolk (eds), *Principles and Practice of Stress Management*, 2nd edn. New York: Guilford Press.

McMullin, R.E. (1986) *Handbook of Cognitive Therapy Techniques*. New York: Norton.

Meichenbaum, D. (1977) *Cognitive-Behavior Modification: an Integrative Approach*. New York: Plenum Press.

Meichenbaum, D. (1985) *Stress Inoculation Training*. New York: Pergamon.

Milroy, E. (1982) *Role-Play: a Practical Guide*. Aberdeen: Aberdeen University Press.

Muss, D. (1991) *The Trauma Trap*. London: Doubleday.

Nelson-Jones, R. (1991) *Lifeskills: a Handbook*. London: Cassell Educational.

Nelson-Jones, R. (1993) *You Can Help! Introducing Lifeskills Helping*. London: Cassell.

Norris, P.A. and Fahrion, S.L. (1993) 'Autogenic biofeedback in psychophysiological therapy and stress management', in P.M. Lehrer and R.L. Woolfolk (eds), *Principles and Practice of Stress Management*, 2nd edn. New York: Guilford Press.

Paffenbarger, R.S. and Hale, W.E. (1975) 'Work activity and coronary heart mortality', *New England Journal of Medicine*, 11: 292.

Palmer, S. (1988) *Personal Stress Management Programme Manual*. London: Centre for Stress Management.

Palmer, S. (1989) 'The use of stability zones, rituals and routines to reduce or prevent stress', *Stress News*, 1(3): 3–5.

Palmer, S. (1990a) 'Assertion', *Journal for Women in the GMB, Northern Region*. Newcastle: GMB.

Palmer, S. (1990b) 'Stress mapping: a visual technique to aid counselling or training', *Employee Counselling Today*, 2(2): 9–12.

Palmer, S. (1990c) 'Uses of biofeedback techniques in cognitive behavioural therapy', *Bulletin of the Association of Behavioural Clinicians*, 8, December, 29–34.

Palmer, S. (1992a) 'Multimodal assessment and therapy: a systematic, technically eclectic approach to counselling, psychotherapy and stress management', *Counselling*, 3(4): 220–4.

Palmer, S. (1992b) 'Editorial: What law of the universe states that you must . . .?', *Stress News*, 4(3): 1.

Palmer, S. (1992c) 'Guidelines and contra-indications for teaching relaxation as a stress management technique', *Journal of the Institute of Health Education*, 30(1): 25–30.

Palmer, S. (1992d) 'Stress management interventions', *Counselling News*, September, 7: 12–15.

Palmer, S. (1992e) *Stress Management: a Course Reader*. London: Centre for Stress Management.

Palmer, S. (1993a) 'The "Deserted Island Technique": a method of demonstrating how preferential and musturbatory beliefs can lead to different emotions', *The Rational-Emotive Therapist*, 1(1): 12–14.

Palmer, S. (1993b) *Multimodal Techniques: Relaxation and Hypnosis*. London: Centre for Stress Management and Centre for Multimodal Therapy.

Palmer, S. (1993c) 'Occupational stress: its causes and alleviation', in W. Dekker (ed.), *Chief Executive International*. London: Sterling.

Palmer, S. (1993d) 'Organisational stress: symptoms, causes and reduction', *Newsletter of the Society of Public Health*, November, 2–8.

Palmer, S. (1994) 'Stress management and counselling: a problem-solving approach', *Stress News*, 5(3): 2–3.

Palmer, S. (1995) 'The stresses of running a stress management centre', in W. Dryden (ed.), *The Stresses of Counselling in Action*. London: Sage.

Palmer, S. and Dryden, W. (1991) 'A multimodal approach to stress management', *Stress News*, 3(1): 2–10.

Palmer, S. and Dryden, W. (1994) 'Stress management: approaches and interventions', *British Journal of Guidance and Counselling*, 22(1): 5–12.

Parrott, A. (1991) 'Social drugs: their effects upon health', in M. Pitts and K. Phillips (eds), *The Psychology of Health: an Introduction*. London: Routledge.

Pease, A. (1984) *Body Language: How to Read Others' Thoughts by their Gestures*. London: Sheldon Press.

Perris, C. (1993) 'Stumbling blocks in the supervision of cognitive psychotherapy', *Clinical Psychology and Psychotherapy*, 1(1): 29–43.

Peveler, R. and Johnston, D.W. (1986) 'Subjective and cognitive effects of relaxation', *Behaviour Research and Therapy*, 24: 413–20. .

Phillips, K.C. (1979) 'Biofeedback as an aid to autogenic training', in B.A. Stoll (ed.), *Mind and Cancer Prognosis*. Chichester: Wiley.

Pitts, M. and Phillips, K. (eds) (1991) *The Psychology of Health*. London: Routledge.

Quick, J.C. and Quick, J.D. (1984) *Organizational Stress and Preventive Management*. New York: McGraw-Hill.

Rachman, S. (1968) 'Phobias: their nature and control', *American Lecture Series, Publication No. 721*. Springfield: Charles Thomas.

Ross, R.R. and Altmaier, E.M. (1994) *Intervention in Occupational Stress: a Handbook of Counselling for Stress at Work*. London: Sage.

Salkovskis, P. (1989) 'Somatic problems', in K. Hawton, P. Salkovskis, J. Kirk and D. Clarke (eds), *Cognitive-Behaviour Therapy for Psychiatric Problems: a Practical Guide*. Oxford: Oxford University Press.

Salkovskis, P. and Kirk, J. (1989) 'Obsessional disorders', in K. Hawton, P. Salkovskis, J. Kirk and D. Clarke, (eds), *Cognitive-Behaviour Therapy for Psychiatric Problems: a Practical Guide*. Oxford: Oxford University Press.

Schmaling, K.B., Fruzzetti, A.E. and Jacobson, N.S. (1989) 'Marital problems', in K. Hawton, P. Salkovskis, J. Kirk and D. Clarke (eds), *Cognitive-Behaviour Therapy for Psychiatric Problems: a Practical Guide*. Oxford: Oxford University Press.

Shapiro, D.A. and Shapiro, D. (1983) 'Comparative therapy outcome research: methodological implications of meta-analysis', *Journal of Consulting and Clinical Psychology*, 51: 42–53.

Sharpe, L., Tarrier, N. and Rotundo, N. (1994) 'Treatment of delayed post-traumatic stress disorder following sexual abuse: a case example', *Behavioural and Cognitive Psychotherapy*, 22: 233–42.

Sloan, S. and Cooper, D. (1986) *Pilots under Stress*. London: Routledge and Kegan Paul.

Smith, M.L., Glass, G.V. and Miller, T.I. (1980) *The Benefits of Psychotherapy*. Baltimore, MD: Johns Hopkins University Press.

Sobel, H. and Worden, J. (1981) *Helping Cancer Patients Cope: a Problem-Solving Intervention for Health Care Professionals*. New York: BMA and Guilford Press.

Steptoe, A. (1981) *Psychological Factors in Cardiovascular Disease*. London: Academic Press.

Stoyva, J.M. and Budzynski, T.H. (1993) 'Biofeedback methods in the treatment of anxiety and stress disorders', in P.M. Lehrer and R.L. Woolfolk (eds), *Principles and Practice of Stress Management*, 2nd edn. New York: Guilford Press.

Trower, P., Casey, A. and Dryden, W. (1988) *Cognitive-Behavioural Counselling in Action*. London: Sage.

Wasik, B. (1984) 'Teaching parents effective problem-solving: a handbook for professionals'. Unpublished manuscript. Chapel Hill: University of North Carolina.

Weishaar, M.E. (1993) *Aaron T. Beck*. London: Sage.

Weiss, T. and Engel, B.T. (1971) 'Operant conditioning of heart rate in patients with premature ventricular contractions', *Psychosomatic Medicine*, 33: 301–21.

Wessler, R.L. (1984) 'Alternative conceptions of rational-emotive therapy: toward a philosophically neutral psychotherapy', in M.A. Reda and M.J. Mahoney (eds), *Cognitive Psychotherapies: Recent Developments in Theory, Research and Practice*. Cambridge, MA: Ballinger.

Wessler, R.L. and Ellis, A. (1980) 'Supervision in rational-emotive therapy', in A.K. Hess (ed.), *Psychotherapy Supervision*. New York: Wiley.

White, J. and Keenan, M. (1990) 'Stress control: a pilot study of large group therapy for generalised anxiety disorder', *Behavioural Psychotherapy*, 18: 143–6.

White, L. and Tursky, B. (1982) *Clinical Biofeedback: Efficacy and Mechanisms*. New York: Guilford Press.

White, J., Keenan, M. and Brookes, N. (1992) 'Stress control: a controlled comparative investigation of large group therapy for generalised anxiety disorder', *Behavioural Psychotherapy*, 20: 97–114.

Wilkinson, J. and Canter, S. (1983) *Social Skills Training Manual: Assessment, Programme Design, and Management of Training*. Chichester: Wiley.

Wolpe, J. and Lazarus, A.A. (1966) *Behavior Therapy Techniques*. New York: Pergamon.

Index

Note: Page references in italics indicate tables and figures.

Index compiled by Meg Davies (Society of Indexers)